Comparative Advertising

Comparative Advertising

History, Theory, and Practice

Fred Beard

LEXINGTON BOOKS
Lanham • Boulder • New York • London

Published by Lexington Books
An imprint of The Rowman & Littlefield Publishing Group, Inc.
4501 Forbes Boulevard, Suite 200, Lanham, Maryland 20706
www.rowman.com

Unit A, Whitacre Mews, 26-34 Stannary Street, London SE11 4AB

British Library Cataloguing in Publication Information Available

Library of Congress Cataloging-in-Publication Data

Names: Beard, Fred K., 1957- author.
Title: Comparative advertising : history, theory, and practice / Fred Beard.
Description: Lanham, MD : Lexington Books, [2018] | Includes bibliographical references and index.
Identifiers: LCCN 2018011612 (print) | LCCN 2018019368 (ebook) | ISBN 9781498560337 (ebook) | ISBN 9781498560320 (cloth : alk. paper)
Subjects: LCSH: Comparative advertising. | Comparative advertising—History.
Classification: LCC HF5827.2 (ebook) | LCC HF5827.2 .B43 2018 (print) | DDC 659.1—dc23
LC record available at https://lccn.loc.gov/2018011612

∞™ The paper used in this publication meets the minimum requirements of American National Standard for Information Sciences Permanence of Paper for Printed Library Materials, ANSI/NISO Z39.48-1992.

Printed in the United States of America

Contents

List of Figures

List of Tables

Acknowledgments

Christina DeWalt, PhD, Assistant Professor, Florida Atlantic University, for assistance in conducting a survey of corporate advertising executives.

MD Nazmul Rony, The Gaylord College, University of Oklahoma, for assistance in analyzing some of the survey data.

Introduction

Have you ever noticed that a lot of companies seem to spend almost as much time talking about their competitors in their advertising as they do their own products or services? One brand of low-cal yogurt was claiming recently that two competitors contain either the artificial sweetener sucralose or the preservative potassium sorbate. Small financial firms have been calling out mega banks like Chase and Bank of America for taking "bailouts," charging high fees, and being "out of touch" with Main Street. And one brand of ready-to-eat soups launched a campaign not long ago in which they told us they make theirs with "TLC," while their biggest competitor uses "MSG" (that's monosodium glutamate).

These kinds of ads were originally called "knocking" or sometimes just "competitive" ads. In the 1970s, advertisers, industry observers, and researchers settled on the term "comparative advertising." Although they're not new, especially in the United States, early businessmen didn't think much of them. That doesn't mean they never used comparative ads, though. In fact, it wasn't all that uncommon for early 20th-century businesses to identify competitors in their ads specifically so they could claim the other guy's products were unhealthy or even dangerous. Much like the contemporary MSG claim, a classic example from the late-1920s was the "Spit" campaign for the Cremo brand of cigar. The Cremo ads warned smokers that whoever rolled that other cigar might have sealed the end with, well, you get the picture (Headline: "Beware: 'SPIT' is a horrid word BUT . . . it's worse on the end of your cigar."). And, yes, just about everybody complained about the Cremo ads.

Still, comparative advertising didn't really take off in the United States until the late 1960s and early 1970s. That's when the government's Federal Trade Commission officially defined comparative ads as those that directly or indirectly compare different brands based on their features or prices and actively began encouraging advertisers to use them. Not entirely convinced it was a good idea, the Big Three TV networks agreed to give them a trial, and their audiences were freed forever from the burden of wondering who "Brand X" was. In fact, the effectiveness of the National Association of Broadcasters' near ban on comparative ads is why some people even today think they used to be illegal in the United States. Even after the networks started allowing them, though, many marketers and other business execs still agreed with legendary adman David Ogilvy, who believed it didn't make much sense to create awareness for a competitor's brand by mentioning it. He was also convinced that people who see a comparative ad tend to get the impression that the sponsor is actually the villain and the target of the attack is the real hero.

Mr. Ogilvy wasn't alone, either. Many ad agency executives and business decision makers still argue that spending time and money talking about a competitor is usually a bad idea. Consider this observation attributed to one of the casualties of the spaghetti sauce war between the Ragu and Prego brands back in the 1990s. After years of open hostilities, he ultimately concluded and admitted that the two companies were "spending $60 million a year to convince consumers that our spaghetti sauce is really crappy" (as cited in Neff, 1999, p. 26). In fact, some of the historical research summarized in this book shows that many comparative advertisers throughout the 20th century often wound up regretting the decision to attack a competitor.

Yet research on the use of comparative advertising in the United States shows it increased significantly during and after the 1970s and is widely used today. Some suggest that as many as one-third of all ads in the United States are comparative. If that's an accurate estimate, it would mean companies in the United States alone are spending somewhere in the neighborhood of $60 billion a year on ads in which they identify, either directly or indirectly, one or more competitors. Estimates of the use of comparative advertising on TV alone are similar if not higher, with one recent study showing that nearly half of all commercials either directly identify a competitive brand by name or indirectly refer in some way to one or more competitors (Beard, 2016b). And it's not just national advertisers. One of my personal favorites is a local furniture storeowner (I'm talking to you, Phil), who just can't resist declaring that, "unlike those other furniture stores," he won't "mess you around" over a few dollars. On the other hand, it's a slightly different story elsewhere in the world. In many other countries, the use of comparative advertising was not only less frequent throughout most of the 20th century, it was actually illegal. That situation changed not all that long ago, in the European Community anyway, with the passage of Directive 97/55/EC, which established that both direct and indirect comparative ads should be allowed as long as they aren't anti-competitive, unfair, or misleading.

As you'd expect, such a controversial yet widely used business practice has attracted a lot of attention from academic researchers, marketing and advertising professionals, and government and industry regulators. Hundreds of histories, practitioner surveys, experiments, literature reviews, meta -analyses, trade journal articles (I've collected nearly 800 of those alone), and opinion pieces on comparative advertising have been published since the 1960s. The purpose of this book—*Comparative Advertising: History, Theory, and Practice*—is to summarize and synthesize this vast body of academic and professional trade literature into a single source for the benefit of anyone who plans, creates, or pays for advertising, as well as those who are simply interested in definitive answers to the following question: Why have so many advertisers relied on a message tactic that research and professional experience confirms they often lacked confidence in and frequently regretted using?

Chapter One

A History of Comparative Advertising

Given the extent to which advertising inserts itself into our lives—someone estimated not too long ago that the average American sees around 5,000 ads a day (Creamer, 2007)—it's probably no surprise that advertising has drawn a lot of historical interest over the past century. The first histories of advertising were actually published in the late 1800s, written by Henry Sampson (1874) (appropriately titled *A History of Advertising from the Earliest Times*) and Charles Hindley (1884) (*A History of the Cries of London*). A few of these older works, like Sampson's, or that of Frank Presbrey (1929), a notable American advertising pioneer and historian, focus on countries other than the United States. As we'll see in a moment, there's also a growing body of recent historical research.

We know quite a bit about the advertising of the 19th and 20th centuries, but things start getting a little murky much before that. As advertising historians Maxine Berg and Helen Clifford (2006, p. 154) confirm, "our knowledge of advertising from the 18th century is at a primitive stage." There are also good reasons to believe that comparative advertising, whether competitors are named or shown or merely referenced indirectly, is not the 20th century phenomenon many assume it is. As researchers Jean Boddewyn and Katherin Marton (1978, p. 3) point out: "Whether done poorly or well, responsibly or not, the use of comparisons in advertising is old; and its prohibition or restriction in many countries reveals that it was practiced but *became* controversial [italics added]."

This brief overview points to a couple of recently identified problems with the body of historical research on advertising and some of the topics related to it, such as branding and brands. Historian Stefan Schwarzkopf (2011), who conducted a review of historical studies on advertising published between 1980 and 2010, concluded that much advertising history is limited by at least two methodological-theoretical norms: "Americanization" and "Modernization." These norms, or biases, have produced the combined views among many marketing and advertising historians and professionals that anything occurring before the late 19th or early 20th centuries or the contributions of anyone other than the American pioneers are unimportant.

Many historians date the dawn of modern advertising and branding to the beginning of the 20th century and tend to fixate on the philosophies and practices of the period's influential Americans, such as Albert Lasker, Claude Hopkins, George Rowell, Francis Wayland Ayer, Harley Procter, James L. Kraft, and J. Walter Thompson. This Modernization bias has partly occurred because historians have focused so much on newspaper advertising. One consequence of that, according to Berg and Clifford (2006, p. 154), is that "in the main, they assume eighteenth-century advertising to be functional, about giving the customer information on the product; its banality, they argue, ultimately gave way to modern advertising with its use of images and entry into modern visual culture."

Yet, as we'll see in a moment, the early Mesopotamians, Chinese, Greeks, and Romans apparently appreciated the value of a good promotion. Iron Age Greek potters used "trade's marks" and mottos to differentiate their brands, and medieval Chinese manufacturers relied on consumer word-of-mouth (WOM) to promote theirs. Point-of-purchase ads are visible on the walls of Pompeii and Herculaneum, and *garum* (a fermented fish sauce) was marketed under several brand names throughout the Roman Empire. Support for the assumptions that any earlier history is mostly irrelevant when it comes to teaching us something about practices like comparative advertising, or that ancient advertising totally lacked visual power or emotional impact, is weak at best.

Most historians also agree that the American advertising industry influenced other countries largely during the 20th century. The widespread adoption of a marketing orientation, marketing research, segmentation, ad agency specialization and professionalization, the agency creative team, ad pioneer J. Walter Thompson's strategic approach, and a heavy reliance on the broadcast media were mainly American contributions. On the other hand, some research shows that industry structures, professional practices, and creative expression often evolved independently from American influence, both before and during the 20th century (Beard, 2016a). Influences flowing from Europe to the United States include an early European consumer culture, advertising-supported print media and marketing ephemera (promotional objects or media executions created for a one-time, limited purpose), poster design and other creative approaches and traditions, as well as the practices of the earliest advertising agents.

The purpose of this chapter, then, is to look for historical evidence regarding the use of comparative advertising on an international scale and to generate some answers to this book's core question: Why have advertisers often relied on a message tactic that research and professional experience confirms they often lacked confidence in and frequently regretted using? To achieve this purpose, the chapter presents an integrative history of comparative advertising that avoids the Modernization and Americanization theoretical and philosophical limitations. First, instead of focusing on a supposedly "modern" era, we'll attempt a more comprehensive analysis of advertising's history in order to identify developmental trends and themes in comparative advertising beliefs and practices. The validity of this approach was captured especially well by magazine editor, author, and advertising historian James Playsted Wood (1958, p. 502): "Over the centuries, advertising has experienced changes in the proportioning of its ingredients, in direction, in application, but something of the first advertisement survives in the latest, and there will be traces of it in the last." Second, rather than focus almost exclusively on the history of comparative advertising in the United States, the chapter relies on a recent and growing body of global advertising history.

PERIODIZATION

Historians often use an approach called "periodization" to segment their writing and research into chronological and sequential time periods with clearly defined beginnings and endings (Hollander, Rassuli, Jones, & Dix, 2005). Periods serve the same conceptual or literary purposes as the chapters in a book or the acts and scenes in a play (Witkowski & Jones, 2006). Historical research typically focuses on the study of a particular topic, such as comparative advertising, and descriptions of a series of events related to that topic. Organizing the description of the events into different periods makes it easier to recognize how practices or beliefs might have changed or remained the same over time and, more important, helps us understand how each period may have provided a unique historical context that influenced the topic.

It's not unusual simply to periodize a historical narrative based on specific calendar dates, such as decades or centuries. Sometimes that's totally appropriate. However, serious historians generally prefer to base their periodization schemes on major turning points, or important events, in the subject matter or topic they're studying. Sometimes, as well, periods are determined before the collection and analysis of historical data (which is called a deductive or *ex ante* approach) or the periods are allowed to emerge from the data on their own and finalized afterwards (called an inductive or *ex post* approach).

The *ex ante* periodization scheme we're going to use in this chapter begins with Schwarzkopf's (2011, p. 539) observation that what is lacking from advertising's history are "more integrative analyses of medieval, early-modern and contemporary advertising communications." So we're relying on classical and European historiographical approaches, with some revisions to accommodate important turning points in advertising's history. The "Ancient and Medieval Period" consists of developments occurring prior to the end of the Middle Ages and, in particular, German goldsmith Johannes Gutenberg's introduction of printing with movable type to Europe around 1449. "Early Modern" advertising refers to a period defined by the end of the Middle Ages to the approximate beginning of the Industrial Revolution, roughly the late 15th to the late 18th century. The definitions of both these periods are mostly consistent with the classical approaches, but it's important to point out that they are still the focus of some debate.

In classical approaches, the "Late Modern" period usually refers to the entire 19th century and up to about 1950. For this advertising periodization scheme, we're going to refer to the Late Modern period as just the 19th century because it captures the maturing of the first and second industrial revolutions and their tremendous impacts on the production and distribution of consumer goods, as well as the major transition to modern advertising thought and practice that took place at the turn of the century. Similarly, while classical approaches to historical periodization generally refer to the Contemporary Period as spanning from the 1950s to present day, our "Contemporary" period refers to the 1900s to the 1950s, and then "Post Modern" advertising consists of the remaining years of the 20th century and beginning of the 21st. This final period is distinguished from the previous one based on three key turning points: advertising's "Creative Revolution" in the 1960s, the significant increase in the use of comparative advertising in the United States toward the end of the 1960s (especially on TV), and the digital and online media revolution that began during the last decade of the 20th century (Tungate, 2007).

ANCIENT AND MEDIEVAL ADVERTISING

Did advertising really exist before the introduction of the printing press to Europe by Johannes Gutenberg? The answer depends to a certain extent on how you define advertising. One of the most widely cited definitions of modern advertising is that of principles textbook authors Courtland Bovée and William Arens (1992, p. 7): "Advertising is the nonpersonal communication of information usually paid for and usually persuasive in nature about products, services or ideas by identified sponsors through the various media." The key distinguishing feature between ancient and modern forms of advertising, then, is the existence of advertising-supported media. So how much of what could reasonably be called "advertising" was there during the earliest periods—Classical Antiquity and before and then Early Modern (roughly the late 15th to the late 18th centuries)—and how similar was it to the advertising of today?

While it may be a bit of a stretch to claim the wall inscriptions on Hammurabi's temple in Uruk are early examples of corporate billboard advertising and that the Rosetta Stone is an early poster (Presbrey, 1929), once you set out to purposely avoid the Modernization paradigmatic perspective of advertising thought and practice, it turns out there was quite a bit of ancient promotional communications that often looked like modern advertising in purpose and design. Some historians have argued that advertising is, in fact, an ancient form of communication that existed thousands of years ago.

Street criers, often blowing horns or accompanied by musicians, roamed the ancient streets of Carthage, Egypt, Greece, and Rome, and the medieval towns of England, France, and Italy (Beard, 2016a). Presbrey (1929, p. 10) tells us that for several centuries in Europe, "Only the barker was used, and he only where it was safe. He was the medium of the first advertising by merchants in Britain, as he had been in southern Europe." Barkers were still busy at work for carnival sideshows and exotic dance clubs throughout the 20th century. In fact, film star Gregory Peck's biographer (Molyneaux, 1995) reports that Peck began his New York acting career barking on behalf of the owner of the "Meteor Speedway" thrill ride and concession at the 1939 World's Fair.

Merchants eventually began sending their barkers throughout town, instead of just posting them in front of their shops, and the shop barker became a commercial town crier. Some of these early advertising professionals had charters from their governments and there were limits in some places on how many could be employed at any particular time. In Paris, criers handed out wine samples from wooden buckets, with the obvious goal of encouraging a grateful patron to follow them back to the tavern for more (Presbrey, 1929). The next time you're at the grocery store and someone offers you a piece of cheese stuck on a toothpick, you might recall the ancient tavern crier and his bucket.

Another early aural form of advertising was organic (that is, naturally occurring) WOM, and there's historical evidence it was quite important at least as early as the Chinese Ming Dynasty (1368–1644) (Eckhardt & Bentsson, 2010). This is one topic in advertising's history that definitely could benefit from additional research because some historians suggest WOM has been important for an even longer time. It would be very interesting to know just how much early merchants relied on WOM and, more important, what they did to actively encourage it. Recently, an author for *BuzzTALK* made such an explicit connection between ancient WOM and electronic word-of-mouth (e-WOM), when she observed that e-WOM is "the oldest type of marketing we know" (Kremers, n.d.). In addition, the importance of WOM remains substantially unchanged today, with the Word of Mouth Marketing Association (2017) declaring it to be the "most effective form of advertising."

Written announcements, offering rewards for runaway slaves and dictated to scribes, appeared as early as 1100 BC in Egypt (Presbrey, 1929). The ancient Egyptians, Greeks, and Romans used signboards to attract the attention of passersby, and it apparently wasn't unusual for them to employ a rebus (a picture used to represent a word or object) if their names or trades lent themselves to such a visual referent (Diamond, 1975). As mentioned earlier, point-of-purchase signs and painted political campaign signs can be seen on the walls of Pompeii and Herculaneum (Presbrey, 1929; Rokicki, 1987), the Roman towns destroyed by pyroclastic flows from Mount Vesuvius in 79 AD.

The first advertising professionals might have been Roman *signatores* or *scriptores* (scribes or sign painters) (Rokicki, 1987). They solicited and serviced clients, created advertising, and arranged for its placement. The *album*, a flat, whitewashed space on a wall, on which they painted in red or black, was their primary medium. Advertising contractors may have controlled some of these Pompeiian *albums*, since they included of a variety of announcements—theatrical performances, baths, gladiatorial contests, and circuses—and locations were apparently chosen for their high volume of traffic (Presbrey, 1929).

The Chinese invented paper during the Han dynasty (206 BC–AD 220), and what followed were the first ads containing words and pictures (Eckhardt & Bentsson, 2010). Movable type printing arrived at least 400 years sooner in China than it did in Europe, and popular promotional items included banners, lanterns, pictures, and printed product wrappers (McDonough & Egoff, 2003). Today, these "below-the-line" expenditures are called promotional products, or advertising specialties, when they're used to reach consumers rather than the trade, such as wholesalers and retailers. How important are they? Typical packaged-goods marketers spend from 65% to 90% of their budgets on below-the-line consumer and trade sales promotions and direct marketing compared to only 10% to 35% on above-the-line expenditures such as advertising, which are intended to drive product and brand awareness, interest, and message retention (Myers, 2014).

Brands and Branding

The history of brands and branding, which advertising historians have claimed as part of their domain of study, is one of the areas in advertising's history that has been significantly influenced by the Modernization and Americanization paradigmatic limitations. Many, if not most, historians have assumed that "true" brands didn't exist until mainly 20th-century American advertisers of soaps and patent medicines strategically crafted them using relentless repetition, psychological branding principles, and the power of the mass media. Until recently, historians would occasionally mention that the origins of brands and branding are ancient, consisting mostly of the burning of a mark on cattle and manufactured goods, but then move quickly on to talk about developments during the late 19th and early 20th centuries.

This history is especially relevant here because one of the main purposes of ancient brands was the same as the frequent use of comparative advertising today—to clearly differentiate products or services from those of competitors. At its simplest, branding involves the use of a tangible mark, sign, or symbol that works to identify a product or service and differentiate it from competitors. Branding as a practice is often traced to ancient Rome, where shopkeepers used pictures to indicate the specialty of their store. However, recent research shows brands are much older than even that. One team of researchers has concluded that brands existed as early as 2250 BC in the Indus Valley through 300 BC in Greece (Moore & Reid, 2008). Another team proposed that differentiated brands existed in Mesopotamia and Egypt throughout antiquity and continuously in China from 2700 BC to present day (Eckhardt & Bentsson, 2010).

Brands and trademarks are related and both are closely connected to the earliest advertising. For example, brands and trademarks encouraged WOM. In addition, from trademarks it's only a short step to one of the earliest forms of advertising—sign-boards on shops. A U.S. Supreme Court ruling in the important 1942 *Mishawaka Rubber & Woolen Mfg. Co. v. S.S. Kresge Co.* court case clearly establishes the important definitional relationships among brands, trademarks, and advertising:

> A trademark is a merchandising short-cut which induces a purchaser to select what he wants, or what he has been led to believe he wants. The owner of a mark exploits this human propensity by making every effort to impregnate the atmosphere of the market with the drawing power of a congenial symbol. Whatever the means employed, the aim is the same—to convey through the mark, in the minds of potential customers, the desirability of the commodity upon which it appears. Once this is attained, the trademark owner has something of value. (as cited in Diamond, 1975, p. 288)

Historians propose that early trademarks also functioned in some of the same ways brands did in the early 20th century. In a functional sense, they were used to control and ensure quality and to inform prospective consumers about the origin and authenticity of goods that were produced in quantity and exported to distant markets. "The maker's mark symbolized both the producer's handiwork and his or her relationship with the customer. Advertisers quickly claimed this venerable history [in the 20th century]: brands assured consumers of quality in every purchase, they argued, since manufacturers would suffer if products failed to satisfy the consumer" (McGovern, 2006, p. 90). Archaeologist David Wengrow (2008) recently discovered evidence that shipping container seals, a branding system used in 4th-century-BC Mesopotamia and elsewhere, possessed many of the same characteristics as modern brands—they offered evidence to consumers of quality, authenticity and manufacturer ownership.

Modern brand theory and management also recognize the role of brands beyond merely functional and as conveyors of image, status, power, and personality. Some research on the history of brands and branding proposes that early brands often had these qualities as well. "We observe a gradual transition from a more utilitarian provision of information regarding origin and quality (in the case of what they call early 'proto-brands') to the addition of more complex brand image characteristics over time, including status/ power, added value, and finally, the development of brand personality" (Moore & Reid, 2008, p. 439). This is probably the key feature that distinguishes what some have called proto-brands from modern ones.

Like other manufacturers in the ancient world, the manufacturers of premodern brands in China, where consumer classes developed several hundred years earlier than in Europe, used visual branding to provide information, establish the origin and quality of goods, and to prevent counterfeiting. However, they also used visual and informational branding elements to portray a more complex image and to enable status seeking on the part of consumers (Eckhardt & Bentsson, 2010; Moore & Reid, 2008). The "white rabbit"—a brand of sewing needles originating during the Song dynasty (960–1279) and strategically chosen for its symbolic and mythological properties—is believed to be the oldest surviving complete brand in the world (Eckhardt & Bentsson, 2010).

How About Ancient Comparative Advertising?

Here's where we really have to dig into the historical research available to us, mainly because so few ads or other promotional messages from this oldest period have survived. There also weren't any ancient "trade journals" for merchants and manufacturers to share what they thought about topics like comparative advertising. That's one reason why the study of printed advertising trade cards, which didn't show up until the next period, has been so popular. There are several very large and important collections of these in the United States and Europe and several books have been written about them. One important reason is that they evolved from the earliest shop signs, which are long gone. Most shop signs were actually outlawed and replaced with street numbers and trade cards in Paris and London by the 1760s, mainly because the signs had the unfortunate tendency to fall and crush people who happened to be passing by at the wrong time.

But there are clues to be found here and there regarding whether or not early craftsmen and merchants directly or indirectly mentioned competitors in their promotional messages. For instance, the author of the preface to early American advertising great Theodore F. MacManus's (1927, pp. ix–x) book, *The Sword-Arm of Business*, identified in the 1927 edition only as "J.B.K.," wrote the following:

> Recent excavations in the sea-ruled site of ancient Carthage have revealed that while the power of Carthage was certainly destroyed, clues to its culture remain. Among these clues were items of household and personal utility, and among these lamps of precise fashion, branded with the name of the maker and with hieroglyphics which their discoverers reverently regarded as of mystic import. Lamps, these, that might have been burned before the fiery, blood-drenched alters of Moloch or in the soft, seductive cloisters of Diana. The secrets hidden in these chaste torch-cups, dulled and macled by the dust of untold centuries, might contain truths to stir the world. Slowly, with infinite labor, archeologists examined these relics of an almost obliterated past. Scholars waited, eager for words of learning, agape for the divulging of tremendous truths. Painfully the twisting graphs were freed from the clinging clay of ages, ponderously white-bearded men bent eye and glass to the task of discernment and translation. And what was the message carved by earth-claimed hands on these hoary vessels of light that illumined the paths of vestals to the sacrifice of ancient altars. Simply this: "Our lamps are the best lamps sold in Carthage."

The modern term for this in advertising that's used almost everywhere in the world is "puffery"—an often-exaggerated, totally non-fact-based claim about a product or service that legally doesn't have to be true because it's presumed no one believes it anyway. But this statement about Carthaginian lamps is also a recognizable type of implied comparative claim, a type we'll look at in greater detail in Chapter 2. What makes it a comparative claim, despite not mentioning any other lamp makers by name, is that it doesn't make any sense unless there are, in fact, other lamp makers in Carthage. So in addition to an amusingly told story, highlighting the difference between the most serious and weighty archeological research you can imagine and the discovery of a somewhat trite and very modern-looking puff (for comparison, consider Pizza Hut's "The Best Pizzas Under One Roof"), "J.B.K." provided us with evidence that 3,000 years ago, when at least one Carthaginian craftsman decided to say something persuasive about his lamps (just like Phil, the furniture store guy I mentioned in the introduction to this book), he couldn't resist the urge to acknowledge competitors and make a claim that his product was better than theirs.

Another ancient example—and this time, an actual direct comparison with an identified competitor—comes to us from Iron Age Greece (825 BC–336 BC), where mottos were often inscribed on pottery to provide additional information about its manufacture and, sometimes, to portray an image to prospective buyers. On one such vase, made by Grecian potter Euthymides, was inscribed a motto boasting it was of "high quality as never [were those of] Euphronios" (as cited in Moore & Reid, 2008, p. 428). Euphronios was another famous Greek vase painter and potter, active in Athens at the same time as Euthymides.

As we already know, there were lots of shop signs in Rome. Such advertising for the baths, an important leisure and social activity for Romans, often included boastful statements of superiority (Rokicki, 1987). As Presbrey (1929, p. 7) similarly points out: "There is evidence that the Romans knew something of advertising psychology. A bathing establishment in a provincial town would not fail to mention that its 'warm, sea and fresh-water baths' were patterned after the baths in the City of Rome." This is a modern comparative advertising approach called "Riding the Coattails," generally consisting of a claim that the advertiser's product or service is just as good as the well-known brand leader. Although many advertisers in the United States during the early 20th century believed Riding the Coattails was unethical and probably should be illegal (as it still is in many other countries), it clearly has a long history of use. Arguably the most important and influential application of the Riding the Coattails approach occurred during the 20th century in the United States—its use to promote product "knock-offs." You'll read more about this development in a little bit.

EARLY MODERN PERIOD

We know street criers and barkers were still at work throughout this period in Europe and the American colonies. One advertising historian colorfully describes what it was like at the time: "Even in the eighteenth century, the noise of criers in the streets was a fair parallel to our noise of autos and fire engines and Coney Island. It was a pandemonium of 'Buy, Buy, Buy'; 'Rally up, Ladies'; 'What d'ye lack?'" (Frederick, 1925, p. 15).

This period's most important event, however, was Johannes Gutenberg's invention of a metal alloy, soft enough to cast and hard enough to endure, which made movable type and widespread printing in Europe possible. Fortunately for Gutenberg's self-esteem, he probably didn't know the Chinese had been printing with movable type since around AD 1040. But thanks to the printing press, it didn't take long for advertising to progress beyond criers, WOM, and shop signs. London printer William Caxton's second print job, after publishing his first book in 1480 or so, was an ad to help sell the book. It was also the first ad printed from type in the English language (called a "tackup" or "siquis bill" in his day). With no advertising media and the refusal of the Royal Mail to carry advertising, Caxton sought the aid of the clergy, who kindly allowed him to tack his ad to their church doors. You can actually view Caxton's ad online as part of The Bodleian Library collection at the University of Oxford (Bodleian Library, 2015). At about the same time in Japan, merchants were posting flyers on the pillars of Shinto shrines, Buddhist temples, fences, and gateposts, and inserting ads into books (Tungate, 2007).

Trade cards, shop cards, and bill heads were the earliest widely circulated form of advertising combining images and printed text in Europe, and the oldest trade card in existence is a French one dated from 1622. These were handed out to customers to serve as a reminder of their shopping experience, among other purposes. In France, trade cards were called *enseignes*, also the term used for shop signs. The term was probably derived from the French verb "to teach" (*enseigner*). Collectors at the time, and there were many of them, had a genteel dislike of the term "shopkeepers," so instead of trade or shop cards, they called them tradesmen's cards. Historians Berg and Clifford (2007) argue they were more central and important to pre-19th century advertising than early newspapers and newssheets, and trade cards were widely used and collected for the next 300 years. As they elaborate:

> We challenge the assumption that pre-19th century advertising was primitive. We argue trade cards, where text and image are interdependent, had a wider impact (via the range of trades represented and the complexity of the messages conveyed) than purely text-based newspaper advertising. (Berg & Clifford, p. 146)

The Modernization paradigmatic limitation in advertising's history is clearly evident in English historian Marjorie Plant's observation that "it can scarcely be said that there was much deliberate advertising before the middle of the seventeenth century" (as cited in Stern, 2006, p. 60). In addition to street criers, shop signs, and trade cards, the use of handbills in many European cities exploded. For instance, the easiest way a theatre patron in Early Modern London could find out what plays were being staged was by reading the ads hanging from the street and door posts (Stern). The printing and posting of playbills began at least as early as 1587 and historians report they were posted throughout London in huge numbers, mainly because they were cheap and the theatre district was located outside of London and far from where most people lived (Stern).

Unfortunately for the homeowners of London, one of the favorite places to post a playbill was on the walls, doors, and doorposts of their homes. Doors and doorposts not only had the advantage of being everywhere, they also protected the playbills from the weather so they'd last longer. It may be a little hard to believe, but playbills were so highly valued, upper-crust theatre patrons would send their servants out to collect them (Stern, 2006). Not everyone thought so highly of them, though. "Players," as one critic wrote, "by sticking of their bils in London, defile the streets with their infectious filthiness" (as cited in Stern, p. 74). Considering the other sources of "infectious filthiness" there must have been in the streets at the time, the criticism seems at least a bit exaggerated. Still, the Lord Mayor of London tried to outlaw posting on people's homes in 1581, but failed.

And who knew we could credit advertising for helping to make early books available to the masses in England? When the number of rich literary benefactors willing to pay for the writing and printing of books declined dramatically in the final decade of Elizabeth I's reign (1533–1603), one of the period's types of advertising was there to save the day. "Printers and publishers—the parties with the greatest financial stakes in printing projects—employed many sophisticated forms of advertising specifically designed to persuade readers into buying books" (Voss, 1998, p. 733). Closely resembling the playbill, ads for books consisted of title-pages, printed separately from the book and then posted. Title-page ads were widely distributed but not everyone was a fan of these, either. English playwright, poet, and literary critic Benjamin "Ben" Jonson famously banned the bookseller responsible for his poems from using title-pages to promote his work (Stern, 2006).

Ad-Supported Media Arrive

As we discussed earlier, the main thing that distinguishes early advertising from modern advertising is the existence of ad-supported media. The first of these, periodicals, arrived in Europe in the late 16th and early 17th centuries in the form of the pre-cursor to the modern newspaper, called a newsbook. The first ad printed in one of these, which is available for viewing in the British Museum, was printed in a German newsbook in 1591 (Rivers, 1929). Surprise! It was about the supposed medicinal properties of a plant. Newsbooks continued to occasionally carry announcements of books or pamphlets, usually religious in nature. The early advertising historian George Burton Hotchkiss (1938) reports these probably weren't paid for, but inserted to help the sale of books that editors approved of. A newsbook called the *Moderate* for March 20–27, 1649, however, may have carried the first ad for which we know the publisher was paid (it was an ad for a lost horse).

The first newspaper to print an advertisement was either the *Mercurius Britannicus*, in 1625 (Presbrey, 1929; Wood, 1958), or London's *Weekly News* (Frederick, 1925), in 1632. Throughout the 1600s, posters and handbills continued to be the main media used for advertising (Hotchkiss, 1938). However, it's important to recognize that none of these early print messages were called "advertisements." That term wasn't used until 1655. Before that they were called "advices," a term that had previously replaced the term "siquis" or "siquis bill." This term came from ancient Rome, where announcements and notices often began with the words "Si quis," meaning "if anybody" or "if anyone" (Frederick, 1925; Presbrey, 1929). By 1750, 75% of the space in some British newspapers consisted of ads (Walker, 1973). It's unlikely most of these early newspapers would have survived without advertising because most people read them in coffee houses, and publishers got little of their financial support from subscribers (Wood, 1958).

The arrival of the earliest newspapers occurred about the same time as the establishment of what were called public registries. Inspired by Frenchman and essayist Michel de Montaigne, Englishmen Sir Arthur Gorges and Sir Walter Cope hoped to set up a public registry office in 1611. Here, people seeking or offering work, buying or selling goods, or making public announcements of all kinds would register their offers and requests, and copies would be distributed to branch offices. Such registries and accompanying periodicals were successfully established by Parisian Théophraste Renaudot in 1630, Englishman Henry Walker in 1649, and Marchmont Nedham in 1657 (Presbrey, 1929). To disseminate this information more widely, Renaudot created the first French newspaper in 1631, which he called *La Gazette* (named after the unit of currency he'd discovered in Italy, the *gazetta*) (Tungate, 2007). Some historians have suggested that the public registry might reasonably be considered the forerunner of the modern advertising agency, since they accepted and circulated advertising (Wood, 1958).

Magazines were the next periodical medium to arrive, although they were unimportant as an advertising medium for another 200 years. What is considered to be the first magazine was *Robinson Crusoe* author Daniel Defoe's *The Review*, in 1704. In 1741, the first issue of Andrew Bradford's *The American Magazine, or a Monthly View of the Political State of the British Colonies* was mailed out. Neither of these magazines carried advertising (Foster, 1967). As Wood (1958, p. 84) notes: "What magazines there were carried no advertising, or little of any account, and were not to run advertising for another half century. Magazines did not become major advertising media until the late years of the nineteenth century."

How About Early Modern Comparative Advertising?

Describing both the advertising and creative expression of this period, Wood (1958, p. 75) reports that some criers resorted to aggressively confrontational comparisons:

> Advertisers shouted until the veins stood out on their necks, or simpered delicately of insinuated delights. Hysterical denunciation of rival peddlers choked some with indignation. Other advertisers ignored their competition. The purpose, matter, manner, approach, tone, often the product, has changed little since the eighteenth century.

We also see the use of comparative messages for a reason that became important during the next period and that still exists today—to address the continuing problems of counterfeiting, intellectual property piracy, and other types of thievery. The use of printers' and publishers' marks on books, called *colophons* or bookplates today, began around 1440. "Originally derived from printers' shop signs and intended to be mainly decorative, they soon evolved to become proprietary identification marks of origin to combat the frequent book piracy of this period" (Diamond, 1975, p. 883). One of the most famous early printers, Aldus Manutius the Venetian, had serious problems with competitors infringing on his dolphin and anchor trademark as early as 1518 (Greenberg, 1951). As Aldus pointed out:

> But they have so managed, that any person who is in the least acquainted with the books of our production, can not fail to observe that this is an impudent fraud. For the head of the dolphin is turned to the left, whereas that of ours is well known to be turned to the right. (as cited in Rivers, 1929, p. 31)

The orb and cross design—discovered in the Great Pyramid at Giza (Diamond, 1975)—was also popular during this period for its use in colophons. Do a Google search for "Nabisco logo" and you'll see an example of the orb and cross that's currently in use and virtually unchanged from hundreds, if not thousands, of years ago. Look for it on your next Oreo cookie, too.

Advertisers of quack nostrums and patent medicines, with limited patent protections, often confronted the problem of counterfeiters during the early 1700s. They aggressively defended their brands and directly attacked their competitors with comparative ads that warned consumers to avoid competitors' products and the shops where they were sold. For example, in 1717 a newspaper ad for a medicinal elixir called "Specifick Tincture" warned consumers that not only would the famous and competitive "Anodine Necklace" (claimed to be composed of beads made from dead people's sculls) fail to cure their STDs or "pox" (Walker, 1973), it was even made by papists! Warnings about counterfeits also turned up in an ad found by historian Thomas Herbert Russell (1910, p. 80) for an early dentifrice: "Most Excellent and Approved Dentifrices to scour and cleanse the Teeth, making them white as Ivory, preserves from the Toothache. . . . The reader is desired to beware of counterfeits" (published in the *Mercurius Politicus*, Dec. 20, 1660).

This famous quotation from British essayist Samuel Johnson also suggests comparative ads were common in the mid-1700s. "In an advertisement it is allowed to every man to speak well of himself, but I know not why he should assume the privilege of censuring his neighbour. He may proclaim his own virtue or skill, but ought not to exclude others from the same pretensions" (cited in Rivers, 1929, p. 60). Not only is there other historical evidence to suggest comparative ads were fairly common, we even have an example of what today we'd call a "comparative advertising war." An ad published in the *London Daily Courant* for January 11, 1705, provides some of the copy (including an obvious puff) from one of these newspaper attacks. The ad is for "Right Venetian Strops" and mentions "the many false shams and ridiculous pretenses, as 'original,' etc., that are almost every day published to promote the sale of counterfeits, and to lessen the great and truly wonderful fame of the *Venetian Strops*, which are most certainly the best in the world" (Presbrey, 1929, p. 66). The Venetian Strops ad was a direct, comparative response to one published by a competitor the prior week, which had proclaimed the following:

> Since so many upstarts do daily publish one thing or other to counterfeit the original strops, for setting razors, penknives, lancets, etc., upon, and pretend them to be most excellent; the first author of the said strops, does hereby testify that all such sort of things are only made in imitation of the true ones which are permitted to be sold by no one but Mr. Shipton, at John's Coffee House, in Exchange Alley, as hath been often mentioned in the Gazettes, to prevent people being further imposed upon. (as cited in Hess, 1922, p. 215)

LATE MODERN PERIOD

Advertising in many countries during the 19th century was encouraged by the continued migration of rural inhabitants to the growing cities, the Industrial Revolution's mass production of consumer goods, geographic and social mobility, the spread of consumer culture, and the continued rise of the newspaper. Concentration of production capacity in greater volumes stimulated the development of more efficient methods of distribution to deliver the goods to consumers. Along with the growth of distribution came the greater use of advertising to create awareness of the availability of these goods.

As with the introduction of printing with moveable type to Europe in the previous period, much of the advertising and media-related progress in the 19th century is also explained by advancements in printing technology (Beard, 2016a). Rotation presses and the halftone process enabled cheaper production and pictorial advertisements (Ciarlo, 2011). Outdoor advertising surpassed mere wooden signs and painted messages in many cities around the world, thanks to the lithography printing process (Foster, 1967) and, in the late 1800s, electricity.

The old street criers, such as the "coster-monger" (fruit seller), could still be found in the streets of London during this period (Hindley, 1884). In fact, there were so many criers in London, and they were so obnoxiously loud, people complained and there was an attempt to ban them. As Hindley (p. 152) writes:

> In our own days there has been legislation for the benefit of tender ears; and there are now penalties, with police constables to enforce them, against "All persons blowing any horn or using any other noisy instrument, for the purpose of calling persons together, or of announcing any show or entertainment, or for the purpose of hawking, selling, distributing, or collecting any article, or of obtaining money or alms."

To help merchants avoid paying taxes for newspaper advertising in England, many other forms of street advertising began to appear. Sampson (1874) colorfully describes the profusion of signs, billboards, sandwich men, sidewalk ads, and advertising processions of London in the first half of the 19th century:

> It was an anarchical melee. Marauding bill posters, "external paper hangers," descended nightly on the city, plastering their signs on every available surface, whether the wall, the sidewalk, or the door of a householder. They vied with each other in happy desecration, racing for the best spots, defacing the work of their rivals, overplastering what they could not tear down. A law was passed in 1839 making it an offense to paste bills on property without permission of the owner. The law could not be enforced. . . . Dynamic signs came with the static. The sandwich man was invented, a man walking with placards attached front and back. This led to processions of sandwich men, each carrying part of the message, like a row of Burma-Shave advertisements going by a stationery motorist in the twentieth-century United States. Floats of a kind were devised, huge mockups of articles for sale paraded through the streets. Inspired advertisers hired troops of derelicts, dressed them in uniforms, and marched a seedy burlesque of the Guards or a company of foot through the streets as an advertising scheme, until a law was passed forbidding such unseemly conduct. (as cited in Wood, 1958, p. 117)

Display advertising, as opposed to what was called the "want-ad style," appeared in the form of theatrical bills, handbills, direct-mail circulars, and in novels early in this period in Great Britain (Presbrey, 1929). However, newspaper ads in Great Britain, Germany, and the United States rarely included illustrations beyond simple woodcuts, even after presses and engraving processes made it easily possible (Ciarlo, 2011). Why? As Presbrey (p. 96) reports, most publishers simply regarded setting type in different sizes or breaking column rules to be a nuisance. They doubted whether this and other forms of "vulgar screeching" by advertisers was worth the trouble of accommodating their creative aspirations. Bold display advertising was common in France, however, in the early 1850s. Mass circulation and penny papers, born in the United States in 1825, encouraged greater use of advertising whenever and wherever they appeared (Ciarlo).

Often exquisitely engraved bill heads and shop bills were still being used to wrap purchases, record transactions, and for public posting during this period (Laird, 1998). Job printers also competed with periodical media by creating marketing ephemera with high-quality typesetting, engraving, and lithography. There are some 40 important collections of these worldwide, with artifacts originating as long ago as the 1700s (Beard, 2017). In 1890s Germany, chromolithographic printing encouraged the widespread use of posters, trade cards, and millions of collectible advertising stamps called *reklamemarken* (Ciarlo, 2011).

Creatively, many advertisers in Great Britain, Germany, and the United States during the 19th century said they favored informational and dignified ads intended to generate sales directly or create brand awareness and were critical of the "circus-style," with its link to the period's "bombast and ballyhoo" creativity. However, the professional tension between these advocates of rational advertising and the spectacular advertising designed to attract attention and trigger emotional responses continued throughout this period (Beard, 2004; Ciarlo, 2011). By 1865, retail advertisers had also discovered the emotional value of creating a sense of urgency (Laird, 1998). Many historians have also concluded that, by the end of the 19th century, U.S. advertisers had redefined abundance and were successfully encouraging consumers to define themselves by way of the products and brands they consumed (Fox, 1984; Leach, 1994; McGovern, 2006).

Despite our goal of avoiding the Americanization paradigm limitation, it's important to acknowledge that some North American advertising pioneers clearly were influential toward the end of this period. Unfortunately, one of them was named P. T. Barnum (1810–1891), and late-19th- and early-20th-century advertisers and their agents spent years trying to get out from beneath the "Barnumesque" shadow he cast over them and their efforts to establish advertising as a serious and dignified profession. Some of the more respectable American figures during this period included George Rowell, John E. Powers, Nathaniel C. Fowler, and Charles Austin Bates. There were, however, important pioneers and thought leaders rising to fame elsewhere, such as France's Charles-Louis Havas and Germany's Rudolf Cronau. During the second half of the 19th century, the use of international advertising campaigns for products such as Germany's Liebig's Extract of Meat and Great Britain's Pears' Soap became common.

In the year 1825, a landmark event in newspaper and advertising history occurred. "The New York *Gazette* imported from Germany a steam-powered press that could print 2,000 newspapers an hour. Such a capacity demanded a much larger circulation and a cheaper price than that of rival papers. In turn, more advertising was required" (Foster, 1967, p. 40). Soaring ad revenues had a positive effect on newspapers and their transition from political organs to commercial and journalistic enterprises (Laird, 1998). At the same time, many manufacturers of consumer goods in the United States were trying to create national markets and gain control of their distribution channels from jobbers and merchants (Beard, 2011). Still, many 19th-century businessmen in Europe and the United States remained skeptical regarding the respectability and value of advertising (Ciarlo, 2011; Laird, 1998; Marchand, 1985; Wood, 1958).

Late Modern Comparative Advertising

Although there isn't much in the historical literature regarding what business decision makers of the day thought about comparative advertising, we do have influential American advertising pioneer George Rowell's advice regarding how advertisers should deal with "rivals." These recommendations for the writing of advertising copy appeared in Rowell's *American Newspaper Reporter* on November 20, 1871, which he titled "Principles of Advertising":

> Honesty is by all odds the very strongest point which can be crowded into an advertisement. Come right down with the facts, boldly, firmly, unflinchingly. Say directly what it is, what it has done, what it will do. Leave out all ifs. Do not claim too much, but what you do claim must be claimed without the smallest shadow of weakness. Do not say "we are convinced that," "we believe that" or "ours is among the best" or "equal to any" or "surpassed by none." Say flatly "the best," or say nothing. Do not refer to rivals. Ignore every person, place or thing except yourself, your address and your article. (as cited in Presbrey, 1929, p. 276)

If you directly asked them, most advertisers at the time would acknowledge that what they called "knocking" copy was all-too-common during this period. As a *Printers' Ink* (advertising's most important trade journal for approximately 75 years) contributor notes:

> In the early days of the art an advertisement was the voice of a single individual proclaiming the merits of his own goods, often coupled with a warning against similar goods sold by competitors. This one-man advertisement is still the commonest form of publicity, but among advertisers nowadays, the knocking of a competitor is considered not only bad form, but bad business. ("Broad-gauge Advertising," 1906, p. 30)

However, it turns out that aggressive comparative advertising was not uncommon in the 19th century, at least in the United States. Toward the end of this period, for instance, manufacturers in the highly competitive and constantly innovating agricultural equipment field frequently went after each other in their print ads in what were called the "Reaper Wars" and "Binder Wars." One of the most antagonistic of these combatants was American inventor and businessman Cyrus McCormick. As historian Pamela Laird (1998, p. 37) notes: "His advertisements attacked his competitors by implication and even by name, which also paralleled patent medicine purveyors' assaults on medical doctors' snobbery, faulty treatments, and expenses."

The Wisconsin Historical Society (2017) further describes the combative nature of McCormick and his competitors' ads: "After each new field trial, the victorious manufacturer boasted of its latest triumph in hastily printed posters that it distributed locally. Losers sometimes produced posters as well, condemning the judges, test conditions and the products and business practices of their rivals." See the example from the Society's collection with its "Caution!" headline in Figure 1.1.

This period's trade cards also reveal many examples of comparative claims and attacks. Merchants often distributed their cards in sets and as premiums, with the goal of attracting customers back to the store so they

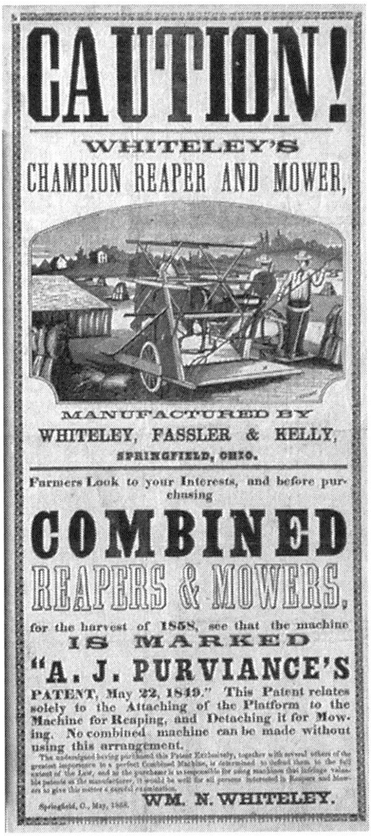

Figure 1.1. Whiteley, Fassler, & Kelly Advertising Handbill (1858). ***Used with permission of Wisconsin Historical Society (WHI-2623).***

could complete their sets. Wood (1958, p. 237) describes the aggressively comparative nature of one set, which purportedly "showed the horrible results which would accrue if people turned to other beverages than the Great Atlantic & Pacific Tea Company's tea and coffee." Sadly, a search for these comparative trade cards failed to uncover them, and it's likely we'll never know just how horrible those results might have been. Two trade cards from the Victorian Trade Card Collection at the Paul J. Gutman Library, however, are shown in Figures 1.2 and 1.3. The Chadwick's includes a claim of superiority over all other brands and the Howard, Goodrich, and Pierce card employs a tactic that became common during the next period—an attack on the truthfulness of competitors' advertising ("NO MATTER what others may advertise . . .").

CONTEMPORARY PERIOD

The full-service advertising agency achieved unprecedented levels of size and importance during the first half of the 20th century in North America and throughout much of Europe. Although many historians emphasize the contributions of entrepreneurs in the United States to the continued professionalization of advertising and agencies, they also point to the influence of other international figures—such as France's Marcel Bleustein-Blanchet, China's Carl Crow, Spain's Pedro Prat Gaballi, and Australia's George Herbert Patterson (Tungate, 2007).

National advertising expanded significantly in many countries and revolutionary, new products appeared almost continuously. Other factors contributing to growth during the first three decades of the 20th century include single-price selling, the development of department stores and supermarkets, nationally branded products, and mail-order merchandising (Church, 1999). The period is also distinguished by the application of marketing research and the social and behavioral sciences to marketing and advertising planning and practice. Advertisers in Germany (Ciarlo, 2011), Great Britain, France (Howard, 2008), and the United States also faced major backlashes against advertising's quantity and qualitative content, as they and their agencies continued the "creep" and "clutter" tactics of earlier periods, leading to messages being placed on almost every possible surface. This period is also distinguished by the emergence of magazines, radio, and then television as major national media in the United States and in some other countries.

Comparative Advertising during the Contemporary Period

Marketing and advertising became big business at the beginning of this century, especially in the United States. They spawned numerous now-defunct trade journals, many of which can still be found today in dusty, bound collec-

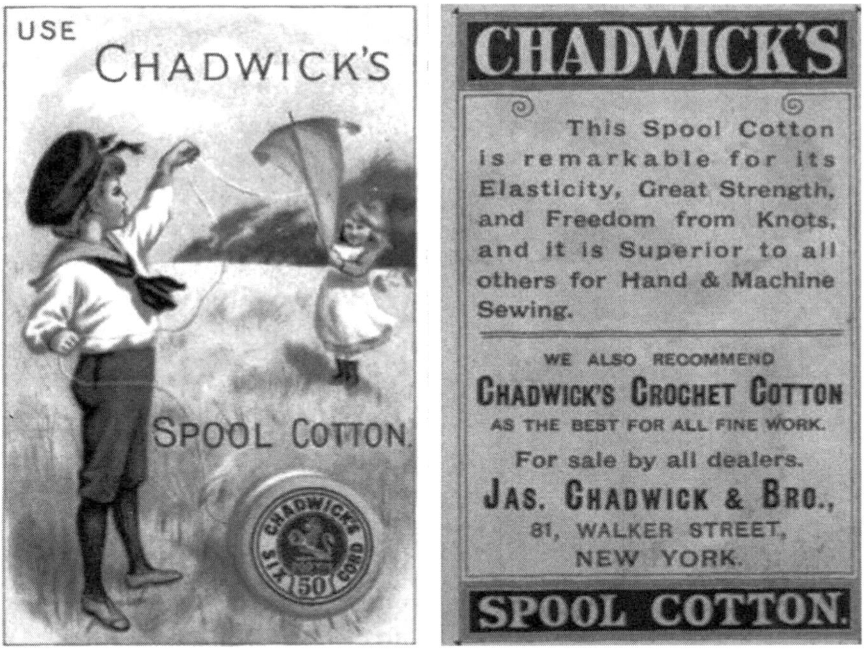

Figure 1.2. Chadwick's Trade Card (Victorian Era). ***Image from the Paul J. Gutman Library, Thomas Jefferson University. Available at http://digitalcollections.philau.edu/cdm/compoundobject/collection/TCards/id/1527/rec/1.***

tions in large city and university libraries or on microfiche and microfilm. Consequently, we know a lot about what the media, industry pundits, advertisers, and other business decision makers thought about comparative advertising, especially toward the latter part of this period.

Problems for Publishers

As the use of comparative advertising expanded during this period and the next, especially in the United States, it's important to understand just how serious a problem it became for newspaper and magazine publishers. Some industry observers at the time suggested that comparative advertising might represent a profitable opportunity for the period's advertising-supported media, as dueling advertisers purchased increasing amounts of space and time to run attacks and counterattacks. For example, in 1901, tobacco monopolist James Buchanan Duke (who created an endowment in honor of his family that still provides funds for Duke University today) acquired a British firm and began a raid on the British tobacco industry, with attacks on two British

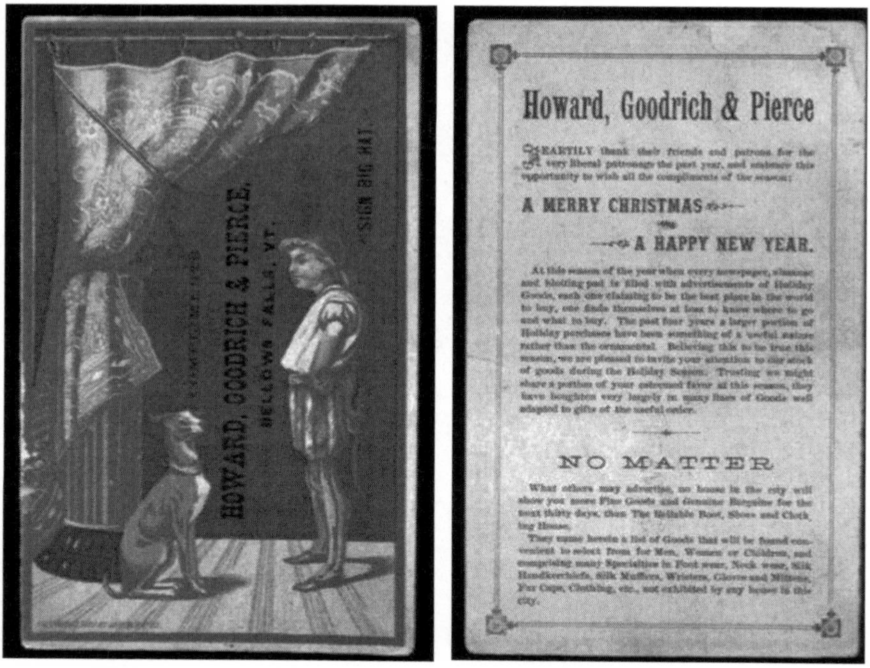

Figure 1.3. Howard, Goodrich, and Pierce Trade Card (Victorian Era). ***Image from the Paul J. Gutman Library, Thomas Jefferson University. Available at http://digitalcollections.philau.edu/cdm/compoundobject/collection/TCards/id/674/rec/1.***

cigarette brands. John S. Grey (1902, p. 16), a frequent contributor to *Printers' Ink*, reports publishers were critical of Duke's aggressive comparative attacks—e.g., "Even the English newspapers that are carrying the advertising of the contending parties are criticizing it editorially." However, as Grey also writes: "It is a golden harvest for the advertising agents and also for the newspaper and periodical publishers" (p. 16).

By the early 1930s, however, publishers and media industry observers in the United States were in near-unanimous agreement that comparative advertising represented a serious business and regulatory problem. Publishers complained bitterly throughout this period about protests from advertisers and their frequent threats to withdraw their own advertising over a competitor's "dishonest" attack (Beard & Nye, 2011). You'll be reading much more about publishers' efforts to deal with comparative advertising in Chapter 4.

Perceptions of Competition

As we've already discovered, whether manufacturers or merchants had any competitors was a motivating factor in the earliest uses of comparisons or even attacks in advertising. As this period began, a majority of business executives and managers actually said they believed competitors should be ignored. As one wrote at the time, the businessman

> cannot rule the weather and the crops, but he can attack the items of neglect of business, extravagance, speculation and incompetence. And, when these black beasts are considered beside the relatively unimportant one of competition, the average business man would better devote his time, energy and advertising space to relentless war upon them, leaving his rivals to their own devices. ("Is it Really Worthwhile...," 1902, p. 36)

Another summarizes the view concisely: "Talk success in your advertising, ignore competitors and make your offering of vital interest to the people whose trade you seek" ("Talk Success in Your Advertising . . . ," 1903, p. 27). Influential copywriter Claude Hopkins (1930, p. 20) perhaps summarized this belief best, especially as applied to advertising: "Rule 1 in all salesmanship courses I have studied is: Never attack a competitor."

Not only did many business decision makers believe competitors should be ignored, many actually agreed that competitors could be helpful. A *Printers' Ink* author summarized this view in his description of an advertising war between two steamship companies. "It dawned upon both lines that it was work meet for even two advertisers to educate the local public to travel more by water. The patronage was not fixed; it could be increased as the public came to understand the pleasures and the benefits of a trip by steamer" (Pickett, 1910, p. 29).

Oddly enough, while growing markets and the potential for increasing the number of customers and their consumption encouraged some businessmen to view competition as unimportant, it encouraged just the opposite belief among many others (Beard, 2011). During this period, there were numerous outbreaks of comparative advertising in U.S. markets characterized by rapidly growing demand. For instance, despite a steady increase in cigarette consumption during the 1920s, R. J. Reynolds, Liggett & Myers, American Tobacco, and P. Lorillard fought an aggressive and damaging advertising war, followed by something even worse—a price war. As described by trade journal *Sales Management* ("How the 'Big Four' Cigarette Advertisers . . . ," 1929, p. 592): "The scramble for increasing shares of the rich cigarette lode has been attended by great advertising campaigns and a retail price war of exceptional sharpness. . . . By 1928 all four companies were in the thick of an advertising melee such as has not often been witnessed."

On the other hand, although there are many examples of comparative advertising use in expanding markets, many advertisers and industry observers who talked about advertising and competition mentioned marketing situations characterized by zero-sum competition. In a zero-sum competitive situation, growth is static and each competitor in a product or service market can only increase sales or market share by stealing them from one or more of the other competitors. For example, in 1939, a Pepsodent vice president described the zero-sum competition he saw among the various brands of toothpaste:

> Years ago when there was very little competition in the dentifrice field, Pepsodent's advertising could be more general. At that time Pepsodent meant 'toothpaste.' Now, the advertising must make Pepsodent mean a specific kind of toothpaste with features not possessed by other brands. . . . Our advertising, therefore, necessarily must be competitive. . . . Every time one brand of dentifrice shows a gain some other brand shows losses. (as cited in Luckman, 1939, pp. 15, 18)

A steady stream of new and improved products during the early 20th century offered another reason why a handful of advertisers concluded that competition—and, in some cases, comparative advertising—weren't necessarily bad things. As one executive observed at the time: "No one will deny the right of the maker of an improved article to call very special attention to the addition which puts his product in a class by itself. Such advertising is really another form of 'competition'" (Leach, 1924, pp. 137–138). Industry leader Joel Benton (1932, p. 53) similarly wrote in *Printers' Ink*: "When a mechanical advance is made in a product there is no reason why the advertiser should not make the most of it, compared with the old-fashioned way. That's the kind of competition we want."

Others, however, complained that such highly competitive advertising on behalf of new entries and against existing ones encouraged a type of comparative approach they disdainfully called "unselling." *Printers' Ink* (1925, p. 144) summarizes this view:

> We fall into the habit of quoting these names as standards, each in its field, until some competitor, tired of having a name flung in his face, says with a touch of easy tolerance "Steinway might have been the leader *once*," or "Victor *used* to be," or "Ivory Soap—you're talking of yesterday." And the first gun is fired in the campaign of unselling.

Printers' Ink quoted an executive on the same topic 10 years later: "We believe that good salesmanship constitutes the selling of one's own product rather than the unselling of another's, although we may be entirely wrong in this" (as cited in "Battle of the Basements," 1935, p. 81).

The Substitution Menace!

As most markets expanded during the first two decades of the 20th century, manufacturers faced the free-rider problem *Printers' Ink* dubbed "The Substitution Menace." After building primary demand with their advertising, these manufacturers would discover often-inferior brands substituted for theirs—sometimes inadvertently, but often purposely—by retailers. One advertiser believed advertising itself was the cause of his substitution problem:

> Our hope of large future growth, general distribution through national advertising, volume production and lowered manufacturing costs is based on the home market. How are we to reach that market effectively with consumer advertising, when advertising attracts cheap competition which takes our market away from us about as rapidly as we create it? ("Why We Stopped Advertising . . . ," 1925, p. 104)

Many others, however, proposed that advertising was the solution for the competitive problem of substitution. Kraft Cheese Co. President John H. Kraft (1927, 142) was an advocate of such brand-building advertising:

> It did not take long for our competitors to follow our lead in bringing out a foil-wrapped 5-pound package resembling ours. . . . We avoided saying "Insist on the Kraft label" or "Beware of Substitutes." We felt that the buying public had been surfeited with that sort of tarnished warning until it had lost its force. So we try in our copy to lead the reader into realizing what our name on a package of cheese stands for.

Printers' Ink editor C.B. Larrabee (1923, p. 112) agreed: "When you get a new idea, broadcast it. In this way you steal a march on your competitors and put it up to them to stamp themselves as imitators."

Why Not Light Up a Lucky?

One especially significant comparative campaign during this period can be traced directly to one of modern advertising's most colorful characters—American Tobacco Company's George Washington Hill. The obsessively competitive Hill is remembered as "the most demanding client in Madison Avenue history" (Meyers, 1984, p. 27). He was also the inspiration for one of advertising's most memorable fictional characters—Evan Llewellyn Evans, played by Sydney Greenstreet in the film version of Frederick Wakeman's novel, *The Hucksters*. Watkins (1953) included one of Hill's "Reach for a Lucky Instead of a Sweet" ads in his book, *The 100 Greatest Advertisements*. The campaign is also ranked 60th among *Ad Age's* (1999) "Top 100 Advertising Campaigns of the 20th Century."

Hill's "Reach for a Lucky . . ." advertising campaign is almost universally despised for being among the first to aggressively encourage women to smoke cigarettes. Adding to the campaign's infamy are beliefs it achieved its goal by capitalizing on the cultural consequences of the suffrage and early feminist movements, while simultaneously exploiting women's fears of gaining weight. However, it also represents one of the first examples of a cross-category comparative advertising campaign. Instead of attacking competitors in his own product category, cigarettes, Hill favorably compared smoking Lucky Strikes to the negative consequences of consuming "sweets."

Most advertising histories fail to capture the sweets industry's outrage over Hill's apparent attack (Beard & Klyeuva, 2010). As one observer notes: "Mr. Connolly [editor of *Candy World*] has done everything but call out the marines. Among others he telephoned and wrote to are: American Tobacco Company, National Better Business Bureau, Federal Trade Commission, Cocoa Bean Brokers, National Confectioners Association and the National Broadcasting Bureau" (Goode, 1928, p. 190). The conflict initially focused on the meaning of the word "sweet," which Hill had evidently meant to refer to anything sweet, such as cakes, candy, and preserves. However, as *Printers' Ink* ("Lucky Strike and the Candy Industry . . . ," 1928, p. 10) reported at the time: "the candy industry contends that the word 'Sweet,' in the public's mind means one thing, and only one thing, candy."

Most historians and industry observers at the time agreed the goal of the "Reach for a Lucky . . ." campaign was to increase sales by targeting women and encouraging them to smoke. Two decades after Hill launched the campaign, Vincent Riggio—a Sicilian-born barber, sales executive, and Hill's friend and successor as president at American Tobacco—told *Printers' Ink*: "Many in marketing today believe that campaign created more women smokers than any other single promotional effort" (as cited in Stephen, 1948, p. 70). On the other hand, Hill directly linked his attack on sweets to his belief in what many business decision makers at the time referred to as "the New Competition." As one advertiser describes it: "Competition today takes on broader dimensions to those manufacturers and retailers who look below the surface. It doesn't do the house furnishing store any good if a family spends more than it needs to at the grocers and less than it ought to at the house furnishing store" (Ross, 1924, p. 10).

While the "Reach for a Lucky . . ." campaign may have been a successful attempt by Hill to obtain his share of a growing market of female smokers by exploiting the implications of the New Competition, the goal of this early cross-category comparative campaign was also to find a unique appeal or message strategy to differentiate Luckies from competitors (Beard & Klyeuva, 2010). Hill explains the strategy:

> Naturally, I am deeply interested in watching the new developments this new competition is going to bring, both from the standpoint of my own business and from the standpoint of other businesses, but it is inevitable that it has come to remain and that it will be an increasing factor in the competition not only of one industry against another, *but in the competition of one business to maintain itself in a highly competitive market.* (as cited in Hughes, 1928, p. 737 [italics added])

The influence of George Washington Hill's comparative tactics may have even traveled across the Atlantic. As one industry observer wrote at the time: "The anti-sweet advertising in America by Lucky Strike, which has been the subject of several articles in *Printers' Ink*, may or may not have inspired some recent copy developments here" (Russell, 1929, p. 12). A popular and extensively advertised brand in Great Britain at the time was called "Black Cat Cigarettes." After packaging two additional cigarettes with the period's standard 10, a competitive brand called "Plus Two" ran an ad featuring a cartoon homeowner scowling out his window at two cats yowling in the moonlight. As Russell (p. 12) points out in his article: "It may have been an accident. Let us hope so. But the target of the awakened sleeper are distinctly and indubitably *black cats*!"

During the Great Depression

At the outset of the Great Depression, there were many signs advertisers were growing more desperate and, consequently, more combative and comparative with their advertising. As advertising historian Roland Marchand (1985, p. 304) points out: "Depression advertisers were not only willing to become more competitive; they were also prepared to become more undignified." A *Printers' Ink* editorialist also suggests that problems with comparative advertising continued throughout the Depression years of the 1930s: "Advertisers of a considerable list of commodities . . . seem to be outdoing each other in unfair, unethical and even untruthful competitive claims. This sort of thing, to state the case with great restraint, is bad for the advertiser. It is equally bad or worse for the publisher" ("Competitive Claims," 1936, p. 8). In reference to an outbreak of comparative advertising wars in several U.S. industries, *Business Week* similarly notes: "With a flash of claims and counter-claims, makers of mayonnaise and salad dressing, steel automobile bodies and wood-and-steel bodies are skirmishing in print, to the slight bewilderment of the readers, and the great glee of the purveyors of white space" ("Word War," 1933, p. 21).

Still, faith in a constructive role for advertising held firm throughout the Depression, and some contributors to *Printers' Ink* continued to argue in favor of mainly constructive and mostly noncomparative advertising. *Print-*

ers' Ink columnist "Groucho" (1934, p. 57) condemned comparative advertising:

> But when several kinds of wire nails are sold in a hardware store, the maker of brand A begins to worry about the sales of brands B and C. . . . Beware of "others"! Don't take a chance of your hencoop falling by building with "ordinary" nails! . . . Advertising is all set to leap ahead, if it can get rid of this nonsense. You've got to chum with competitors as well as customers to have good times.

An advertising executive similarly explains what happened when he abandoned a comparative campaign: "We threw out all comparison and began to confine ourselves to direct statement of what our material would do. . . . Competitors have appeared—new as well as old—and they are all doing a satisfactory volume of business" (McGarry, 1931, p. 28).

This period, however, also produced what is widely considered to be a breakthrough comparative ad, both then and now—adman J. Sterling Getchell's "Look at All Three" for the Plymouth automotive brand. The original ad ran in April of 1932 as a full page in many big-city newspapers and several contemporary industry observers have acknowledged its significance (historyofadvertising, 2018). Author Julian L. Watkins devoted a chapter to the ad in his book, *The One Hundred Greatest Advertisements: Who Wrote Them and What They Did.* President of ad agency Cunningham & Walsh Inc. Anthony Chevins (1975, p. 32) referred to the ad as the "grand-daddy of all specific comparative ads."

Beliefs in favor of ignoring competitors and criticisms of the Depression's comparative advertising continued into the 1940s and 1950s. A J. Walter Thompson ad agency executive revealingly spoke for many when he wrote: "if you study the record you'll find that many an advertiser who turned from quality in favor of black, dirty headlines and throat cutting policies came to rue the day" (Stone, 1951, p. 130). "Aesop Glim" (*Printers' Ink* columnist George Laflin Miller) agreed: "Old Aesop Glim believes that—more often than not—it is sound practice to ignore your competition. . . . Tell your own story—exclusively, positively—give your copy sound construction, sequence and conviction—and you'll get your share of the market" (1945, p. 25).

An Early Development in Europe

In the early 1950s, an important court case involving the French-language version of *Reader's Digest* highlighted the substantially different path the Europeans were going to take when it came to comparative advertising. The magazine's publishers had hired a research company to conduct a survey of magazine popularity. They then compiled the findings into a report—which named 14 competitive titles and showed that *Digest* was the most popular—and sent it to 200 advertising agencies. The other magazines sued, arguing that the survey, while purported to be scientific, actually wasn't, and that the report sent to the agencies was, in fact, a "commercial promotion" (that is, an ad).

What's more important and revealing about this case is the Belgian Court's ruling that "A competitor has the right to insist that one not speak of him, even to speak the truth, in such a way as to harm his future business" (Digges, 1953, p. 38). By extension, the ruling implied that publishers had a right to privacy when it came to their circulation numbers and nobody else had the right to say anything about them without their permission. Things were, and are, far different in the United States and this ruling helps explain some of the differences in comparative advertising use in the United States versus many other countries for the next 40 years.

Comparative Advertising Outcomes, Strategies, and Tactics

Among the first beliefs to emerge regarding what the outcomes of a comparative ad or campaign might be was that they were very effective for attracting attention and creating awareness. Advertisers and industry observers, however, also often acknowledged that the competitor mentioned in the ad would probably benefit in the same way. As suggested by *Printers' Ink* in an editorial devoted to a comparative ad that mentioned and actually complimented a competitor: "One danger which a compliment shares with a knock is that of informing the ignorant of the existence of the competitor" ("The Little Schoolmaster's Classroom," 1928, p. 208). And as *Printers' Ink's* Aesop Glim (1947, p. 74) warned comparative advertisers some 20 years later: "In a left-handed way, you are inviting some of your prospects . . . to look into your competitor's proposition."

By the 1930s, many advertisers had decided that comparative advertising could also be informative. After all, if a shocking comparison got people's attention and created awareness, then there was a good chance they'd also learn something and remember it later. On the other hand, many others during this period expressed the belief that comparative advertising would cause not informed consumers, but confused ones. One problem was the inevitably conflicting claims in comparative ads—how, for instance, could everybody be "the best"? Another was the simple belief that many readers didn't pay enough attention to an ad to remember who the sponsor actually was. This was, of course, quite consistent with the belief that mentioning competitors and their products and brands just created awareness for them.

As one might expect, given the many concerns and criticisms about comparative advertising during the first half of the 20th century, the majority of advertisers' views regarding its believability were negative. Comparative advertising's lack of believability was linked to three frequently mentioned problems and criticisms—(a) implications or outright claims that all an advertiser's competitors were dishonest in their advertising, (b) blanket condemnations that everyone else's products were inferior, and (c) that comparative advertising threatened the believability of not just advertising in specific industries and product categories, but all advertising (Beard, 2013a). Many publishers and media managers, in fact, shared the prevalent belief that comparative advertising was responsible for damage to the believability of all advertising.

Advertisers and industry observers also overwhelmingly agreed during much of this period that comparative ads would likely cause negative attitudes toward the advertiser and brand. Some identified the cause of these negative attitudes as backlash, linked, in turn, to consumer perceptions that mentioning a competitor was bad sportsmanship. Advertising attorney Morton J. Simon (1951, p. 81) captured this view in an *Advertising Agency* piece about the legal implications of what he referred to as "acrimonious advertising warfare" and disparagement: "Someone has said: 'I hate the man who builds his name, On the ruins of another's fame.'" There was a small minority, on the other hand, who proposed that comparative ads could reflect positively on their sponsors, but with a *caveat*—the advertising's tone had to be positive and not excessively negative.

The majority of advertisers and industry observers during this period also agreed the ultimate problem with a comparative ad is that it would fail to cause a sale. One *Printers' Ink* contributor summarizes this view in the following way: "There is no need to refrain from attacking a competitor, directly or indirectly, on ethical grounds. It is enough if you once get it clearly in your head that it doesn't pay you" (Hitchcock, 1927, p. 152). Some even argued that along with negative effects on attitudes toward individual brands and their sales, comparative ads could damage the sales of entire industries or product categories. Regarding an especially early and vicious advertising war between Calumet baking powder and other brands marketed by a "trust," which included the equally popular Royal brand, a *Printers' Ink* author notes: "Can one be blamed if the suspicion gets around, and gathers force with the passage of years, that all baking powders are bad, and that the less one uses any of them the better it will be for his health. . . . What can such a condition be laid to except this persistent campaign of attack and counterattack?" (Hill, 1910, p. 24). Note the description of "Cheap Baking Powder" in Figure 1.4's example from the Calumet campaign.

Advertisers and industry observers offered few strategic or tactical recommendations regarding what might contribute to the effectiveness of comparative advertising during the first three decades of the 20th century, probably because so few advertisers had anything favorable to say about it. However, one advertiser, in an open forum on the topic, offered a recommenda-

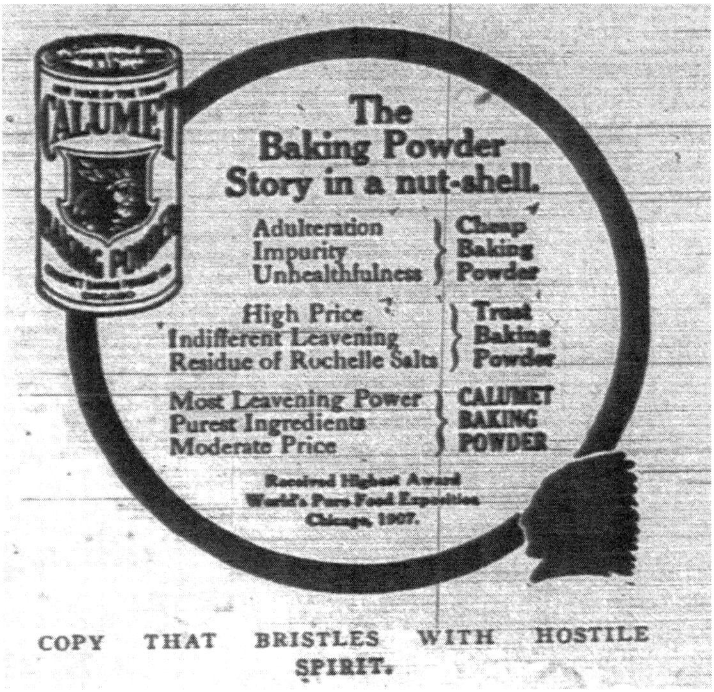

Figure 1.4. Calumet Baking Power Advertisement (1910). ***Hill, F.T. (1910). Attacks upon competitors shown to be poor policy,*** **Printers' Ink,** ***71(1), 23–25.***

tion that would remain consistent to present day—that a well-substantiated comparative claim made about a product of superior quality would be both believable and effective. As he declared: "Gentlemen, what better and more convincing campaign arguments can I possibly assemble than that I build my product with the greatest possible care, out of the best materials, and that my competitors do not?" (Leach, 1924, p. 137).

Many critics of comparative advertising similarly linked its ineffectiveness to advertisers' frequent failures to mention salient consumer benefits or claims in reference to them. Much of this problem, however, was also associated with the problem that first appeared during the previous period—that of attacking what competitors said in their advertising instead of the features or benefits of their products or services. Adman William Wisdom (1930, p. 114) perfectly summarizes this view: "In drawing attention to his competitor's advertising he is keeping the competitive product before their eyes and omitting to tell them how good his product is and what makes it good. . . . If you and I go out to shoot rabbits and start shooting at each other, we are not going to get many rabbits."

Perhaps as a consequence of the desperate and occasionally vicious comparative advertising of the 1930s, many industry observers and decision makers also recommended limiting excessive negativity or, better yet, avoiding it altogether. Advertising executive and marketing textbook author Edward E. B. Weiss (1951, p. 39) referred to the importance of maintaining a positive tone and avoiding an audience perception of bad sportsmanship. As he wrote:

> Now it strikes me that the American public has given abundant evidence of our love of good sportsmanship. It was this national characteristic that helped make Plymouth's *Look at All Three* such an instantaneous success. Competitive rivalry, until then, had publicly displayed little sportsmanship.

A related issue that would contribute to substantial conflict over comparative advertising during the 1960s and 1970s emerged for the first time toward the end of this period. This was the belief that any reference to competitors, even indirectly, was synonymous with disparagement.

Finally, an important strategy to appear during this period in terms of a comparative ad's creativity is best defined as "opportunism." Moreover, competitors themselves were often the source of an opportunity to exploit, such as a problem or limitation with their products or services or, worse yet, some purposeful change in their marketing strategies. As the dispute over the comparative strength of all-steel versus wood-and-steel auto bodies heated up in the 1930s, for example, Chevrolet ran an ad illustrated with a cartoon elephant sitting on top of a Chevy, declaring that "if your elephant wants to ride on top, it's all right with a Chevrolet." A group of Houston, Texas, Ford dealers quickly exploited the opportunity with a tongue-in-cheek advertising response, offering a $500 reward to anyone who would take an elephant for a ride on his or her Chevrolet. Around the same time, both Chevrolet and Chrysler Corporation were quick to take comparative advertising advantage of Henry Ford's refusal to sign on to President Franklin D. Roosevelt's National Industrial Recovery Act (NIRA) automobile code during the Great Depression.

POSTMODERN PERIOD

Many marketers and their ad agencies developed increasingly fragmented approaches to market segmentation during this period, as much of the industrialized world experienced favorable economies in the 1960s and consequential increases in advertising. Advertising took a turn creatively—and to a certain extent, internationally—with the arguably short-lived "Creative Revolution" in the 1960s. By the 1980s, American-style, postmodern consumer cultures were fully in place throughout much of the industrialized world, including Spain and Italy (Arvidsson, 2003; Tungate, 2007).

A global advertising industry had fully emerged by the end of the 1970s, and during the 1980s the industry consolidated as a result of ad agency acquisitions and mergers (Beard, 2016a). The largest companies—such as the UK's Saatchi & Saatchi, Japan's Dentsu, and the United States's Young & Rubicam and Omnicom Group—evolved to become the global communications firms they are today, integrating marketing services far beyond advertising, including direct response, public relations, sales promotion, and digital marketing (Arndorfer et al., 2005; Tungate, 2007). Elsewhere, however, advertising and agencies matured more slowly, such as in the 1960s and 1970s in Brazil (Tungate) and Italy (Ciarlo, 2011). The emergence of integrated marketing communications in the 1980s, the Internet and World Wide Web, digital and mobile media, and new forms of promotions, such as "branded entertainment" and "experiential" or "engagement" marketing, substantially distinguishes the postmodern period from the earlier ones.

Two of the most important events in the history of comparative advertising occurred during this final period. First, during the 1970s, there was the U.S. Federal Trade Commission's (FTC's) initiative to encourage advertisers to "name names," which, in turn, led to the FTC's attack on industry self-regulation codes and advertising media policies that limited or even outright banned direct comparisons with identified competitors (Beard, 2012). The use of comparative advertising in the United States increased significantly during and following the 1970s. Indeed, *Advertising Age* columnist Sidney A. Diamond declared in 1978 that "Brand X now is just a historical curiosity" (p. 66). The second event occurred some 20 years later, when the EU passed Directive 97//55/EC, which established that comparative advertising should be permitted as long as it was used responsibly; that is, it was neither unfair nor misleading.

Comparative Advertising during the Post Modern Period

Perceptions of competition and positive versus negative economic conditions continued to offer explanations for attitudes in favor of or against the use of comparative advertising. In the United States, for instance, the belief that competitors should be ignored almost disappeared from industry trade journals during the second half of the 20th century. When it was mentioned, it was almost always linked to the recommendation that market leaders or major brands should avoid it. As one agency executive told *Advertising Age* ("Unsolicited Ad Idea Problems . . . ," 1975, p. 3): "We know of no psychological theory that suggests that a leader will benefit from naming a competitor." A conflicting statement, however, was offered to explain a spate of attack advertising among several business publications. One author, citing the director of communications for *Forbes*, wrote at the time: "*Business Week* carries more ads than anyone else, and when you are No. 1, you have to find somewhere to grow" (as cited in Emmrich, 1982, p. M1).

In the 1990s, the major telecommunications companies in the United States—AT&T, MCI, and Sprint—waged advertising war over expanding markets for long distance services, much like Verizon, Sprint, T-Mobile, and AT&T did throughout the second decade of the 21st century for wireless services. As one source explains: "Telecommunications usage is exploding worldwide, via new usage surging for telephone lines carrying voice, data, facsimile, cellular and wireless signals" (Fitzgerald, 1993, p. 12). Ultimately, the combatants concluded the war was futile, at least as far as long-distance services were concerned, as efforts to differentiate parity offerings merely created what one source described as "'the spinner,' something of a hybrid of a switcher and a price buyer that changes long-distance carriers as often as every three months" (Koprowski, 1995, p. 22). The major wireless carriers in the United States seemed to be heading down the same path in the mid-2010s as smartphone sales leveled off and heavy spending on comparative ad campaigns and price promotions started to eat into profits.

Many industry observers, on the other hand, linked combative or comparative advertising with zero-sum competition throughout the remainder of this period. As early as 1978, Boddewyn and Marton had already concluded that an ideal time to use comparative advertising was "when the market is static and comparison may be the ultimate weapon in order to get a bigger share of it" (p. 99). Describing a Burger King comparative campaign in the early 1980s, for instance, a source notes: "Like soft-drink companies, fast-food marketers are dealing with a slow-growth industry, where market share gains are the driving force behind any expansion" (Kreisman & Marshall, 1982, p. 1). As an auto executive similarly observes, "Each of the companies is fighting for a bigger share of a smaller pie. The key word is 'fighting.' If a customer is not going to buy our car, he's going to buy someone else's" (as cited in McClain, 1983, p. M1). In fact, comparative automotive advertising at the time became so combative, the creators of a Toyota TV spot featuring "the blowing up of a generic American station wagon" (Serafin, 1985, p. 76) missed what would seem to have been a fairly obvious thematic connection to the Japanese attack on Pearl Harbor.

Similar beliefs were expressed in the 1990s by ad agency BBDO/LA CEO Steve Hayden: "In a recession year, with everyone in a blackened mood, we'll see harsher competition because everyone's struggling for market position" (as cited in Jaben, 1992, p. 36). Again, in the highly combative auto industry, advertisers unanimously referred to the zero-sum competition they perceived to exist and consistently argued the need for product differentiation. As one industry observer noted at the time: "Nissan's out to sell 100,000 Maxima units in model year 1995, an ambitious goal in a no-growth market, outsiders say. To meet it, the carmaker will need to steal share from competitors" (Garcia, 1994, p. 2). At about the same time, advertising researcher Tahi Gnepa (1993) conducted a study of comparative advertising in U.S. magazines and confirmed that slow industry growth rates over time were, in fact, statistically associated with the more frequent use of aggressive and confrontational comparative ads. As Gnepa concluded: "once the industry growth improved enough to accommodate all participants, peaceful coexistence among competitors became the rule, [and] the frequency of DCA [direct comparative advertising] markedly declined" (p. 71).

Executives and observers during this period also consistently linked the use of comparative advertising to recession, the existence of parity products, the need for brand differentiation, and the failure of brand-building image campaigns. Describing a return to comparative advertising among technology marketers, an Ogilvy & Mather creative director told *Advertising Age*: "There's always this sense of softness, like branding is somehow soft. . . . In hard times, the units get smaller and the ads get shriller" (as cited in Wasserman, 2001, p. 8). Jack Trout, of "Positioning" fame, revealingly told *Advertising Age*: "When hard times hit, the singing, dancing and emotional ads go out the window, and clients say, 'How do I nail my competitor?'" (as cited in Vranica, 2008).

Along with zero-sum competitive situations, comparative advertising was also frequently associated with a desperate desire to slow slumping sales or to blunt a competitor's overwhelming success. A perfect and early example was VW's popularity in the United States during the 1960s, which painted a big advertising bull's-eye on the "peoples' car." As one competitor explained at the time, "Everybody in the foreign car market is trying to cut Volkswagen down to size. . . . The reason for this blasé reaction is seen in the fact that two-thirds of the more than 500,000 foreign cars sold in this country last year were Volkswagens" (as cited in Meyers, 1966, p. 4). Sales successes on the parts of McDonald's and Wendy's International in fast foods, Prego spaghetti sauce in the 1990s, and Tito's Vodka in 2017 were also cited as motives for comparative attack advertising by Burger King Corp., Ragu Foods, and the Diageo-owned Smirnoff brand.

Problems for the TV Networks

By the early 1970s, national advertisers in the United States were increasingly naming names and expecting the Big Three TV networks and their affiliates to run their comparative ads. For years, the networks' own policies had all but banned them. NBC was the first to change policy in 1965 when it began accepting "substantiated comparative ads" (Danielenko, 1973, p. 56). The entire network spectrum opened up in early 1972, however, when the FTC asked ABC and CBS to give comparative ads a one-year trial.

Unfortunately, by 1975, the old problem with advertiser complaints reappeared, this time for the networks and their affiliates, who were in overall agreement that the comparative trial was a disaster. John E. Hinton, CBS's director of commercial clearance, told an American Association of Advertising Agencies (AAAA) panel that "comparative advertising has become a 'great headache,' and expressed the hope that 'it goes away'" ("Unsolicited Ad Idea Problems, Other Woes Get Four A's Airing," 1975, p. 3). His counterpart at ABC, Alfred Schneider, confirmed that the flood of comparative advertising was causing "great consternation" for the networks and the National Association of Broadcasters as "complaints and challenges mount from those companies mentioned adversely in a rival's ad" ("ABC Censor Raps Trend to Naming Rivals in Ads," 1975, p. 98). You'll be reading much more in Chapter 4 about the problems comparative advertising created for both media and advertising regulators during this period.

As the U.S. networks looked for a way out of their predicament, unfortunately for them, the first of the postmodern period's "Analgesic Wars" broke out. When Bristol-Myers launched the Datril pain reliever in mid-1975, it was with a price that was half that of Johnson & Johnson's (J&J's) Tylenol. The company then went to the TV networks with a comparative campaign that directly compared the two brands' prices. Upon learning of these plans, J&J executives invested $20 million to send 700 "detail men" scurrying across the United States to mark down every Tylenol package they could find. The goal was to nullify the Datril price claim before the campaign was launched. With price cuts and rebates, Tylenol's new price was one cent less than Datril. ABC and NBC had aired Datril's price comparisons, but then dropped them on the heels of the cut. CBS had not aired the ads and rejected them once the price cut took effect (Giges, 1975).

The Datril campaign would have a long-term influence on the practice of comparative advertising in the United States. Speaking about comparative advertising at a U.S. Trademark Association seminar, a J. Walter Thompson VP-legal counsel told participants he suspected

> that the networks had been preparing to tell FTC the naming of competitors had not helped consumers, had, in fact, caused even more confusion and was becoming extremely costly and sometimes impossible for the networks to monitor. But along came Datril and the subsequent price cut for Tylenol, a definite advantage for the consumer, and the networks no longer had an argument. (as cited in "Tylenol Exec Speaks Out on Datril Price Ad," 1976, p. 115)

The Analgesic Wars would continue for several more years—including a Bayer Aspirin attack on Tylenol, a Tylenol counterattack targeting "the millions who should not take aspirin" and an extraordinary confrontation between Tylenol and Advil—and eventually reach an unprecedented level of viciousness, bordering on irrationality (Beard, 2010).

Thanks to the FTC and its desire for more direct comparative advertising, and the Big Three networks' almost total capitulation to it, advertisers in the United States, according to advertising historian Stephen Fox (1984, p. 325), "made comparative advertising the most characteristic technique of the 1970s." Famous examples from the period include 7-Up's dramatic increase in sales after targeting Pepsi and Coca-Cola with the "Uncola" brand position and Procter & Gamble Co.'s attack on Listerine for giving its customers "medicine breath." P&G's Scope campaign also included a 1970s state-of-the-art advertising innovation—scratch 'n' sniff magazine ads.

The Age of the Comparative Ad War

Beginning in the early 1960s, a groundbreaking comparative ad war broke out between rental car companies Avis Inc. and Hertz Corporation. Avis famously repositioned itself with the campaign theme and slogan "When you're only no. 2, you try harder." You can view one of these classic comparative ads online at adwomen.org (2012). Although the implied comparative advertising (competitor Hertz wasn't identified) initially tested poorly in research commissioned by agency Doyle Dane Bernbach (Fueroghne, 2017), years later, *Advertising Age* (1999) recognized the campaign with position number 10 on its list of the "Top 100 Campaigns of the 20th Century." Consequently, it's probably not surprising the company continued to use the slogan for the next 50 years. It took several years for Hertz to counterattack, and their early rejection of this strategy led to an advertising agency change. However, they eventually did with the following copy: "For years, Avis has been telling you Hertz is No. 1. Now we're going to tell you 'why.'"

Entire books could be written about the comparative advertising wars waged from the 1970s to the 1990s. Just a few of these included the "Burger Wars" fought by McDonald's, Burger King, and Wendy's ("Where's the beef?"); the "Spaghetti Sauce War" between Ragu Foods and Campbell Soup Co.'s Prego; the "Long-Distance War" between AT&T and MCI; the "Credit Card Wars" among foes Visa USA, American Express, and MasterCard; and the "Pizza War" between Papa John's and Pizza Hut. At least three books actually have been written about the "Cola Wars" (Enrico & Kornbluth, 1986; Louis & Yazijian, 1980; Oliver, 1986). The consequences of the Cola Wars were, in fact, so significant, a 60-foot granite monument was erected in Washington D.C. to acknowledge "the advertising executives who lost their families and jobs in the most bitter advertising war in U.S. history" ("Ad Industry Veterans Honored," 1997). OK, there's no monument. But *The Onion*'s satirical homage to the ad wars between Coke and Pepsi clearly highlights the unique place they hold in the history of comparative advertising, not just in the United States, but around the world.

This period's comparative ad wars also produced one of the most surprising historical revelations regarding advertisers' decisions to use comparative advertising—the extent to which they so frequently expressed their regret that they'd ever gotten involved in a comparative campaign in the first place (Beard, 2010). Although advertisers during the first half of the 20th century occasionally mentioned that an ad war could turn out bad, it's almost shocking how consistently such views were expressed in the second half. By then, it had become obvious there were consequences that would almost inevitably lead to this kind of regret. First, there was a tendency for hostilities to escalate, with claims on either side becoming increasingly vicious. Second, there was a tendency for the escalation of hostilities to cause damage to all the combatants. Few wars more perfectly illustrate hostility escalation and its consequences than Tylenol versus Advil. As an *AdWeek* contributor concluded at the time: "The main educational benefit of the Tylenol-Advil war has been to teach the public that you can't believe anything you hear, that the world is unsafe, and that drug companies, behaving like cynical cutthroats, are no better than, well, politicians" (Goldman, 1996, p. 25).

The Knock-Off Craze

The Riding the Coattails approach took on an entirely new and significant twist in the United States in 1968, when a U.S. court of appeals ruling affirmed a California perfume distributor's right to use competitor Chanel's registered trademark "Chanel No. 5" in ads for his own products. The ruling undoubtedly legitimized this form of name-naming and encouraged the subsequent comparative product "knock-off" phenomenon of the 1970s and 1980s. Adman Herschell Gordon Lewis (1992, p. 32) offers this insightful description of the period's marketing and advertising phenomenon:

> A sniff-alike perfume calls itself a "version" of Giorgio or Opium. An inexpensive watch used successfully as a premium has this descriptive line: "No, it isn't the $2,000 museum watch—but your friends will think it is." This type of comparison is, really, coattail-riding. The comparison gains credibility through association (or deliberate) confusion with a similar item whose position is admittedly superior.

By 1987, more than two-dozen firms were marketing knock-off fragrances, and the trend had spread to other product categories, including, especially, fashion and personal care products. Among perfume industry advertisers and observers, the belief was almost unanimous that—while the knock-offs captured some sales from the more expensive, upscale competitors they compared themselves to—they gained most of their sales from the mid-priced, mass-market brands that were not the target of their comparisons. As one upscale brand Oscar de la Renta executive notes: "Really, it has no effect on us at all. . . . Our customers don't shop at K mart" (as cited in Fisher, 1988, p. 70).

Other upscale brands, such as Calvin Klein, however, resented the knock-offs and attacked these coattail riders for two reasons. One is that they viewed the exploitation of their brand names and registered trademarks as infringement. A second, which was explained by an attorney on behalf of Calvin Klein Cosmetics, was the concern that "a consumer who wants Obsession but first tries a copycat fragrance might never buy Obsession if the imitation is lower quality" (Sloan, 1987, p. S14). You'll read more about this type of comparative advertising and other variations of "coattail-riding" in Chapters 4 and 6, and we'll see why they've long been illegal just about everywhere other than the United States.

U-Haul International Inc. v. Jartran, Inc.

The most famous legal case involving comparative advertising, and perhaps any advertising, took place in the United States during the mid-1980s. In *U-Haul International Inc. v. Jartran, Inc.*, 793 F.2d 1034 (9th Cir. 1986), a federal district court ruled that Jartran, Inc. was responsible for a maliciously false comparative campaign targeting its main competitor, U-Haul. In more than 2,000 print ads in 160 cities around the United States, from June 1979 to December 1980, Jartran ran newspaper ads featuring a series of false rental price or equipment comparisons. In one of the ads, Jartran photographically reduced a larger U-Haul truck so it would look the same size as a smaller Jartran truck, which the company subsequently attempted to claim was just "puffery." Prosecuted under the Lanham Act (which you'll be reading much more about in Chapter 4), the outcome of the lawsuit was an unprecedented punitive judgment that ultimately cost Jartran some $40 million (the equivalent of nearly $90 million in 2017 dollars) in damages and the cost of corrective advertising.

Two important legal principles resulting from the Jartran ruling were that (a) no proof of actual malice would be required for damages to be awarded if a competitor were injured by comparative advertising and (b) findings of liability under the Lanham Act would also be sufficient to support a claim that a tort of unfair competition by disparagement had also occurred. Moreover, the court ruled that a false comparative ad didn't even have to "directly or explicitly" identify another product or service and disallowed claims that comparative ads should always be considered mere "puffery." While some at the time believed that the size of the record-setting false-advertising judgment against Jartran would likely lead to a chilling effect on the use of comparative advertising, others noted that this was unlikely because the falsity of the claims was so blatant. As we'll see, that was clearly the case.

Global Developments

In Europe and throughout much of the world, policies and regulations continued down the path of discouraging comparative advertising. In the early 1960s, Great Britain's now-defunct agency for the regulation of TV advertising, the Independent Television Authority, outright banned comparative laundry detergent commercials. The ban led to criticisms from some British advertising professionals. As Sinclair Wood, president of the Institute of Practitioners in Advertising, complained at the time: "If motor car A achieves higher mileage to the gallon than motor car B, it seems reasonable and desirable that its maker should be allowed to point out the fact in his advertisements. But he may not do so" (Wood & Fowle, 1961, p. 32).

A few years later, Bristol-Myers Co. ran into legal problems in Greece, where hostility toward comparative advertising was even greater, with a comparative price ad for Mum deodorant ("Mums the Word on Competitive Copy in Greece," 1968). A headline asking, "Why pay more?" and subhead claiming "Mum deodorants. Excellent quality. Best price." were enough to encourage a lawsuit from an angry competitor. Bristol-Myers dropped the ad after running it twice.

During the mid-1980s, attempts by U.S. marketers to run comparative campaigns outside the United States continued to run into trouble. In Germany, for instance, Procter & Gamble Co. discovered that merely claiming Valencia orange juice "tastes just like fresh squeezed orange juice" was sufficient to run afoul of the country's rigorous fairness test for comparative claims. Frequent comparative advertiser Wendy's International postponed a rollout of a comparative campaign in Italy, while waiting for a new comparative advertising law to take effect in 1985.

By the mid-1990s, however, things were loosening up enough outside the United States for Pepsi-Cola International to attempt a global comparative advertising campaign with an emphasis on its youth appeal. The campaign began in the United States with a Super Bowl spot featuring two chimpanzees undergoing a laboratory experiment in which one drinks Pepsi and the other drinks Coke. This commercial is also available on YouTube (Barbara Poplits, 2014). After six weeks, the Coke chimp had developed a "remarkable improvement in motor skills," while the Pepsi chimp was partying and cruising the beach with pretty girls ("Pepsi Dares . . . ," 1994). For the many countries that still discouraged or banned comparative advertising at the time, Pepsi produced a second version featuring a can marked "X."

An earlier Pepsi attack outside the United States, however, ran into legal problems when Coke bottlers took exception to the Pepsi claim that drinking Coke would render rapper M.C. Hammer incapable of singing anything other than the very uncool ballad "Feelings" (you can also find this commercial on YouTube [SmartAdvertising, 2009]). This international comparative advertising episode took an even more amusing turn when Coke executives actually approached some advertising regulators with demands for medical and legal substantiation that drinking Coke would produce such a detrimental effect on Hammer's singing voice and performance style. Still, the author of an article in *Beverage World* reported that the courts mostly rejected lawsuits against it "helped open Italy, Spain and Greece to comparative ads" ("Pepsi Dares . . . ," 1994, p. 18), and Pepsi itself claimed that it boosted sales in Japan by 50%.

The introduction of the European Union's Council Directive No. 89/104/EEC relating to trademarks in 1988, the passing of the UK's Trade Marks Act of 1994, and, of course, the EU's Directive 97/55/EC on comparative advertising led to less hostility toward comparative advertising in many countries. Significant comparative campaigns and wars, which were attributed mainly to intensifying competition, took place in the UK (Cable & Wireless PC vs. British Telecommunications PC and Ryanair Limited vs. British Airways) and the Netherlands (Gillette vs. Wilkinson). Even so, not long ago a 30-second TV commercial for the consumer home carbonation soft drink system SodaStream—while successfully running in the United States, Australia, Sweden, and several other countries—was banned in the UK. Clearcast, the organization currently responsible for pre-approving most British TV commercials, concluded that showing competitors' bottles exploding was disparaging and denigrating. It's also worth mentioning that CBS refused to run the spot in that year's Super Bowl broadcast (SodaStream, 2013). You'll be reading much more about international developments and their practical and legal implications in Chapter 6.

Comparative Advertising Outcomes, Strategies, and Tactics

The belief that comparative advertising greatly enhances attention and awareness was overwhelming during this final period among advertisers and industry observers. In reference to Taco Bell's comparative campaign featuring real-world spokesmen named "Ronald McDonald," *Advertising Age* contributor Ken Wheaton (2014) pointed out that what viewers "will remember is that Taco Bell had the gumption to not only turn a waffle into a taco—American ingenuity and gluttony at its best—but to also stick its fingers right in McDonald's eyes. And it does so without managing to be a big jerk about it."

Moreover, toward the end of the period, some advertisers began mentioning a new connection—they proposed that the initiation of a lawsuit often enhanced the awareness created by a comparative campaign. As an *Advertising Age* contributor reported in 2009: "Marketing experts were quick to criticize AT&T for taking legal action against Verizon's 'Map for That' ads. While AT&T wanted the ads pulled, what the lawsuit was more likely to do is bring attention to the ads, and AT&T's weakness: its iPhone-taxed 3G network" (Klaassen, 2009). As during the previous period, a majority of advertisers acknowledged that comparative ads often create attention and awareness for the competitor as well.

The belief that comparative advertising could be informative was also widely held during this period. McCann-Erickson executive David Ramsey, responsible for General Motors advertising at the time, explains: "Buyers are looking for more product information, comparisons. I like it when it is done fairly; when it is an honest-to-goodness free-for-all. Where it is done right, it is extremely helpful. It makes good reading" (as cited in McClain, 1983, p. M). Many who argued in favor of the informativeness of comparative ads suggested they were the most effective tactic for communicating a feature of similarity or difference. This belief was summarized well by *Advertising Age* columnist Sid Bernstein (1989, p. 16): "I have always considered the technique a useful one, definitely serving the interests of consumers, because comparing Product A with Brand B is essential in almost every buying decision—especially in an economy with endless numbers of look-alike, taste-alike, cost-alike and perform-alike products."

Advertisers during this period made scores of references to the problem of comparative advertising confusion. They also offered specific reasons for it: (a) consumers were unfamiliar with the target of the comparison; (b) the target of the comparison was a dissimilar product (e.g., a comparative Super Bowl ad that pitted Diet Coke against the sugared Pepsi flagship brand); (c) the ad lacked sufficient identification for the sponsoring brand; and (d) the old problem with directly conflicting claims in an ongoing advertising war (Beard, 2013a).

Similar to their contemporaries during earlier periods, advertisers questioned the likability of comparative ads, although this belief was not as prevalent. Unlike the previous period, the mere identification of a competitor was never mentioned as a cause of negative attitudes toward comparative ads. On the other hand, the belief that comparative advertising causes especially negative attitudes among the users of the comparison brand was mentioned frequently. John Goodchild, chief operations officer of ad agency Weightman Group, spoke for many with this observation: "Even the lowest brand has fans who resent being ridiculed by a rival's advertising. . . . But it's just plain dumb to trash a brand in a mean-spirited fashion and offend the millions who know it and love it" (as cited in Chang & Parekh, 2009). Despite the prevalent use of comparative advertising, the belief that the tactic could lead to damage to all the competitors in a product category was frequently mentioned during this period. However, in each of these cases, ongoing advertising wars were said to be the cause of the problem.

The belief that comparative advertising could successfully create sales occurred simultaneously during this period with the widely held belief that it might often cause negative attitudes toward the advertiser, possibly the brand, and the product or service category overall. There are also many examples of comparative campaigns to be found in the trade literature for which authors cited actual increases in market share or sales.

During this final period, how to strategically and tactically execute an effective comparative campaign was discussed fairly often. Numerous advertisers and other decision makers mentioned their belief that comparative advertising works most effectively for smaller competitors, whether it was a new product launch, Riding the Coattails or "Twisting the Tiger's Tail" (a tactic that involves a smaller competitor claiming not similarity, but superiority over the larger one). In 2014, for example, numerous community banks, regional financial firms, and credit unions touted their strengths in comparative campaigns targeting the banking behemoths, such as Chase and Bank of America. Nissan also did some interesting coattail-riding in a 2016 TV spot, in which the company and its Titan XD pickup paid an homage to three iconic Ford, Chevrolet, and Dodge models. This spot can also be viewed on YouTube (Atazoth, 2016). Gnepa's (1993) earlier study had, in fact, confirmed this "underdog hypothesis," with a finding that advertisers who ran direct comparative magazine ads had, on average, significantly smaller market shares than the competitors they attacked by name.

As during previous periods, advertisers frequently referenced their belief that comparative advertising would most likely be effective if the product or service possessed a true feature of superiority. This faith was probably captured best in this statement near the end of the period, attributed to industry observer Roger Entner, a senior vice president with research company Nielsen Telecom, with regard to a Verizon attack on the iPhone: "This strategy can work quite well if you have a device that is truly better than the iPhone. . . . As long as you can back it up. If not, you lose a lot of credibility" (as cited in Shields, 2009, p. 36).

Also during this period, advertisers continued to express their belief that the feature or selling point that was the focus of a comparative claim needed to be salient to consumers. Related to the importance of salience, numerous advertisers acknowledged how easy it was for comparative advertising to distract them from a proper focus on it. Moreover, among the most widely held views, as it was during the previous period, was the believability of product demonstrations.

Advertisers and industry observers continued to lament the negativity and aggressiveness of this period's comparative advertising, and many advertisers continued to view it as somewhat unseemly. For instance, in 2016, when yogurt maker Chobani ran a comparative campaign contending that the makers of Dannon and Yoplait use potassium sorbate, a common food preservative, "to kill bugs," a spokesman for General Mills told *Advertising Age*: "The statements made by Chobani in their latest attempt to sell more yogurt are entirely misleading, and we don't think consumers appreciate that kind of approach" (as cited in Strom, 2016).

Related recommendations address how to execute comparative advertising and avoid the consumer perception of excessive negativity, such as the tactical use of humor to maintain a positive tone. Perhaps one of the most insightful observations in this regard was offered by Apple's Steve Jobs, in response to a question about the long-running "Mac versus PC" campaign: "The art of those commercials is not to be mean, but for the guys to like each other" (as cited in Kerwin, 2007, p. 49).

This period also revealed numerous examples of comparative advertising creative based on opportunism. Comparative ads or campaigns that exploited a limitation or weakness of a competitor or a marketing misstep were employed in numerous industries and product categories. One of the most famous comparative ads of all time—Pepsi's "The Other Guy Blinked"—is an obvious example of the latter. The ad ran in national newspapers on April 23, 1985, as Pepsi celebrated, and exploited, its apparent victory in the Cola Wars, with Coco-Cola's announcement of a reformulation of their flagship soda. Two other excellent examples took place at the end of this period, when (a) plus-size clothing retailer Lane Bryant launched its "#ImNoAngel" campaign in response to a controversy over a lack of plus sizes and models in Victoria's Secret catalogues and (b) Sprint took advantage of Verizon's decision to replace actor Paul Macarelli ("Can You Hear Me Now?") after nearly a decade and hired him to appear in Sprint's own comparative ad campaign.

SUMMARY AND CONCLUSIONS

One conclusion seems fairly clear. Making a direct or indirect comparison with the goods or services of a competitor is as old as inscribing a motto on a piece of pottery, shouting a sales message in the street, tacking up a handwritten or crudely printed flyer, or buying an actual ad in an early newspaper. The comprehensive history we have in this chapter offers substantial evidence to support the recent observation of one academic researcher: "The history of Comparative Advertising dates back to the beginning of commerce itself. It has always been normal for a trader to attempt to enjoy pecuniary benefits by drawing a comparison between the qualities of his products/services and a competitor's" (Singh, 2014).

Another conclusion is that the simplest answer to the question we began with—why have advertisers so frequently used such a risky approach—shares much the same explanation for the emergence of advertising in the first place—the existence of competitors. In fact, in most of the explanations we have for both comparative advertising in ancient times and the beginning and escalation of advertising wars in modern times, are based at least in part on competition in its various forms. Going back thousands of years, manufacturers and merchants initially began branding their goods and referencing competitors in their promotional messages simply to distinguish them from others or to make a clear statement as to quality (for example, "Our lamps are the best lamps sold in Carthage.").

Next to appear, however, were both direct and indirect references to competitors to alert potential customers to the existence of inferior products, counterfeiters, and intellectual property thieves. And this provides another answer to our question. Such warnings in print appeared as early as 500 years ago and steadily continued, with warnings to avoid counterfeit books, plays, patent medicines, and razor strops (when was the last time you saw one of those?). This motivation for comparative advertising was revealed again as part of the 20th century problem of The Substitution Menace.

As the Industrial Revolution–inspired product innovation and mass production fully kicked in during the 19th century, new forms of competition took place and, as we've seen, for some manufacturers, in the United States especially, comparative advertising was almost always the solution to their competitive problems. While at least a handful of manufacturers seemed to view the correct way to compete in expanding markets to be cooperation with competitors (or the very least ignore them), others concluded the best way to get their share of a rapidly expanding market was to attempt to take out competitors as quickly and completely as possible (somewhat like political attack advertising is used today in the United States).

It also turns out, though, that comparative advertising was frequently seen as the correct approach when the opposite situation occurred—intensifying competition in static or slow-growth markets characterized by two or more "me-too" competitors and, often, a corresponding need for brand differentiation. So another way to look at this conclusion is that, while the existence of intense competition has obviously and frequently encouraged advertisers to go on the attack, it doesn't seem to matter all that much what type of competition it is.

As advertisers began sharing their beliefs about advertising strategies and tactics in the trade journals of the 20th and 21st centuries, they also began to reveal more about the appeal of comparative ads and campaigns. For instance, advertisers in the 21st century believe just as strongly as their contemporaries in earlier periods that comparative ads encourage high levels of attention and recall. Although many linked this belief to the novelty of comparative ads, especially ones that name or otherwise directly identify a competitor, advertisers in the United States still believe in the attention and awareness outcome, even though comparative advertising became much more common in the 1970s. More recent explanations for these beliefs include secondary exposure caused by lawsuits, self-regulation challenges, and buzz via social media (Beard, 2013a).

Advertisers during nearly every period expressed the belief that comparative ads were informative because they often highlighted the differences between competitive products or services. It's worth pointing out that the main reason the FTC in the United States began encouraging advertisers to identify competitors was because the agency thought it would lead to better informed consumers. We'll also see in Chapter 6 that the informational value of comparative advertising has been one of the primary arguments in support of its expanding use around the globe.

However, the findings also support an important conclusion regarding when comparative advertising will not be informative—many advertisers throughout the past 100 years acknowledged that comparative ads often cause confusion. It's also evident that many advertisers thought comparative ads would be more believable, although just as many others thought just the opposite. Problems with believability seem to focus on two main issues: (a) advertisers believe comparative ads won't be believable if competitors are making directly contradictory claims and, especially, if these occur as part of an ongoing advertising war; and (b) the practice of attacking a competitor's advertising or responding directly to it that began in the 1930s.

Advertisers often recognized several strategic and tactical advantages to campaigns that compared new, less popular, or low-end products with well-known, often higher-priced competitors. For instance, advertisers of new products often favored the Riding the Coattails approach simply because it attracted attention, exploited the larger advertising expenditures of brand leaders, or because associating a product with a popular competitor was an effective way to quickly inform consumers about its features, uses, and benefits (Beard, 2013a). Other tactical advantages are attitudinal and persuasive, such as establishing value or upgrading brand image.

It's also likely that the more frequent and tactical uses of comparative advertising in the United States were influenced during the second half of the 20th century by changes in the law. It's obvious that a government agency, the FTC, played a major role in the loosening of media clearance standards that paved the way for the more frequent use of comparative television advertising in the early 1970s. As we also know, public policy, the law and industry regulations have played a key role in the acceptance of comparative advertising in countries other than the United States. We'll get into these issues in greater depth in Chapters 4 and 6.

Perhaps the most interesting explanation for why advertisers have so often relied on comparative ads and campaigns is their use to exploit a marketing or advertising opportunity, whether it was the discovery of a limitation in the design or formulation of competitors' products or something they said in their advertising. Today's advertisers would do well to remember New Coke. The reformulation of that iconic American product not only outraged millions of loyal customers, it was also seen by many to be synonymous with waving a white flag in the Cola Wars.

Finally, it's important to remember that the choice of a particular message strategy is often up to a small handful of decision makers or even a single businessman or -woman. The fact is, some people are more competitive than others, some more confrontational. Anger and frustration, as well as other emotions, certainly help explain the escalation of ongoing comparative ad wars, as well as why it seems that advertisers have so frequently found it difficult to follow their own advice about excessive negativity. So another good historical explanation for why comparative advertising has often been seen as a solution for just about any problem is that it ultimately reflects the attitudes and experiences of the people who make the message decision. *Advertising Age* ad reviewer Ken Wheaton (2015) captured this idea very nicely in his explanation for a Budweiser beer attack on "fussy craft brews" in the 2015 Super Bowl: "Budweiser was simply doing what tons of smart, sophisticated advertising folks have been counseling for the past decade. It was taking a stance. It was establishing passion points and offering a point of view."

Chapter Two

Theoretical Foundations and Empirical Research

Since the 1970s, researchers have produced a large body of research with the goal of understanding how comparative advertising affects a variety of (a) cognitive (attention, message recall, and brand-name recall), (b) affective (attitude toward the ad [A_{ad}] and attitude toward the brand [A_{br}]), and (c) conative (purchase intention [P_i] and initial trial) objectives and outcomes. Moreover, this growing body of empirical research shows these effects often differ according to many situational factors or variables. Among them are whether the comparative advertiser's brand has a small or large market share, whether claims are well substantiated, or the brand is new to the market.

The purpose of this chapter is to review what the empirical research published in scholarly journals has revealed about how the uses and effects of comparative advertising differ from noncomparative and to explore theoretical explanations for these differences. We'll rely extensively on two major efforts to summarize the research literature up to 1997 (Grewal et al., 1997; Rogers & Williams, 1989) and then from there focus on what's been reported in scholarly research journals since then. We'll also focus on some of the theories researchers have relied on to explain how comparative advertising works and why people respond to it the way they do. Although the emphasis will mainly be on research that has compared directly comparative ads (that is, those that explicitly identify competitors by naming or showing them) with noncomparative ones, the chapter concludes with a look at what empirical researchers have discovered about the effectiveness of different types of comparative ads.

COMPARATIVE ADVERTISING AND OBJECTIVES AND OUTCOMES

The model in Figure 2.1 summarizes what has been reported in the scholarly research literature about the direct effects of comparative advertising versus noncomparative and how they're affected by what are the most important situational factors. So why these particular objectives and outcomes?

First of all, you may have noticed that many of the model's outcomes match up pretty well with what Chapter 1's history suggests are the most important ones for advertisers (that is, attention, brand-name recall, A_{ad}, A_{br}, and P_i). Advertisers have always been concerned about whether their ads are catching people's attention, creating awareness for what they have to offer, encouraging people to have positive feelings about their ads and offerings, or stimulating some kind of action or behavior. In fact, advertising's oldest process model of advertising outcomes and effects—AIDA (Attention-Interest-Desire-Action)—captures these objectives very well.

Later so-called "hierarchy-of-effects" models, such as Lavidge and Steiner's (1961), offer similar but increasingly comprehensive explanations for how advertising works by informing consumers about a product or service (cognition or "learning"), then by persuading them to like it (affect or "feeling"), and finally by encouraging a purchase or some other behavior (cona-

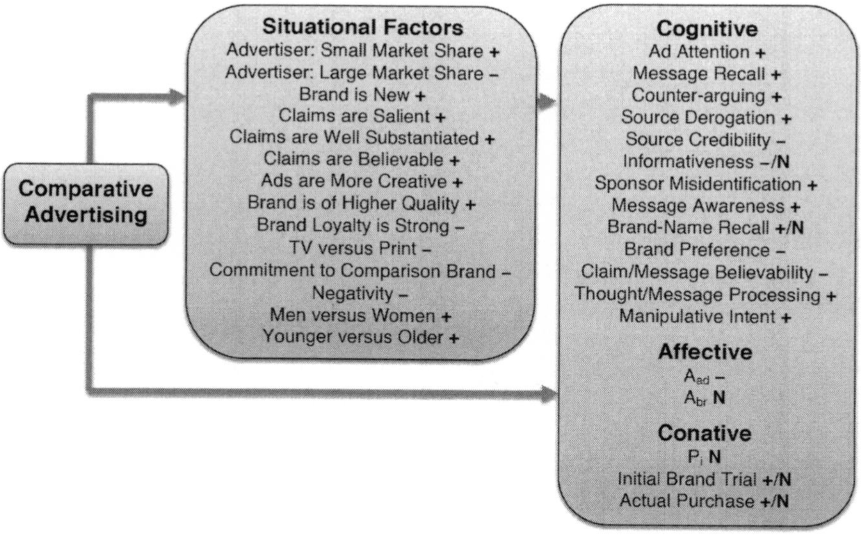

Figure 2.1. Comparative versus Noncomparative Advertising: Summary and Synthesis of Empirical Research Results. ***Figure courtesy of author.***

tion or "doing"). Even more recent and sophisticated models—namely the FCB Grid (Vaughn, 1980) and Rossiter-Percy Grid (Rossiter, Percy, & Donovan, 1991)—propose consumers don't always look for or process information in the sequence predicted by the classic high-involvement Learn-Feel-Do hierarchy. They may, for example, try the product first, learn about it that way and later decide how they feel about it (the Do-Learn-Feel hierarchy). Another possibility is the Feel-Learn-Do hierarchy, which begins with an attitude change, proceeds through information acquisition, and then ends with a purchase. Which process is likely to describe a particular product purchase decision depends on the level of involvement in making a choice (high versus low) or whether the motivation to purchase is mainly rational versus emotional—"thinking" versus "feeling" purchase decisions in the FCB Grid and "informational" versus "transformational" decisions in the Rossiter-Percy Grid.

When it comes to choosing a service provider, rather than a material good, there's a fourth process, Feel-Do-Learn, that may more accurately describe the sequence consumers follow to reach that purchase decision (Young, 1981). Some research has, in fact, shown that emotional and transformational appeals are often used in services advertising. This, of course, makes perfect sense if the purchase decision process begins with a change in attitudes or feelings (Abernethy & Butler, 1992; Cutler & Javalgi, 1993; Firestone, 1983; Mortimer, 2008).

THE MODEL

Figure 2.1's model includes what could reasonably be considered the most important comparative advertising versus noncomparative advertising effects and outcomes, based on empirical research over the years as well as the beliefs of advertising professionals. The model presents a summary and synthesis of three important sources and streams of research findings and results. First, before John Williams and Terrell Rogers (1989) conducted their widely cited survey of U.S. ad agency creative directors about comparative advertising, they reviewed the 42 studies that had been published up to 1987. Second, we have the results of Dhruv Grewal and his colleagues' (1997) also widely cited meta-analysis. Meta-analysis is a sophisticated statistical approach that can be used when there are a fairly large number of studies on a topic and researchers want to combine all those findings and results. Grewal et al. found 77 studies (54 published and 23 unpublished) that were conducted between 1976 and 1996 and that directly compared comparative with noncomparative advertising.

For the third source, we have conclusions based on a review and synthesis of 80 articles on comparative advertising published between 1997 and 2017.

Unfortunately, while many researchers studied and measured the same important objectives and outcomes we're interested in for both practical and theoretical reasons—for example, message recall and awareness, A_{ad}, A_{br}, and P_i—they didn't always report how comparative versus noncomparative advertising directly affected these outcomes, but only how they were affected by two or more other situational factors at the same time. In experimental research and statistics, these additional factors are called *moderator* variables and the way they affect each other are called *interactions*. The increasing sophistication of the research literature in regard to new and important situational factors and complex factorial experimental designs represent researchers' efforts to build on prior research and theory development and provide more rigorous and complete explanations for how comparative advertising actually works. Unfortunately, it also means some of their research results aren't directly comparable to what our other two sources reported.

Consequently, as with Rogers and Williams's (1989) review and conclusions and Grewal et al.'s (1997) analysis, the more recent research results were only included in the development of the model when a study found in the literature directly compared the effects of comparative versus noncomparative advertising on an objective or outcome or how they were affected by just one of the situational factors at a time. We will, though, also look at some of the most important and recent research reporting complex interactions and explore how they may help explain some of the nonsignificant or neutral conclusions you can see in the model.

For the review of the most recently published research literature, conclusions were based on the same procedures Rogers and Williams (1989) followed. They're based on a simple count of positive, negative, or nonsignificant research results. So if three studies reported positive results and five studies reported nonsignificant or neutral ones, the overall conclusion would be that the direct effect of comparative versus noncomparative advertising or the effects of a situational factor in that case are neutral. The literature's theory articles, histories, and game/theory works were not included in the development of the model.

In addition, situational factors and outcomes were included in the model if any of the three sources reported a conclusion regarding it. For example, only Rogers and Williams (1989) reported effects on source derogation and counter-arguing (two negative and unintended outcomes associated with comparative advertising you'll be reading more about in a bit). On the other hand, only Grewal et al. (1997) reported the effects of comparative versus noncomparative advertising on source credibility and message awareness. In Chapter 3, we'll take this review and synthesis one step further and compare these empirical research conclusions about the effectiveness of comparative advertising versus noncomparative and how they are affected by other situational factors with the beliefs of advertising professionals.

COGNITIVE OBJECTIVES AND OUTCOMES

Rogers and Williams (1989) concluded that comparative versus noncomparative advertising has a positive effect on message recall, but also two other outcomes called counter-arguing and source derogation. Recall is obviously good. Counter-arguing and source derogation, however, are not. It's difficult to appeal favorably to people or persuade them when they're going over in their minds all the reasons they don't like you and why they think what you're telling them isn't true. Rogers and Williams also concluded that the effects of comparative advertising on informativeness are negative. However, they concluded comparative ads have a positive effect on another unintended consequence that we discovered in Chapter 1 is a major comparative advertising concern—consumers' tendencies to confuse the comparison brand and the sponsor ("sponsor misidentification" in the model). They also reported a majority of the studies published at the time had reported a nonsignificant or neutral effect on brand-name recall. In addition, though, it's also important to note here that some studies analyzing the content of comparative ads—such as Harmon, Razzouk, and Stern's (1983) early study of U.S. magazine advertising—have reported that comparative ads actually do contain more information cues than noncomparative ads. They argued that the findings "[support] the original intent of the FTC when it encouraged comparison in advertising in order to provide the consumer with more information" (p. 17).

Grewal et al. (1997) concluded that the effects of comparative ads versus noncomparative are all positive on attention, message awareness, brand-name awareness (which is closely related to a consumer's ability to recall a brand), and thought/message processing, although they didn't report an effect on message recall. A recent study conducted in Spain by del Barrio-Garcia and Luque-Martinez (2003) is one of the very few to report no difference in attention between a comparative and noncomparative ad.

Two other studies have investigated the direct effect of comparative versus noncomparative advertising on message recall. Donthu (1998) found that both unaided and aided recall were significantly greater for a comparative ad among research participants in the United States, Canada, Great Britain, and India. On the other hand, Manzur, Uribe, Hidalgo, Olavarrieta, and Farias (2012) studied a sample of Chilean college students and reported no difference in the effect of a noncomparative, direct comparative, or indirect comparative ad on message recall.

There are a couple of reasons why the often-negative information in comparative advertising enhances cognitive message outcomes and effects. One is that comparative ads are simply relevant to more people because they mention more than one brand (Wilkie & Farris, 1975). A second and similar reason comparative ads encourage more attention is that they are often believed to contain more information than noncomparative ads (Muehling, Stoltman, & Grossbart, 1990).

Theoretically, Petty and Cacioppo's (1986) and Petty, Cacioppo, and Schumann's (1983) Elaboration Likelihood Model (ELM) offers a useful framework for explaining the effects of comparative ads on cognitive outcomes. The ELM argues there are two routes to persuasion—one *central* and one *peripheral*. The central route predicts that when people are *motivated* to think about a message (for example, they are highly involved or the message is especially relevant) and *able* to think about it (for example, the message is fairly easy to understand), then they'll cognitively elaborate on the claims in the ad (basically, think about them) and be persuaded by issue-relevant arguments.

The ELM's peripheral route, on the other hand, predicts that people may still be persuaded even if they are unmotivated or unable to process the information in an ad. Message elements unrelated to the product (called *peripheral cues*), and which people already have positive attitudes about, can be used to associate those positive attitudes with the product or brand, leading to a weaker and temporary kind of persuasion. What are common peripheral cues in advertising? Celebrities, attractive models, catchy music, appealing visuals, and humor.

Another theoretical explanation for the effectiveness of comparative advertising is referred to as "negativity bias." Research in advertising, communication, and political science has shown that negative information is often more memorable and influential, compared to positive information. This may happen because it's more unexpected and novel, less ambiguous, more credible, appeals to emotion rather than logic, and because people assign greater weight to negative information when making evaluations in social settings and about other people. Moreover, negativity bias predicts comparative ads activate the ELM's central route to persuasion, that some consumers will form supportive arguments and, consequently, be persuaded by the ad (Priester et al., 2004). However, since comparative ads also tend to encourage more counter-arguing and source derogation, especially if the source lacks credibility or the ad is not believable, some consumers will not be persuaded. In the case of neutral responses, or when consumers are unmotivated or unable to process the message, peripheral cues, such as humor, music, or likable spokespersons will become relevant and the ad may produce a weak and likely temporary change in attitudes.

Believability

Rogers and Williams (1987) reported that research at the time showed the effects of comparative advertising on claim or message believability are negative. Grewal et al.'s (1997) analysis, however, didn't reveal a significant difference in ad, or message, believability between comparative and noncomparative ads. Two later studies reported that comparative ads and their claims were significantly more believable than noncomparative ads (Barone & Miniard, 1999; Barone, Palan, & Miniard, 2004), although it's important to point out that the comparative ads in both these studies were "partly" comparative ads (that is, the test ads included both comparative and noncomparative information). Researchers del Barrio-Garcia and Luque-Martinez (2003) found that comparative advertising versus noncomparative had a negative effect on claim believability among Spanish consumers. A study of comparative services advertising conducted a few years ago (Beard, 2015) also reported that study participants rated a comparative ad as significantly less believable than a noncomparative one. Finally, Manzur et al. (2012) reported that a noncomparative ad was more believable than either a direct or implied comparative ad. The empirical research literature strongly supports a conclusion that comparative ads and their claims, versus noncomparative ones, are less believable.

Rogers and Williams (1989) didn't find any studies that had investigated source credibility. The findings of Grewal et al.'s (1997) meta-analysis, however, led them to conclude that source believability is lower for comparative ads versus noncomparative ads. This conclusion is obviously consistent with the two conclusions that comparative ads encourage counter-arguing and source derogation.

An outcome similar to believability and credibility that has received some recent attention is called "perception of manipulative intent." Some research suggests advertising that encourages high levels of attention, like comparative advertising, also causes people to believe the advertiser is trying to manipulate them (Campbell, 1995). In a study conducted by Chang (2007), he found that comparative versus noncomparative ads did indeed score higher on perception of manipulative intent. He also found a significant difference between men and women. You'll read more about that in a bit.

AFFECTIVE OBJECTIVES AND OUTCOMES

As we discussed earlier, affective outcomes emphasize how advertising can generate positive feelings toward an ad or brand. Some research, however, suggests consumers don't think much of comparative ads. Online survey firm Ask Your Target Market (Pilon, 2012) conducted a survey of consumers not long ago on the topic of comparative advertising. Some 46% of their respondents said they see comparative ads often, 59% said they thought the ads could be effective, and 81% said they thought they were especially effective when delivered via TV. On the other hand, 64% agreed comparative ads can be too negative and alienate potential customers, 27% thought many are too negative, and, probably worst of all, 42% reported a comparative ad encouraged them to try the comparison product or brand and not the advertiser's. A study of European consumers similarly reported that only 34% agreed it was acceptable for advertisers to criticize each other, while 62% were against it (as cited in Brabbs, 2001).

Rogers and Williams (1989) reported that researchers, at the time, had failed to identify either a positive or negative effect of comparative advertising, versus noncomparative, on either A_{ad} or A_{br}, but they did find one study that reported a negative effect on brand preference. Grewal et al. (1997), on the other hand, concluded that while comparative ads generate more negative A_{ad} than noncomparative ones, they encourage more favorable A_{br}.

Since 1997, eleven studies have reported the direct effect of comparative versus noncomparative ads on A_{ad}. Five reported a negative effect (Beard, 2015; Chakravarti & Xie, 2006; del Barrio-Garcia & Luque-Martinez, 2003; Donthu, 1998; Shao, Bao, & Gray, 2004), four reported no significant difference (Chang, 2007; Choi & Miracle, 2004; Kalro, Sivakumaran, & Marathe, 2017; Manzur et al., 2012; Thompson & Hamilton, 2006) and only one reported a significant positive effect (Zhang, Moore, & Moore, 2011). It seems highly likely, then, that the effect of a comparative versus a noncomparative ad on A_{ad} is negative.

Ten recent studies have also reported the direct effect of comparative versus noncomparative ads on A_{br}, with seven reporting nonsignificant differences (Chang, 2007; del Barrio-Garcia & Luque-Martinez, 2003; Jeon & Beatty, 2002; Manzur et al., 2017; Muthukrishnan, Warlop, & Alba, 2001; Thompson & Hamilton, 2006; Zhang et al., 2011), two reporting a significant positive difference (Barone & Miniard, 1999; Miniard et al., 2006) and one reporting a negative effect (Beard, 2015). Across all the sources, then, our conclusion has to be that the effect is neutral.

So why might comparative ads encourage negative consumer attitudes? Perhaps in much the same way most of us instinctively dislike people who always seem to be running other people down, Dröge (1989, p. 194) concluded that comparative ads are perceived to be "impersonal, less friendly and pleasant, more aggressive and intense, and less believable and honest." Sorescu and Gelb (2000, p. 26) similarly note that the principal downside to comparative advertising is "the perception that it's unfair or in some other way undesirable."

Researchers Karen James and Paul Hensel (1991) offer some helpful suggestions as to when and how a comparative ad, in which a competitive brand is identified merely for the purposes of claiming superiority over it, is likely to be perceived as especially negative. The two are best differentiated based on (a) the degree to which the targeted brand is identified, (b) whether the direction of the comparison is differentiative vs. associative (that is, the brands are presented as different rather than similar), and (c) the extent to which consumers perceive the advertising to be particularly malicious or unfair.

Researchers Michael Barone and Robert Jewell (2012) recently extended the line of theory development on perception of manipulative intent to help explain why consumers might respond to comparative advertising with negative attitudes. They conducted a multi-experiment study of how "persuasion knowledge" moderates the effectiveness of comparative advertising by encouraging suspicion and discouraging believability, especially for advertising perceived to be excessively negative. They then took this one step further and hypothesized that direct comparative advertising would have a negative effect on attitudes toward the advertised brand if it were used in a product category in which it wasn't typically used (that is, "in violation of category norms"). Their experiments showed that such a "persuasion penalty" can happen when comparative advertising is viewed by consumers as atypical for the product category and consequently inappropriate.

Theoretically, Barone and Jewell's (2012) research offers a deeper explanation for one of the common problems associated with comparative advertising—the "backlash" effect. However, they also found that the negative effect on brand attitudes didn't hold for everyone and was moderated by yet another variable. Some people actually like things that violate category norms, called "counter-conformity." The "counter-conformists" among their experiment participants responded with more favorable brand attitudes when they viewed a comparative ad that was atypical for the product category.

So what product categories would qualify as typical versus atypical for a comparative ad? Thanks to a recent content analyses of comparative advertising on TV in the United States (Beard, 2016b), we have an answer to that question. Comparative advertising was used significantly more often for beverages (72.3% comparative), followed by non-prescription drugs (68.8%), automotive (almost exclusively cars, trucks, and dealers) (66.7%), prescription drugs (65.5%), personal care items (52.7%), other consumer durables (48.5%), fast food and pizza restaurants (47.7%), household products (45.2%), consumer services (40.0%), restaurants (38.9%), and retailers (37.3%). Perhaps more important, direct comparative advertising, versus implied, was used most often for automotive products (18.4%), followed by non-prescription drugs (11.7%), prescription drugs (3.4%), beverages (3.1%), other consumer durables (3.0%), and consumer services (2.2%).

Those findings are quite similar to a less detailed study of TV advertising in the United States conducted decades ago. Researchers Stephen Brown and Donald Jackson (1977) reported that direct comparative advertising was used most often for drugs, household products, foods, consumer durables (which included automotive products), and personal care items, in that order. Research findings for comparative magazine ads also provide similar findings. Researcher Tahi Gnepa (1993), for instance, reports that direct comparative magazine ads were used most often for automotive products (14.5%), drugs (13.9%), tobacco products (11.1%), and telephone services/equipment (5.4%). It seems fairly clear, then, that "typical" product categories for comparative advertising would certainly include automotive products (including cars and trucks) and prescription or non-prescription drugs and atypical would include most food products, clothing, retailers, services (not counting consumer information and technology), and restaurants (not counting fast food).

CONATIVE OBJECTIVES AND OUTCOMES

Rogers and Williams (1989) found two studies reporting a positive effect on purchase intention but four with neutral results. They similarly found one study with a positive effect on actual purchase but two with neutral results. So they concluded at the time that the effects on both were neutral. Grewal et al. (1997), on the other hand, concluded comparative ads appear to increase both P_i and purchase behavior more than noncomparative ads.

Since 1997, no studies have investigated the effects of comparative versus noncomparative advertising on either brand trial or actual purchase behavior. However, nine studies have been published reporting the direct effect on P_i, with six reporting no significant differences (Chang, 2007; Choi and Miracle, 2004; del Barrio-Garcia & Luque-Martinez, 2003; Gotlieb et al., 2013; Manzur et al., 2017; Thompson & Hamilton, 2006), two reporting positive findings in favor of comparative advertising (Barone & Miniard, 1999; Jeon & Beatty, 2002), and one reporting a negative effect (Beard, 2015). Consequently, for now, our conclusion has to be that the effects of comparative advertising versus noncomparative on P_i are neutral, while the effect on brand trial or actual purchase could be either positive or neutral.

SITUATIONAL FACTORS

As the discussion above suggests, one explanation for the neutral or inconclusive findings regarding the effectiveness of comparative versus noncomparative advertising that you see in the model is that its effects differ according to the many other factors that may be at work in any particular marketing or advertising situation. When they conducted their meta-analysis, Grewal et al. (1997) analyzed the effects of six situational factors (or *moderators*), some of which you can see were included in the model. Since then, researchers have studied the effects of literally dozens of additional factors. Some of them are message-based, such as the strength of an ad's arguments (Miniard et al., 1998), the type of product attribute featured in a comparative ad (Jain, Buchanan, & Maheswaran, 2000; Markman & Loewenstein, 2010; Zhang,

Kardes, & Cronley, 2002), the amount of comparative versus noncomparative information included in an ad (Manning et al., 2001), the positive versus negative "framing" of comparisons (Jain & Posavac, 2004; Shiv, Edell, & Payne, 1997), and the type of comparative claim (Jain, Agrawal, & Maheswaran, 2006).

Other factors are consumer-based, such as whether consumers use the comparison brand (Putrevu & Lord, 1994; Sorescu & Gelb, 2000), how consumers process the information in comparative ads (Miniard et al., 1998; Priester et al., 2004; Thompson & Hamilton, 2006), the measures used to evaluate the persuasiveness of comparative versus noncomparative ads (such as relative measures that use the comparison brand as a point of reference and those that don't) (Rose et al., 1993), regulatory focus (whether consumers focus on maximizing the likelihood of positive outcomes when processing the information in ads versus avoiding negative ones) (Jain et al., 2006; Jain et al., 2007), and implicit theory orientation (which proposes individual differences that exert a powerful effect on how consumers interpret and evaluate their world, including ads) (Jain, Mathur, & Maheswaran, 2009).

The model in Figure 2.1 includes 14 situational factors that both theory and the practical experiences of advertising professionals suggest are the most important. They also include those for which we have the most conclusive empirical research results. Based on the findings from their literature review, for instance, Rogers and Williams (1989) concluded comparative ads are more effective when the advertised brand has a small market share or when it's new, and less effective when the brand has a large market share or loyalty to the comparative advertiser's brand is already strong. A study conducted a few years later confirmed that the sponsors of comparative magazine ads actually did have statistically significantly smaller market shares than the competitors they identified in their ads (Gnepa, 1993).

Rogers and Williams (1989) also concluded comparative advertising is more effective when claims are made on salient product benefits, claims are well substantiated, claims are believable, when ads are more creative, and when the brand is of higher quality than those of competitors. They also reported that comparative advertising is less effective than noncomparative when used in TV commercials versus print ads. Nye, Roth, and Shimp's (2008) study is one of the few to report that comparative advertising was more effective for a well-known, established brand than a new one (in their study, A_{br}).

Grewal et al. (1997) similarly concluded that comparative advertising is more effective than noncomparative when the advertised brand's market share is smaller than the comparison brand's, the comparison brand is the market leader, when claims are well substantiated and for brands new to the market. In their research, claim substantiation took the form of "credibility enhancers," which include the use of credible sources, two-sided messages or the support of claims with factual information. Although they concluded the use of credibility enhancers does not increase message awareness nor ad believability, they did find that enhancing the credibility of comparative ads leads to more favorable A_{br} and greater P_i. The content analysis of comparative TV ads that I conducted and mentioned earlier (Beard, 2016b) showed that comparative commercials actually do include substantiation for their claims significantly more often than noncomparative ones do.

Grewal et al. (1997) also concluded comparative advertising is less effective when the advertised brand is the market leader, which certainly isn't unexpected. As some advertising professionals strongly suggested in Chapter 1, nobody wants to see a Goliath deliver a smackdown on a David. Another researcher, Chattopadhyay (1998), similarly reported that comparative ads sponsored by an unknown brand are more effective in changing consumers' brand attitudes than noncomparative ads.

Commitment to the Comparison Brand

One thing that probably comes as no surprise is that the people who use and are psychologically committed to the brand targeted by a comparative ad aren't going to respond very favorably to it. One of the early and most widely cited studies of comparative advertising reported that comparative ads are indeed less believable (for both source and message), but especially for users of the comparison brand (Swinyard, 1981).

It's likely comparison brand users respond negatively because comparative ads challenge their existing beliefs and suggest they regularly make bad purchase decisions. Commitment to a brand is believed to be a good predictor of brand loyalty and likely to cause a defensive reaction to information that conflicts with that loyalty (Chaiken, Liberman, & Early, 1989). Brand-committed consumers are also expected to pay more attention to comparative ads because they have greater personal involvement. This is expected to lead to more thought processing. All of this is probably the reason researchers have found, and as the model shows, comparative versus noncomparative ads encourage more counter-arguing and derogation of the message source.

More recently, Sorescu and Gelb (2000) set out to investigate the effects of commitment to the comparison brand by exploring how the users of sponsored brands, comparison brands, switchers, and the users of third brands differ in response to comparative ads. They began with the assumption that advertisers who target one or more of their competitors are most interested in reaching and attracting third-brand users and switchers. In their study, aspirin was compared unfavorably to Tylenol. Aspirin users (that is, users of the comparison brand) had significantly lower evaluations of the comparative ad than the three other usage categories and significantly lower ratings of the Tylenol brand. On the other hand, both third-brand users and switchers expressed more favorable responses on approval and believability, compared to aspirin users. In addition, third-brand users rated aspirin lower than did aspirin users, and both third-brand users and switchers rated the Tylenol brand higher than did aspirin users.

Pillai and Goldsmith (2008) also found that comparative and noncomparative ads affected A_{br} differently depending on whether or not their research subjects were committed to the comparison brand. However, here again, this effect was moderated by yet another variable—whether the product attribute emphasized in the ad was considered typical or atypical. A typical attribute is one that is often associated with well-known or mainstream brands in a product category. For example, a typical product attribute for snack foods would be taste or crunchiness, while an atypical one would be "low fat" (Desai & Ratneshwar, 2003).

If a comparative ad focuses on a typical attribute, Pillai and Goldsmith (2008) predicted that brand-committed consumers would be more likely to adopt defensive strategies and counter-argue more than if the attribute was atypical. Why? The reasoning is that if a comparative ad claims superiority over a comparison brand based on an atypical attribute, it doesn't challenge the existing beliefs of the comparison brand-committed users. Their research results were consistent with this prediction and helpfully reveal quite a bit about whether or not a comparative ad will be more effective than a noncomparative one when targeting the users of a comparison brand. For example, if advertisers want to target the loyal buyers of the comparison brand with an emphasis on typical product attributes, they shouldn't use comparative ads. On the other hand, comparative ads emphasizing typical product attributes will likely be more effective with non-committed consumers. Yet another possibility is that advertisers might effectively target consumers committed to the competitor's brand with comparative advertising if they emphasize an atypical product attribute. Of course, it would be important to keep in mind that comparative ads are believed to be more effective than noncomparative ones when the claims they make about the advertised brand are salient (that is, relevant or important) to consumers.

Even more recently, researchers Akshaya Vijayalakshmi, Darrel Muehling, and Russell Laczniak (2015) extended the research on brand commitment to comparative "attack" ads, which they defined as direct comparative ads that rely on especially harsh statements about the weaknesses of the comparison brand rather than on the strengths of the advertised brand. They relied on "persuasion resistance theory" (Tormala & Petty, 2004) to explain why people respond negatively to comparative attack ads, especially if they are attacking a brand to which consumers are committed.

Persuasion resistance theory captures many of the expected effects and outcomes we've already discussed. When a comparative ad challenges the favorable attitudes committed brand users have toward their brand, they will cognitively reject the claims and they won't be persuaded. However, this theory goes a step further and helps explain the prevalent problem of backlash toward comparative ads. Not only will consumers committed to the comparison brand reject the negative claims about their brand, they'll become even more certain and confident that they're right and their brand actually is better. In addition to findings consistent with others in the literature focusing on consumers committed to a comparison brand, Vijayalakshmi et al. (2015) extend our understanding regarding the interaction of brand commitment and negativity in comparative ads with the following results and conclusions:

- Committed consumers of a comparison brand in a comparative ad will respond with more favorable attitudes toward that brand after being exposed to a negatively framed comparative ad than will less-committed consumers.
- Committed consumers of a comparison brand will respond with significantly more negative thoughts in response to a negatively framed ad than will less-committed consumers.
- Committed consumers of a comparison brand will generate more negative thoughts in response to a negatively framed comparative ad than a positively framed ad.
- The attitude confidence of committed brand users who are exposed to negatively framed comparative ads will be greater than the attitude confidence of less-committed consumers who are exposed to the same ads at a similar time.

Across all the research investigating the use of comparative advertising and commitment to the comparison brand, we can expect that targeting the loyal or committed users of a competitor's brand is likely to lead to a negative effect on most if not all the positive outcomes and objectives in Figure 2.1's model.

Negativity

The history we covered in Chapter 1 showed that advertisers have long recognized that excessive negativity can be a real problem in comparative advertising. Contrary to that belief, we also learned that excessive negativity is a trap that many advertisers over the years have failed to avoid, especially after becoming engaged in increasingly violent and bitter comparative advertising wars.

Given the seriousness of the problem, it's at least a little surprising that no academic researchers had tackled the problem of trying to understand the effects of negativity in comparative advertising until Alina Sorescu and Betsy Gelb did in 2000. Relying on theory and research from—yes, political campaign advertising—their research results confirmed that a high-negativity comparative ad scored much lower on measures of believability, fairness of content, approval of content, informativeness, and overall ad evaluation compared to a low-negativity comparative ad and a positive one.

A few years later, Shiv, Britton, and Payne (2004) found that the effect of positive framing on A_{br} was more effective than negative framing when message processing motivation is low. When processing motivation is low, people don't pay much attention to the message claims in an ad and are relatively unconcerned about making accurate judgments. In contrast, and consistent with negativity bias, negative message framing can be more persuasive when processing motivation is high. The same year, Jain and Posavac (2004) conducted three experiments demonstrating that comparative ads perceived as containing more negative and derogatory references to competitors resulted in more counterarguments, fewer support arguments, lower believability, more associated perceived bias, and lower brand attitude scores than ads perceived as more positive and less derogatory. Consequently, and as the model shows, we can expect that the more negative a comparative ad is perceived to be by most consumers, the less effective it will be.

Gender and Age

A survey of European consumers found that men thought it was much more acceptable for advertisers to criticize each other, at 42%, compared to just 27% of women. The same survey reported that younger consumers (16 to 24 years old), versus older ones, minded much less if a brand criticized a competitor, with 42% agreeing it's acceptable and 57% disagreeing (as cited in Brabbs, 2001). A study of negative political advertising similarly found that older and more highly educated Americans were more likely to respond negatively (that is, perceive the advertising as "unfair or in some other way undesirable") (Garramone, 1984). When I conducted my study of comparative versus noncomparative advertising for automotive repair services (Chevrolet and Ford) (Beard, 2015), I found that younger consumers responded to the two ads almost identically, while older subjects in the experiment produced significantly lower ratings on A_{ad}, A_{br}, and P_i when viewing the comparative version. They even reported they'd be less likely to recommend the service to someone else.

Finally, remember perception of manipulative intent? Researcher Ching-ching Chang (2007) found that comparative advertising encouraged higher levels of brand-evaluation involvement among men versus women, while it also encouraged higher levels of the perception of manipulative intent among women. As Chang (p. 21) explains:

> For men, the greater brand-evaluation involvement brought about by comparative appeals led to more favorable ad and brand evaluations and greater purchase intentions. For women, the heightened perceptions of manipulative intent brought about by comparative appeals resulted in negative ad and brand evaluations and reduced purchase intentions.

Consequently, and as the model shows, men likely respond more favorably to comparative advertising than women do.

Other Important Message-based Factors

Let's take another look at Grewal et al.'s (1997) meta-analysis results and consider some of the other important situational factors that weren't included in the model. Table 2.1 is a summary of all the situational factors they investigated and their effects on five message objectives and outcomes. As we've already learned and included in the model, their analysis showed comparative advertising to be more effective than noncomparative when the sponsored brand is new, if the sponsored brand's market share is less than the comparison brand's, if a smaller competitor is attacking a market leader and if comparative claims are well substantiated. In contrast, a comparative ad is likely to produce a negative effect on A_{br} if the comparative advertiser's brand is the market leader.

Grewal et al.'s (1997) study also offers several other interesting and informative results. For example, comparative advertising isn't merely more effective than noncomparative for new brands. It also helps if either the sponsor of the comparative ad or the comparison brand are well established in the product category. Similarly, if a comparative advertiser's market share is about the same as that of the comparison brand or even greater, a comparative campaign might encourage attention and P_i, but Grewal et al.'s results show it would likely have a negative effect on A_{ad} and A_{br}. These more detailed research results likely help explain the prevalence of advertising wars between well-known brands, since comparative campaigns between such competitors could produce a mix of some negative outcomes but also some positive ones.

Grewal et al. (1997) concluded that comparative ads containing factual information, rather than evaluative information, account for higher P_i than noncomparative ads although they also generate lower A_{br}. Conversely, in their study of consumers in France, the Netherlands, and the United States, Nye et al. (2008) found that comparative ads containing factual versus evaluative messages generated more favorable A_{br}, but significantly more so in markets where comparative advertising is novel (in their study, France and the Netherlands) and especially for established brands rather than new ones. In the United States, where comparative advertising is not novel, evaluative messages generated more favorable A_{br}. They also found that factual message

Table 2.1. Grewal et al. (1997) Situational Factors and Effects

Comparative advertising is more effective…	*Message Aware.*	*Inform.*	*Similarity.*	*Believe.*	A_{br}	P_i
if the sponsored brand is new	NS	+	+	NS	+	NS
if the sponsored brand is established	NS	+	+	NS	+	NS
if the sponsored brand is the leader	NA	NA	NA	NA	–	NS
if the comparison brand is new	NA	NA	NA	NA	–	+
if the comparison brand is established	+	NS	NS	NS	+	+
if the comparison brand is the leader	+	NS	NS	NS	+	+
if the sponsored brand's relative market position is less than the comparison brand's market position	+	NS	NS	–	+	+
if the sponsored brand's relative market position is equal to or greater than the comparison brand's market position	+	NS	NS	–	–	+
if claims are well substantiated (use of credibility enhancers)	–	NS	NS	NS	+	+
if the ad contains factual rather than evaluative claims	NA	NA	NA	NA	–	+
if relative measures are used versus nonrelative (absolute)	NA	NA	NA	NA	+	+

* + = Comparative advertising superior, – = Noncomparative advertising superior, NS = Not significant, NA = Not applicable.

content generated more positive A_{br} among brand switchers. Whether a comparative ad had a factual or evaluative message made no difference for consumers who were loyal to the comparison brand.

Sorescu and Gelb (2000) similarly concluded that attacking a competitor's product is less risky than attacking the company itself. In fact, the effects should be similar to the difference between factual and evaluative information, since an attack on a product and its features should be perceived as more factual than evaluative. Sorescu and Gelb compared a negative image ad attacking Toyota's competitors for exporting U.S. jobs with a negative product feature ad and a positive comparative ad. The negative image ad generated lower ratings on all their measures—approval of the message, fairness, believability, and informativeness—among all four groups of consumers they studied, including those who drove a Toyota. These experimental research results are completely consistent with Chapter 1's historical research. There we learned that advertisers in the past often regretted becoming involved in increasingly bitter advertising wars that ultimately ranged far from attacks on competitors' product or service attributes or benefits and began focusing on the competitors themselves and their advertising. Some research on political attack advertising also supports the conclusion that attacks on political issues generally encourage more favorable attitudes toward the sponsoring candidate and the ad than do attacks on opponent images or character.

There are also theoretical explanations for why attacking a competitor's products may be less risky for an advertiser, rather than images or reputations. Citing Kelley's (1973) application of attribution theory, James and Hensel (1991) argue that people are more influenced by information they obtain from someone else about a third entity if that information pertains to the entity's factual performance or actions. Sorescu and Gelb (2000) also argue that negative comparative ads appeal to emotion, rather than logic, and that people accord more weight to negative information when evaluating social situations and forming evaluations about others, which could certainly include the comparison brand in a comparative ad.

Comparative Advertising Intensity (CAI)

Up to this point, we've been looking almost entirely at how comparative ads work compared to noncomparative ones. That's what many of the studies in the literature have focused on, and it's also what Grewal et al.'s (1997) research results and summary table are based on as well. It's time to consider what the empirical research literature tells us about different types of comparative ads.

Most researchers have focused on the types proposed and investigated by Brown and Jackson (1977) and Jackson, Brown, and Harmon (1979). "Strictly" comparative ads make explicit comparisons with competitors that are shown, named, or both shown and named. Barry (1993), Stewart and Furse (1986), and most experimental researchers have referred to such advertisements as direct or explicit. These comparative ads include those that show a "look-alike" packaged good that is identical to the comparison product in color, size, and shape.

Implied comparative ads, or what many have called indirect or implicit, are those that allude to, claim superiority over, or criticize one or more competitors by referring to them but not showing or naming them (for example, "other brands," "your brand," "One of the top five brands . . .") or by naming or showing a "generic" or unbranded competitor (e.g., "the phone company" or "DSL"). I prefer to call these ads "competition implied-brand." The reason is that there's a third important type of implied comparative ad that has occasionally been discussed by researchers but rarely studied. These comparative ads acknowledge or imply the existence of competitors but don't refer to them either directly or indirectly. For example, they often include something like "The value only we deliver . . ." or "We're the most dependable . . . in the state."

Such comparative ads are often consistent with one of Stewart and Furse's (1986) definitions of puffery, that is, advertisements that may acknowledge the existence of competitors and claim either superiority or parity with them, but without mentioning an attribute as a basis for it. However, many of these ads also make comparisons or claims that require the existence of competitors to be valid and do include a salient point of difference. A great example is National Car Rental's slogan, "Only National lets you choose any car in the aisle and go." Although National doesn't directly compare itself to competitors or even refer to "the other guys," their claim doesn't make any sense unless there are, in fact, other car rental companies. I call this second type of implied comparative ad "competition implied-category" to capture a type of ad that advertisers use to compare their products or services with all the others in their categories and which, it turns out, is frequently used but rarely singled out for study.

One approach to attempting to explain the neutral and often-varied direct effects of different types of comparative advertising has been referred to as "comparative advertising intensity" (CAI). Donthu (1992), for instance, developed a scale to measure intensity based on four TV commercial characteristics: (a) whether the comparison brand is identified in the ad, (b) whether the comparison is general ("our brand is better") rather than regarding a specific product or service attribute, (c) whether the comparison is two-sided (negative and positive) versus one-sided only (for example, "we cost a little more but work better" versus "we cost less and work better"), and (d) how much of the content of the ad is devoted to making the comparison. He found that the more comparatively intense the commercial, the more it was recalled. In contrast, the most intense commercial had the lowest A_{ad}.

Researchers Cheris Chow and Chung-Leung Luk (2006) also studied five types of comparative ads, ranging from an implied ad (which mentioned the "other guys" but no other brand by name) and four they developed based on Donthu's (1992) scale (CAI = 1 to 4). They found that attitudes (based on a single measure that combined A_{ad}, A_{br}, and P_i) were most positive either when there was no brand comparison (the minimum condition, or "the other guys") or when the comparative ad was moderately intense (CAI = 2 or 3). However, there was a small difference depending on whether study participants were low-CE or high-CE. CE, or "cognitive elaboration," measures the extent to which people tend to think about, or cognitively process, new information. Compared to the low-CE subjects in their experiment, high-CE participants actually responded the most negatively toward the CAI = 1 comparative ad (one that merely mentioned the comparison brand but included no other claims or arguments). They also responded much more favorably toward the CAI = 3 ad than the low-CE subjects did.

Chow and Luk (2006) pointed out three especially important implications regarding their results and conclusions. First, marketers of familiar or established brands, all other things being equal, should be able to safely use moderately comparative ads. The relationship between CAI and negative attitudes isn't directly linear, which is what Donthu's (1992) results suggested. Second, no advertiser should ever use an intensely comparative ad. Period. Third, although the low-CE condition is probably how most people view ads, CE is something that can be predicted or encouraged. For example, most people cognitively elaborate more when product involvement is high versus low; moreover, high-CE could be stimulated by an ad itself, with the inclusion of personally relevant information.

Kenneth Manning and his colleagues (2001) conducted a study to investigate the kinds of relative versus nonrelative mental representations created by comparative ads. Relative representations describe mental impressions about an advertised brand that are held with reference to the comparison brand. This mental representation can be implicit (for example, "Coke's the best brand") or explicit (for example, "Coke is better than Pepsi"). A nonrelative impression, by contrast, represents an impression of the advertised brand without mentally comparing it to the comparison brand (for example, "Coke's a good brand"). They also sought to test the assumption that comparative advertising almost always encourages consumers to perceive how the advertised brand and comparison brand are similar rather than different, regardless of whether the claims in the ad are associative or disassociative in nature.

Manning et al. (2001) confirmed that comparative ads, versus noncomparative ones, do cause more relative mental representations about an advertised brand than nonrelative ones and that differentiative comparative ads generate more disassociative mental representations. However, more important for the present discussion are their results regarding CAI. They hypothesized that a high-intensity comparative ad (containing only comparative claims) would encourage more relative brand impressions and fewer nonrelative impressions compared to a low-intensity ad (one containing both comparative and noncomparative claims).

Manning et al.'s (2001) results supported their hypotheses. The more intense comparative ad in their study did generate a significantly greater number of relative impressions, while the low-intensity ad generated more nonrelative impressions. Their research results are especially important for at least one reason. As we'll learn in Chapter 3, advertising professionals believe comparative advertising is especially effective for positioning brands relative to their competitors. These results regarding relative and disassociative mental impressions speak directly to that effectiveness. Moreover, the results suggest that a high-intensity comparative ad would likely be more effective for this goal than a low-intensity one. This means that for the "Riding the Coattails" approach we learned about in Chapter 1, comparative advertising would be especially effective if the message is associative and the ad has a high CAI (at least in regard to how it was measured here, solely in terms of comparative versus noncomparative content).

Hwang (2002), building on Lamb et al.'s (1978) original typology of comparative ads, also compared experimental subjects (Korean college students) who were exposed multiple times to a noncomparative ad with subjects exposed to low-, medium-, and high-intensity comparative ads. He also compared these four groups to a group that was exposed to an "increasing" comparative ad sequence—instead of just one of the ads, this group was exposed to all three of the comparative ads. This last group of subjects, the ones exposed to the "increasing" schedule of ads, responded with significantly favorable A_{br} and P_i, compared to the noncomparative and low-CAI groups.

Researchers Arti Kalro, Bharadhwaj Sivakumaran, and Rahul Marathe (2013; 2017) conducted two studies of the effects of direct versus implied comparative ads in India. In the first study, they found that direct comparative ads, versus indirect ones, reduced perceived manipulative intent, and increased A_{ad} and the perceived differences between brands, but only for people who use analytical information processing modes (using reason and semantics) versus imagery ones (using nonverbal, sensory representation of perceptual information). Their second study produced similar results. They reported that a direct comparative ad decreased perceived manipulative intent and increased A_{ad} when the ad referenced multiple brands and not the market leader. The practical implications of these results suggest that advertisers should use direct comparative ads when they want to target multiple brands (such as when the category is very fragmented) and they should use indirect when they want to compare their brand with a market leader (that is, implicitly referring to the leader brand but not by directly naming it).

Across-class Comparative Advertising

In addition to direct versus implied comparative ads, there's one more distinct type that's important and frequently used. Researchers Stuart Van Auken and Arthur Adams (1998, 1999, 2005, 2006) carried out a series of studies on "across-class" comparative advertising. Basing their research on assimilation theory, they reported that comparative ads creating across-class associations with a leader in a more prestigious class (for example, luxury import cars) but within the same product category (for example, four-door sedans) can increase the perceived value for the comparative advertiser's brand. In addition, the development of such associations with a leader in a more prestigious class can also result in differentiation from within-class rivals.

Van Auken and Adams (2006) also report that such effects on the part of an across-class comparative advertiser can be moderated by a number of other factors, such as whether the manufacturer of the comparison brand has a quality reputation. The use of across-class comparative ads has been especially prevalent in automotive advertising over the years. Excellent example campaigns include Chrysler comparing its LeBaron with BMW and Mercedes in 1985, Subaru comparing its models to Mercedes-Benz and Volvo in 1989 and Ford comparing its Edge SUV with BMW and Lexus in 2007. In addition, in Chapter 7 you'll be reading a mini-case study focusing on DiGiorno Frozen Pizza's across-class comparative campaign targeting their "delivery" competitors.

CONCLUSIONS

When J. J. Boddewyn and Katherin Marton published their landmark book on comparative advertising in 1978, researchers were just getting started in their efforts to understand what we learned in Chapter 1 is an ancient and often controversial persuasive communication tactic, but one that gained much greater acceptability in the late 1960s. They noted that research was needed to address a number of questions about comparative advertising. For example, they wondered about the effects of competitors' brand positions, levels of brand loyalty, the type or nature of the comparative claims, and advertisers' attempts to "upgrade by association." As we can see by the summary and synthesis of the empirical research presented in this chapter, and by the literature's steady progress in regard to conceptual and methodological rigor and sophistication, researchers have made tremendous progress toward answering these questions as well as many others.

However, the increasing sophistication of the research literature, especially in the form of the dozens of situational factors that have been found to moderate the effectiveness of a comparative ad versus a noncomparative one, points to a strength and a weakness of Figure 2.1's model. On one hand, the model offers a useful summary of what might be expected to happen "on the average" or "all other things being equal."

On the other hand, the relationships shown in the model should also be considered a simplification. The model's 14 situational factors are arguably the most important ones and those for which we have the greatest amount of consistent research support. Yet the results of the many studies summarized in this chapter show there are scores of other important factors. And if that doesn't sufficiently complicate things, the research literature shows there are many complex interactions among the situational factors included in our model and the dozens of others studied by researchers during the past 20 years or so. Consequently, the best advice for anyone considering the launching of a comparative campaign would be to begin organizing expectations around the relationships shown in the model, but then to take a closer look at the research summarized in this chapter and how many of the other factors might also apply to his or her specific marketing situation.

Chapter Three

What the Professionals Say

As we learned in Chapter 2, the findings of more than 40 years of systematic, empirical academic research on comparative advertising have given us some pretty good ideas about when and why it will probably be more effective than noncomparative advertising. But as we learned in Chapter 1, the amount of confidence advertising professionals have expressed when it comes to their experiences and beliefs about whether it's a good idea to identify a competitor and launch a comparative campaign has varied considerably over time and from one professional to another.

As we also know, there's quite a bit of historical evidence to suggest excessively confrontational comparative advertising can lead to problems for advertisers and their ad agencies. For example, Jartran Inc.'s ad agency almost got in serious legal trouble along with their client over Jartran's historically disastrous (and fraudulent) comparative campaign back in the 1980s. In addition to such prevalent concerns that naming competitors can give their awareness an unnecessary boost or that comparative ads are widely disliked, some researchers have recently proposed that excessively confrontational or combative advertising can lead to indifferent consumers who don't develop a preference for any brand (similar to the voter apathy many believe political attack advertising encourages). They also argue that combative advertising can cause an intensified level of competition that actually leaves all the competitors worse off (Chen et al., 2009). We saw obvious examples of this very consequence in Chapter 1's history, such as the comparative ad wars in credit card services and, more recently, wireless services.

And if you were looking for additional reasons why advertising professionals might question the wisdom of identifying competitors, there are many others. For example, comparative ads often cause trouble for U.S. advertisers with the Federal Trade Commission (FTC) or challenges from industry self-regulatory bodies, such as the National Advertising Division (NAD) of the Council of Better Business Bureaus. And if that's not bad enough, there's also a good chance that a competitor might be sufficiently annoyed by a comparative ad to launch a lawsuit. In fact, industry observers report that both lawsuits and complaints to the NAD over disputed claims linked to comparative advertising campaigns began climbing nearly 10 years ago, presumably in response to the greater use of comparative advertising (York, 2010). You'll read more about these kinds of legal and regulatory problems in Chapter 4.

On the other hand, what's also pretty obvious at this point is that advertisers and their agencies do a lot of comparative advertising. Moreover, as the empirical research literature we looked at in Chapter 2 shows, identifying competitors and making comparisons in advertising certainly seems to be quite effective in achieving certain objectives and when carefully executed in certain ways.

So, if you could directly ask them, what would the people responsible for all this comparative advertising say about what they believe comparative advertising is good for or when it's most likely to be effective? The purpose of this chapter is to get at answers to this question, as well as several related ones. We'll do it by (a) identifying what the beliefs of advertising agency creative professionals in the United States are regarding when a comparative ad will probably be more effective than a noncomparative one; (b) assessing in what ways the beliefs of advertising's creative leaders have changed during the past approximately 25 years; (c) taking a closer look at how the beliefs of today's advertising agency creatives differ, or not, from those of their clients and corporate contemporaries; and (d) looking at how the beliefs of advertising professionals match up with the findings of decades of empirical, scholarly research on the topic.

EARLY STUDIES OF ADVERTISING PROFESSIONALS

Researchers began asking advertising professionals what they thought about comparative advertising not long after the FTC launched its campaign in the United States to encourage it in the early 1970s. Perhaps because of the much slower acceptance of comparative advertising around the world during the second half of the 20th century, a search turned up no surveys of advertising professionals elsewhere.

Thomas Barry and Roger Tremblay (1975) conducted what appears to be the earliest study of advertising professionals on the topic of naming competitors, when they sought the opinions of 16 Dallas and Houston corporate and ad agency executives. Despite the fact that advertisers were increasingly naming competitors starting in the mid- to late-1960s, and things really took off in the 1970s, Barry and Tremblay discovered mostly negative attitudes toward comparative advertising. These negative attitudes were primarily based on some of the historical concerns we discovered in Chapter 1—comparative advertising gives free exposure to competitors, could increase the likelihood of damage to a brand's reputation, or even all the competitors in an industry, and often simply leaves consumers confused.

The next study of advertising professionals, conducted by Robert Hisrich in 1983, surveyed a random sample of 200 corporate executives. He found they were generally favorable toward comparative advertising, especially when competitors are clearly identified and the comparisons are direct or explicit.

In 1989, researchers Darrell Muehling, Donald Stem, and Peter Raven substantially replicated Hisrich's (1983) study with a survey of advertising executives from the 100 largest U.S. ad agencies, along with 100 advertising executives representing the largest U.S. advertisers and 51 executives from media and industry regulatory groups. They found the practice of comparative advertising was fairly widespread, with nearly half the advertisers and more than 80% of the ad agency respondents reporting they had used or created a comparative campaign during the previous five years. Similar to what Hisrich (1983) found, all three groups held significantly more favorable attitudes toward direct (or explicit) comparative ads, compared to implied ones or "Brand X" comparisons. The only survey respondents favoring ads that make general comparisons with all competitors or no comparisons at all (which they grouped together into a fourth type) were the media industry regulators.

More important, Muehling et al. (1989) found that agency executives, compared to their corporate clients and the ad regulators, held significantly more favorable attitudes toward both direct and implied comparative advertising. It's probably no surprise they also found the agency professionals were more inclined to disagree that "comparative advertising reduces the credibility of the advertiser" and "should not be allowed," while they expressed stronger agreement that it "is an essential type of advertising," "results in better products offered to consumers," and "presents a true picture of the product advertised" (p. 43). None of Muehling et al.'s respondents agreed that comparative ads should be further regulated by the FTC.

The same year, John Rogers and Terrell Williams (1989) published the findings of their survey of creative directors at the 500 largest U.S. ad agencies. There were several good reasons why they chose to ask agency creative directors about comparative advertising. First, creative directors are advertising's communication and persuasion strategists and artists. Creative teams of copywriters and art directors report to creative directors, so they are significantly involved in every facet of an advertising campaign, including what the advertising message strategy is going to be and how it's executed. Second, because message strategies and tactics are so critical to the success of an advertising campaign, creative directors are also often among the top executives in ad agencies, holding the ranks of partner, president, and CEO. And third, because they are among the agencies' top leaders, their beliefs and opinions about message strategies and tactics likely both influence and reflect those of just about everybody else.

On their questionnaire, Rogers and Williams (1989) defined comparative advertising as "that which contains specific references to competing brands by name," in other words, direct or explicit comparative advertising. Then they asked their creative director respondents to think about a situation in which they might consider using a comparative campaign. Next, they asked them to rate when they thought comparative advertising would be significantly more effective (for example, encouraging purchase intention [P_i] or initial brand trial), noncomparative would be more effective (for example, encouraging a positive attitude toward the ad [A_{ad}] or brand [A_{br}]) or neither (for example, creating brand awareness or obtaining brand-name recall). We'll take a closer look at what they found, and compare their findings with a more recent survey, in the next section.

ADVERTISING CREATIVES AND COMPARATIVE ADVERTISING OBJECTIVES

The ad agency creative executives Rogers and Williams (1989) surveyed were the first ones to reach their levels of leadership and professional practice experience during and following a period when comparative advertising was strongly encouraged by the FTC in the United States and, subsequently, extensively used. That, of course, is why it was important to survey them. But what about 25 or 30 years later? Might the beliefs and attitudes regarding comparative advertising have changed somewhat after, say, another couple of decades of experience with identifying competitors? As we know, a lot happened with comparative advertising in the United States during the 1980s and 1990s.

So what do today's advertising professionals think of comparative advertising? That's an important question, especially when you consider that not only were the last surveys of advertising agency professionals conducted in the late 1980s, there were only 43 (Muehling et al., 1989) and 56 (Rogers & Williams, 1989) ad agency respondents included in those surveys. While Muehling and his colleagues achieved a survey response rate of 43%, which is very good these days for a mail survey, they started with a sample of only 100 agency executives. And while Rogers and Williams had a sample of 500 agency creatives, their survey response rate was only 11%. So for many years, our best insights into what ad agency professionals think about comparative advertising—besides what we see in the advertising and marketing trade media, like *Advertising Age*, or what we've learned from historical research—was mainly based on survey responses from 43 agency executives and 56 creative directors.

To address the first two goals of this chapter—discovering what creative directors think about comparative advertising and seeing how it may or may not have changed over time—we're going to look at the findings of a replication of Rogers and Williams's (1989) survey (Beard, 2013b) and then compare those findings with theirs. For that survey, I followed the same sampling procedures Rogers and Williams did. I identified the 500 largest agencies in an annual agency report, published by the industry's leading trade journal, *Advertising Age*. Creative executives were then identified using listings provided in an industry publication called the *Standard Directory of Advertising Agencies*. I went one step further than the pre-Web Rogers and Williams did, however, and supplemented the *Directory* listings with a search of agency Web sites, with the goal of developing the most up-to-date list of creative directors in the United States as possible.

So how do you get busy professionals to respond to a mail survey? Especially advertising creative directors, many of whom you also know are ad agency partners and presidents, and, who Rogers and Williams (1989, p. 27) point out, have a "tendency . . . to respond poorly to surveys." A good start would be with a personalized pre-notification letter, emphasizing how professional views of comparative advertising's effectiveness have varied over the past century, as expressed by some industry notables. Here's a good example: "As an advertising practitioner I believe that naming names is always a creative cop-out" (Andrew Kershaw, chairman, Ogilvy & Mather, 1976, p. 26). Next, you might send them a full mailing, which includes a copy of the questionnaire and a reply envelope, followed by a reminder post card, and then a final mailing, with another copy of the questionnaire. Finally, fully aware that Rogers and Williams only got a response rate of 11%, you might include an uncirculated U.S. Mint Native American $1 coin as an inducement. Yes, this really works, even with highly paid professionals, but the key is that it has to be delivered with the questionnaire. If you promise to send survey respondents something if they return a questionnaire, it doesn't work nearly as well.

The attitudes and beliefs of the respondents for our replication were measured using the same scales Rogers and Williams (1989) used. The creative directors were asked to indicate their beliefs regarding the relative effectiveness of comparative versus noncomparative advertising using what Rogers and Williams called a modified Stapel scale. This means respondents rated comparative advertising more effective than noncomparative by placing a checkmark on a point on a scale that corresponded to +1, +2, or +3, with +3 being the most effective. They rated noncomparative more effective with responses corresponding to –1, –2, or –3, with –3 being the most effective. The midpoint of the scale, indicating neither was more effective than the other, corresponded to a value of zero.

These procedures paid off with a response rate more than double that of Rogers and Williams (1989), at 27%, or 130 completed questionnaires, after following the standard survey procedure of subtracting the 18 that came back as "undeliverable." As you'd expect with a sample of top agency executives, they reported a lot of experience in advertising, with an average of 23 years. The respondents worked for agencies ranging from tiny to huge, with annual revenues ranging from $100,000 to $286 million, with an average of $17,030,569. They also employed an average of 78 people with staffs ranging from 1 to more than 650.

Survey Findings: Extent of Comparative Advertising Use

The simplest and easiest way to ask advertising agency professionals how much of a certain type of advertising they create or use is to ask them how much of it they billed to their clients the previous year. Forty-one percent of the creative directors for our replication reported that their agencies billed some comparative advertising for consumer products and 26% said they billed some for industrial products. Forty-four respondents (or 33.8%) reported that they had billed no comparative advertising at all.

These findings are similar to those of Rogers and Williams (1989). They reported that 46% of their 56 creative directors had billed comparative advertising for consumer-products advertising and 36% for industrial-products advertising. They also reported that 43% of their respondents had billed no comparative advertising at all during the previous year. Despite the fact there are some differences in the percentages of creative directors who reported that they did or didn't use comparative advertising, if you test the differences between the two samples using what's called a *Z*-test of proportions, it turns out none of them are statistically significantly different. That means we can't reject chance as an explanation for the differences between them and suggests the amount of comparative advertising being created by advertising creatives in 2015 could be exactly the same as it was some 25 years before that.

Rogers and Williams (1989) reported that 93% of their respondents agreed comparative advertising could be more effective than noncomparative "under some circumstances." A similar and overwhelming percentage of the present sample of creative directors, at 96%, also agreed that comparative advertising could be more effective at accomplishing at least one of the objectives and outcomes that you can see listed in Table 3.1. In addition, Rogers and Williams also reported that 25% of their creative directors rated comparative advertising more effective than noncomparative, "per se," although they didn't say how they produced this finding. One way to produce a comparable finding is to create a single measure of comparative versus non-comparative effectiveness by averaging and then combining the ratings for all the objectives and outcomes. If a creative director had a positive score on this measure, it would mean he or she thinks comparative advertising is more effective overall. If it's a negative score, it means the respondent thinks noncomparative is more effective. The result was that nearly 40% of the creative directors rated comparative advertising more effective than noncomparative overall.

The next important thing we'd like to know is which of the objectives and outcomes the creative directors think comparative advertising is or isn't more

Table 3.1. Comparative versus Noncomparative Advertising: Objectives and Outcomes

Advertising Objective/Outcome	*Survey (2013) M*	*Rogers & Williams M*	*t-values and sig.*
Competitive brand positioning	+.62*	+1.28*	3.94**
Initial brand trial	+.62*	+1.20*	3.78**
Attribute recall	+.34*	+.66*	1.95
Claim/message believability	+.33*	+.54*	1.36
Brand preference	−.22	+.51*	4.78**
Message involvement	+.41*	+.45*	.31
Purchase intention	+.43*	+.41*	.16
Ad interest	+.31*	+.30*	.07
Message recall	+.34*	+.30*	.29
Brand interest	−.05	+.28	2.26*
Brand comprehension	−.25	+.24	3.06**
A_{ad} (ad attitude)	−1.42*	−.82*	4.65**
Brand-name recall	−.92*	−.50*	2.75**
A_{br} (brand attitude)	−1.28*	−.44*	5.74**
Brand loyalty	−1.05*	−.36*	4.77**
Repeat purchases	−.41*	−.30*	.88
Brand awareness	−.82*	−.26	3.43**

* $p < .05$; ** $p < .01$; all tests were two-tailed *t*-tests; + indicates comparative more effective, – indicates noncomparative more effective; within-sample means were tested for significant difference from 0, indicating no difference in the effectiveness of comparative versus noncomparative advertising; between-sample means were tested for significant differences from each other.

effective for accomplishing. If the average agreement scores for each objective and outcome are statistically significant (and you can see from all the asterisks [*] in Table 3.1 that most of them are), it means we can have a great deal of confidence that they really do represent agreement or disagreement and that they really aren't positive or negative just based on chance. As the findings in column one of Table 3.1 show, for our replication, creative directors rated comparative advertising more effective for achieving the following objectives and outcomes: (a) competitive brand positioning, (b) initial brand trail, (c) P_i, (d) consumer involvement, (e) message recall, (f) attribute recall, (g) claim/message believability, and (h) ad interest. They rated noncomparative advertising (the ones with the negative mean scores) significantly more effective for achieving almost all the rest of the objectives and outcomes, including the especially important ones of (a) A_{ad}, (b) A_{br}, (c) brand loyalty, (d) brand awareness, and (e) brand-name recall.

The second column in Table 3.1 consists of Rogers and Williams's (1989) findings for each of the same objectives and outcomes. By comparing their findings with our replication, we can address the second goal of this chapter—finding out how the attitudes of advertising creative professionals have changed over the past 25 years or so. To start, these comparisons show that today's creative directors rated comparative advertising more effective for accomplishing nearly all the same objectives and outcomes as Rogers and Williams's respondents. Our current sample of creative directors also rated noncomparative advertising significantly more effective for accomplishing almost all the same objectives and outcomes as Rogers and Williams's respondents did, including the key ones of A_{ad} and A_{br}.

However, there's another important pattern you may have noticed among the differences between the two samples of creative directors. It's fairly obvious that today's creative executives reported considerably less agreement with the effectiveness of comparative advertising (lower mean scores) and greater agreement with the effectiveness of noncomparative advertising (higher mean scores), compared to Rogers and Williams's (1989) respondents, nearly across the board. In addition, many of the *t*-tests of the differences between the two samples of creative directors are statistically significant (Table 3.1's third column), which means they are too large to have occurred by chance. For example, Rogers and Williams's respondents agreed much more that comparative advertising would be effective for achieving brand positioning, brand trial, and brand preference. On the other hand, the current sample of creative directors agreed much more that noncomparative advertising would be more effective than comparative advertising for achieving positive ad and brand attitudes and brand-name recall. These findings suggest the beliefs and opinions of today's creative directors might not be quite as favorable toward comparative advertising as they used to be.

Summary: Attitudes toward Objectives and Outcomes

As the most recent survey findings show, fewer creative directors reported billing comparative advertising for both consumer and industrial products, and fewer also reported billing no comparative advertising at all, compared to Rogers and Williams's (1989) ad agency creative directors. Likewise, the percentage of comparative consumer-product advertising is also substantially less, although the percentage of comparative industrial-product advertising is slightly greater. It's important to keep in mind, though, that none of the differences in the use of comparative advertising are statistically significant. These findings, taken together, support a conclusion that there hasn't been either a significant increase or decrease in the use of comparative advertising since 1989, at least from the perspective of the creative executives who are responsible for creating, or at least approving, the majority of it in the United States.

We have to keep in mind, though, that for this survey and Rogers and Williams's (1989), comparative advertising was defined as that which directly identifies competitors by naming or showing them. This may have led to an underestimation of its use, as well as the differences between both sets of survey findings and content analyses of the use of comparative advertising in the media. Don't forget, there are studies suggesting as much as 40% of all ads in the United States qualify as comparative and as much as 50% to 80% of all TV ads (Beard, 2016b; Donthu, 1992).

The survey findings also show that all of today's creative directors believe comparative advertising could be more effective at achieving at least one of the objectives and outcomes, and nearly 40% rated comparative more effective than noncomparative advertising overall. They also rated comparative advertising to be significantly more effective for achieving 8 of the 17 objectives and outcomes. So it's also reasonable to conclude that the beliefs of top creative professionals in the United States remain quite favorable toward the use of comparative advertising.

One of the most important of the recent survey findings is that respondents rated both comparative and noncomparative advertising effective for achieving almost exactly the same objectives and outcomes that Rogers and Williams's (1989) respondents did. On the other hand, they also consistently rated comparative advertising less effective and noncomparative advertising more effective. These findings support two conclusions. First, the beliefs of advertising creative professionals regarding the objectives and outcomes for which comparative advertising will be more effective changed very little between the late 1980s and when this more recent survey was conducted. These findings from a replication of Rogers and Williams's survey add quite a bit to support both the validity and reliability of their original findings.

A second conclusion, based on our more recent survey findings, is that today's creative professionals are somewhat less confident in the effectiveness of comparative advertising and more confident in noncomparative advertising, compared to those from some 25 years ago. A decline in favorable beliefs regarding the effectiveness of comparative advertising—or, at least the absence of an increase in positive ones—is a little surprising for a couple of reasons. First, although there were few content analyses of comparative advertising frequency of use published in the academic literature from the late 1980s and into the 2000s, those that were (Al-Olayan & Karande, 2000; Beard, 2016b; Robinson, 1994), as well as reports by industry observers (Flint, 1990; Levy, 1987; York, 2009), suggest an increase during this period. Second, the available surveys of practitioners, beginning with Barry and Tremblay in 1975, also suggest very positive views of comparative advertising, especially among agency professionals.

One explanation for the differences between the two studies is that the present sample is quite a bit larger and, for this reason, represents a more accurate and precise description of a population of U.S. ad agency creative directors. Another explanation for a possible decline in favorable beliefs toward comparative advertising effectiveness is a growing body of both historical and empirical research suggesting that aggressively combative advertising often produces some unintended consequences. In fact, concerns about risks associated with comparative advertising were frequently mentioned in the open-ended responses to our most recent survey, which you'll see below.

A decline in favorable beliefs regarding the effectiveness of comparative advertising versus noncomparative advertising could also be explained by another set of findings from the survey. Several of the objectives and outcomes that respondents rated noncomparative advertising more effective for achieving, compared to Rogers and Williams's (1989) creative directors, are brand-related (A_{br}, brand loyalty, brand-name recall, brand awareness). In addition, brand preference is the only objective for which there was a major difference between the two samples (from positive to neutral). This suggests that advertising creative professionals have grown somewhat more concerned that comparative advertising could conflict with their efforts to build strong, appealing brands.

ADVERTISING CREATIVES AND SITUATIONAL FACTORS

As we learned in both Chapters 1 and 2, the effects comparative advertising may have on a particular intended or unintended advertising objective or outcome can be affected by other variables, such as the competitive positions of the comparison or sponsored brand or even features of the product or advertising itself, such as whether the advertised product has a true feature of superiority, whether the advertising does or doesn't attempt to communicate that or how negative in tone an ad is perceived to be. As we learned in Chapter 2, in a scientific experiment, these third variables are called *moderators* because they moderate the relationship between an independent variable—in this case, a comparative versus noncomparative ad—and a dependent variable—in this case, and as an example, A_{ad}. Another more practice-oriented name for these third variables, however, which Rogers and Williams (1989) used, is "situational factors."

Survey findings for what the creative directors think about the effects of various situational factors on the effectiveness of comparative advertising are shown in Table 3.2. A statistically significant positive mean score (one with an asterisk [*]) means the creative directors agreed comparative advertising would be more effective than noncomparative in that situation. A statistically significant negative score indicates they disagreed.

The summary of Rogers and Williams' (1989) findings in the second column of Table 3.2 shows what their sample of advertising creative directors thought about the situation in which comparative advertising might be more effective (for example, when the advertised brand has a relatively small market share or when advertising claims are well substantiated), when it would be less effective (for example, if the advertiser has a big advertising budget or if the advertised brand has a large market share), and those likely having no effects on its effectiveness (for example, if there is no clear market leader).

Table 3.2 also includes comparisons of the survey findings from our replication with those of Rogers and Williams (1989). The differences between them were tested for statistical significance using *t*-tests. As you can see, the more recent sample of creative directors expressed significantly greater agreement that comparative advertising would be more effective in most of the situations listed in Table 3.2. Many of these findings are very consistent with what we learned earlier in Chapters 1 and 2. For example, creative directors today expressed even greater agreement that comparative advertising will be more effective than noncomparative if the claims they make about the advertised product or service are well substantiated, believable, unique, and strong. They also believe comparative advertising will be more effective for smaller competitors and less effective for larger ones (the "Davids" versus the "Goliaths"). Moreover, the statistical significance of the differences between the two samples confirms we can be quite confident that we really did find meaningful differences and it's unlikely that they occurred by chance.

Table 3.2. Situational Factors Affecting Comparative Advertising Effectiveness

Comparative advertising is more effective	*Survey (2013) M*	*Rogers & Williams M*	*t-values and sig.*
Effectiveness related to market/advertiser characteristics			
if the advertised brand has a small market share	+.98**	+.57*	4.61**
in more price competitive markets	+.82**	+.44*	4.80**
if loyalty for the advertised brand is strong	–.44**	+.06	4.47**
if there is no clear market leader	+.20	–.24	3.97**
if the advertiser has a large advertising budget	–.38**	–.28*	1.00
if the advertised brand has a large market share	–.84**	–.79*	.48
Effectiveness related to advertisement characteristics			
if claims are made on salient product benefits	+1.01**	+1.17*	1.80
if claims are well substantiated	+1.21**	+.71*	5.76**
if claims are believable	+1.21**	+.53*	8.08**
if ads are more creative	+.66**	+.44*	1.87
if comparative claims are strong	+1.19**	+.02	15.51**
over a large number of exposures	+.29*	–.22*	5.31**
for TV commercials as opposed to print ads	+.19	–.30*	5.10**
Effectiveness related to the nature of the product advertised			
if compared feature is unique to brand	+.83**	+.77*	.55
if the advertised brand is of higher quality	+.44**	+.23*	1.96
for a brand new to the market (novel)	+.59**	+.06	5.33**
for consumer durables	+.22*	+.06	2.09*
for products priced lower than competing brand	+.58**	+.04	6.39**
for industrial or BtoB products	+.25*	–.04	2.80**
for low-priced, frequently purchased consumer products	+.24*	–.18	3.52**

Comparative advertising is more effective	*Survey (2013) M*	*Rogers & Williams M*	*t-values and sig.*
for more innovative products	+.43**	−.21	4.87**

* $p < .05$; ** $p < .01$; all tests are two-tailed *t*-tests; means were calculated from scores: SA = 2, A = 1, N = 0, D = −1, SD = −2; + indicates comparative more effective, − indicates noncomparative more effective; within-sample means were tested for significant difference from 0, indicating no difference in the effectiveness of comparative versus noncomparative advertising; between-sample findings were tested for significant differences from each other.

Summary: Attitudes Regarding Situational Factors

One fairly obvious conclusion regarding situational factors is that the creative directors surveyed most recently substantially agreed with Rogers and Williams's (1989) survey respondents as to which ones are likely to encourage the success of a comparative versus noncomparative advertising campaign. The stability of these findings across a period of some 25 years also means we can be fairly confident they really do show what creative professionals believe. In fact, there were really only a few big changes in opinion—for example, today's creative directors believe much more strongly that comparative advertising is less likely to be effective than noncomparative if brand loyalty is already strong and more likely to be effective if the brand is new to the market, more innovative, or has a lower price.

A second conclusion is that, while today's advertising creative professionals generally express less confidence regarding which objectives or outcomes comparative advertising will be more effective for achieving compared to noncomparative advertising, they also have significantly greater confidence regarding the situations in which it will be more effective. This is evident in the fact that the scores for their ratings of agreement are consistently higher for almost all the situational factors. The simplest explanation for this finding is that another 25 years of experience has helped our population of advertising creative directors gain a better understanding of when comparative ads and campaigns are likely to be successful.

ADVERTISING CREATIVES VS. CORPORATE PROFESSIONALS: COMPARATIVE ADVERTISING OUTCOMES

The next thing we want to look at is how advertising agency creatives might differ from their corporate clients. You'll recall that Muehler and his colleagues found that, back in 1989, advertising agency professionals had a much more positive attitude toward both direct and implied comparative advertising than corporate professionals did. It's important to understand this for a couple of related reasons. First, both agencies and their corporate clients are involved in the decision regarding the advertising message for a particular campaign. Second, as a service provider in a somewhat tenuous relationship with a client—the average length of a client-ad agency relationship has declined from more than seven years in the 1980s to less than three in 2013 (The Bedford Group, 2017)—ad agencies would certainly like to make and keep their corporate clients happy. In fact, some research conducted back in the 1990s showed that ad agency clients' perceptions that they were in conflict with their agency representatives were strongly and negatively correlated with their satisfaction with the relationship with their agency and even their beliefs that their agency was doing a good job (Beard, 1996).

For this survey, in mid-2016, I selected a sample of 500 executives and managers holding the titles of Advertising Manager, Advertising Director, Advertising Executive, Director of Advertising, and VP Advertising from a sampling frame of nearly 5,500 U.S. professionals, purchased from a commercial list service. This survey was conducted as a hybrid, using both postal and Web-based questionnaires. Respondents received multiple postal and e-mail reminders, and, to encourage responses, a $1 Native American Code Talkers coin.

Measurement was identical to that used in the two surveys of ad agency creatives. Respondents indicated their views regarding the relative effectiveness of comparative advertising—which was defined as that which explicitly identifies the competitor by name—versus noncomparative advertising using a modified Stapel scale. Scale values ranged from +3 (comparative advertising most effective) to –3 (noncomparative advertising most effective), with a midpoint of zero, indicating neither was more effective.

Unfortunately, the survey sample list of e-mail addresses contained a large number of incorrect addresses (70); these "undeliverables" were subtracted from the total sample to calculate a response rate of 13% (56 usable questionnaires out of 430). The response rate is fairly low for a survey and, ironically, it produced exactly the same number of survey respondents Rogers and Williams (1989) had nearly 30 years ago.

On the other hand, descriptive statistics show we wound up with a very experienced sample of corporate advertising professionals. They reported an average of nearly 24 years of experience in advertising (almost exactly the same, in fact, as the average years of experience for our replication survey of ad agency creative directors). Mean annual advertising expenditures for the sample were almost $14 million (with a median of $325,000). They were also experienced with comparative advertising. Some 37.5% of the respondents reported that at some point in their career they had been involved with an explicit comparative ad campaign (that is, which identified one or more competitors by name). Moreover, on average, about 16% of their expenditures the previous year were on directly comparative ads and campaigns.

The main findings of the survey and comparisons with the more recent survey of agency creative directors are shown in Table 3.3. The findings show the corporate client respondents believe comparative advertising is more effective than noncomparative for establishing a brand position and encouraging initial brand trial. They also rated comparative advertising significantly more effective for encouraging attribute recall, ad interest, and message recall. On the other hand, their attitudes are more strongly in favor of noncomparative advertising when it comes to encouraging A_{ad}, A_{br}, brand loyalty, repeat purchases, and brand awareness. It's especially interesting to note here that there was only one statistically significant difference between these respondents and our sample of agency creative directors. Creative directors are far more concerned that comparative advertising will have a negative effective on brand-name recall. It's also worth noting that the difference between the two groups on competitive brand positioning was almost statistically significant.

Advertising Creatives versus Corporate Professionals: Situational Factors

Next, we want to consider what the corporate advertising professionals think about the situational factors that contribute to the success of a comparative campaign and how they might differ from the beliefs of the ad agency creative directors. As you can see in the first column of Table 3.4, the corporate professionals expressed significantly greater agreement that comparative advertising would be more effective in almost all the situations listed in the table. In addition, there are three significant differences here between corporate and agency professionals. Corporate professionals agree significantly more that comparative advertising will be effective when the brand is of higher quality and when it is new, whereas the agency creatives agree noncomparative advertising will be more effective if the advertiser has a large market share (that is, what we'd probably call a "Goliath").

Summary: Agency Creatives versus Corporate Professionals

Corporate advertising professionals rated comparative advertising effective for achieving almost all the same objectives as the ad agency respondents did. There were also few significant differences in their views regarding the situations that likely contribute to effective comparative campaigns. If you're in the advertising agency business, these findings should be good news. The decision as to whether it's a good idea to employ a comparative campaign to achieve certain objectives in a particular situation should produce little conflict between agencies and their clients. In addition, and more important, the levels of agreement between these two groups of advertising professionals

Table 3.3. Clients versus Creatives: Advertising Objectives and Outcomes

Advertising Objectives/ Outcomes	*Clients (2016) M*	*Creatives (2013) M*	*t-values and sig.*
Competitive brand positioning	+1.16**	+.62*	1.82
Initial brand trial	+.80**	+.62*	.65
Attribute recall	+.42*	+.34*	.27
Claim/message believability	+.20	+.33*	.47
Brand preference	+.20	−.22	1.53
Message involvement	+.37	+.41*	.16
Purchase intention (P_i)	+.47*	+.43*	.16
Ad interest	+.55*	+.31*	.91
Message recall	+.45*	+.34*	.44
Brand interest	−.20	−.05	.56
Brand comprehension	−.08	−.25	.58
Attitude-Ad (A_{ad})	−1.02**	−1.42*	1.62
Brand-name recall	−.23	−.92*	2.35*
Attitude-Brand (A_{br})	−1.22**	−1.28*	.26
Brand loyalty	−1.25**	−1.05*	.76
Repeat purchases	−.58*	−.41*	.71
Brand awareness	−.41*	−.82*	1.39

* $p < .05$; ** $p < .01$; all tests were two-tailed *t*-tests; + indicates comparative more effective, – indicates noncomparative more effective; within-sample means were tested for significant difference from 0, indicating no difference in the effectiveness of comparative versus noncomparative advertising; between-sample means were tested for significant differences from each other.

also adds considerably to the amount of confidence we can have in the findings of both surveys.

OPEN-ENDED SURVEY REPONSES

Survey questionnaires with closed-ended items are a great way to collect a lot of information from a large group of people. Surveys also lend themselves to producing straightforward and unambiguous findings, especially when we can use statistics that allow us to reject chance as an explanation for what we found. The biggest problem is that closed-ended questionnaire items don't let the respondents tell us something we didn't already know. In other words,

Table 3.4. Clients vs. Creatives: Situational Factors Affecting Comparative Advertising Effectiveness

Comparative advertising is more effective	*Clients (2016) M*	*Creatives (2013) M*	*t-values and sig.*
Effectiveness related to market/advertiser characteristics			
if the advertised brand has a small market share	+.94**	+.98**	.25
in more price competitive markets	+.94**	+.82**	.88
if loyalty for the advertised brand is strong	–.09	–.44**	1.80
if there is no clear market leader	+.48**	+.20	1.48
if the advertiser has a large advertising budget	–.14	–.38**	1.36
if the advertised brand has a large market share	–.20	–.84**	3.45**
Effectiveness related to advertisement characteristics			
if claims are made on salient product benefits	+.87**	+1.01**	.95
if claims are well substantiated	+1.20**	+1.21**	.07
if claims are believable	+1.06**	+1.21**	1.05
if ads are more creative	+.36*	+.66**	1.52
if comparative claims are strong	+1.09**	+1.19**	.75
over a large number of exposures	+.23	+.29*	.36
for TV commercials as opposed to print ads	+.13	+.19*	.35
Effectiveness related to the nature of the product advertised			
if compared feature is unique to brand	+1.08**	+.83**	1.37
if the advertised brand is of higher quality	+1.00**	+.44**	3.09**
for a brand new to the market (novel)	+.92**	+.59**	2.00*
for consumer durables	+.44**	+.22*	1.62
for products priced lower than competing brand	+.86**	+.58**	1.92
for industrial or BtoB products	+.48**	+.25*	1.33

Comparative advertising is more effective	*Clients (2016) M*	*Creatives (2013) M*	*t-values and sig.*
for low-priced, frequently purchased consumer products	+.47**	+.24*	1.18
for more innovative products	+.65**	+.43**	1.01

* $p < .05$; ** $p < .01$; all tests were two-tailed t-tests; means were calculated from scores: SA = 2, A = 1, N = 0, D = –1, SD = –2; + indicates comparative more effective, – indicates noncomparative more effective; within-sample means were tested for significant difference from 0, indicating no difference in the effectiveness of comparative versus noncomparative advertising; between-sample findings were tested for significant differences from each other.

respondents can tell us whether they think something is true or false, or how much they disagree or agree with it, but they can't tell us whether there's something else that's just as important. So it's a common strategy with a survey to include an opportunity for respondents to add anything else they think might be important.

Seventy-eight of our 130 agency creative directors and 30 of our 56 corporate ad executives responded to an open-ended invitation to share any additional thoughts they had about the topic of comparative advertising. As surveys go, that's good. It suggests the respondents had quite a bit of interest in the topic, which is also a good sign—it implies the respondents gave some serious thought to how they answered the items on the questionnaire.

Although the respondents' open-ended comments and observations ranged fairly widely, there were a handful of especially interesting themes among them. The first one emphasizes what we've already talked about numerous times, and those are the inherent risks involved in running comparative advertising campaigns. Several respondents, for example, mentioned the risk of legal problems. "Get a good lawyer," tersely observed one executive creative director. We'll explore in greater depth why he believes that's the case in Chapter 4.

Another interesting risk survey respondents mentioned—and one that didn't exist back in 1987—is the potential for damage to the comparative advertiser's brand caused by the availability and spread of information via the Web and social media. As one agency creative wrote: "In today's online world the customer can research the comparative issues and determine if there are flaws in the comparisons or previously unconsidered strengths in the competitive product/service." Another made the point even more directly: "Done well, it can be extremely effective. However, especially now, the competitive/comparative claim MUST be iron-clad or you will be torn to shreds by social media." Other insightful observations regarding risks include the following (you'll notice that many of these match up perfectly with some of the historical concerns we discovered in Chapter 1):

- "The biggest danger comes from possible 'brand confusion,' whereby the consumer isn't sure *who* sponsored the ad. I see that as a possible shortfall of a lot of automotive campaigns."—Agency Creative Director
- "Unless you are a lower priced newcomer—like Dollar Shave Club for example . . . why give 'free' publicity to another brand. When Coke mentions Pepsi . . . it's zero gain."—Corporate Advertising Executive
- "I look at comparative as a powerful weapon of last resort—the nuke of advertising. It will work, but *could* annihilate both brands."—Agency Senior Vice President and Creative Director
- "Frankly, comparative advertising has more negatives than positives, making it an ineffective strategy. There have been exceptions but too few. Branding is about creating your own story. Attacking a competitor detracts from that and also gives your brand a negative impression. We advise against it 99 out of 100 times."—Agency Creative Director
- "Don't fall for it. Customers are likely to remember the competitive brand. And you can give the competitors cause to innovate/reformulate to kick your ass."—Agency Director
- "All in all, I think it's a waste of time and strategy to talk about 'the other guy.'"—Agency Director-Creative
- "These types of ads can come back to bite you if you are naming an aggressive and talented competitor. Especially if they have a large advertising budget. They can often turn the tables on you and attack your entire product line so be aware and pick your battles."—Corporate Advertising Executive
- "Approach comparative ads with caution. Be on solid legal ground with your claims. Copy test with consumers before running the ad. Be prepared to respond if the competition fires back."—Agency Executive Creative Director

Another interesting theme among the open-ended comments has to do with the creative directors' clients—the corporate advertising professionals. A lack of client enthusiasm for comparative advertising was a prevalent theme. As one creative director lamented somewhat: "I wish clients were more inclined to do comparative ads. They are extremely reluctant because of their fear of competitive reprisal." One linked the lack of client enthusiasm back to the risk of legal problems: "Most clients are afraid of comparison advertising because of legal issues."

As the survey findings also revealed, both creative and corporate executives believe comparative advertising will be more effective than noncomparative when the competitive claim possesses certain attributes, such as being especially strong or salient to consumers. The importance of the claim was another consistent theme among the open-ended responses. One creative director summarized the beliefs of many with this observation: "If there truly are product features that outshine the competition's, I see power in extolling those virtues in a comparative advertising campaign." That statement, of course, is strikingly similar to this one from Chapter 1, written by an advertiser in the United States nearly a century ago: "Gentlemen, what better and more convincing campaign arguments can I possibly assemble than that I build my product with the greatest possible care, out of the best materials, and that my competitors do not?" (Leach, 1924, p. 137). Several other insightful observations regarding the importance of the comparative claim, such as its believability, are summarized below:

- "When the benefit or function is truly better than a leading competitor, it's a strong move, and should be served up in an educational manner. But other times, it's best to go your own way."—Agency Executive Creative Director
- "It works best when you have a substantial advantage. One that really matters to consumers."—Agency Executive Creative Director
- "Comparative advertising is best used as a tactic to enhance a brand, not as a brand-building strategy. If you're using comparisons make them believable. Don't overreach, e.g., comparing a Ford Grenada to a Mercedes."—Agency Creative Director
- "Only use it if you can make true claims that are truly beneficial to the consumer. If your house brand is comparable to a name brand, say it. If not, sell on your own brand's attributes."—Agency Executive Director-Creative

Other respondents linked the importance of a selling point or feature of true superiority with the value of having research to support it: "If market research proves a key benefit of your product matches or fills the particular need of your target audience and your brand is new or an underdog, then comparative ads help to level the playing field and ensure your brand is part of the audience's considered set." Some other observations regarding support for comparative claims or how to execute a comparative ad are summarized below:

- "Your claim has to be meaningful, substantiated, and communicated in a way that resonates with your target audience."—Agency VP & Creative Director
- "If market research proves a key benefit of your product matches or fills the particular need of your target audience and your brand is new or an underdog, then comparative ads help to level the playing field and ensure

your brand is part of the audience's considered set."—Agency President & Creative Director

- "If comparative advertising is done by demonstration of benefit, I think this is absolutely the strongest way to go, especially if the competitor (by name) is shown to fail next to your product."—Agency President & Creative Director
- "Most times comparison ideas take the form of a demo, an indirect comparison. I feel these can be equally effective at times."—Agency VP/ Creative Director

Finally, and it probably comes as no surprise, today's ad agency creatives and corporate advertising executives consistently mentioned the trap that our history in Chapter 1 revealed so many comparative advertisers have trouble avoiding—excessive negativity. As one corporate ad executive succinctly wrote: "It only works if your message is not negative about [your] competitor. You just have to beat them on higher ground." Here's an insightful sampling of other observations on going too negative:

- "In general, I think it can rally an already loyal customer based (e.g., Mac vs. PC), but otherwise often comes across as untrustworthy and creating a bad name for advertising."—Agency Associate Creative Director
- "If you are the market leader, comparative advertising is not effective. The brand can come across as a bully. Why stoop that low. You are the market leader for a reason, advertising the positive."—Corporate Ad Director
- "In all consumer research and focus groups we do, we find most consumers *do not* like comparative advertising."—Agency Partner and Creative Director
- "PLAY NICE! PLAY FAIR. DON'T LIE."—Agency Co-Founder & Executive Director-Creative
- "Comparative advertising is rarely needed. In a broad sense it limits unique brand positioning. Slice it how you want, mudslinging is mudslinging."—Agency VP & Director-Creative
- "The tone of the comparison is key to effectiveness. I feel comparative ads work best when promoting new or 'underdog' products or brands (Apple vs. PC)."—Agency Assistant Director-Creative
- "As you can see by my responses, I'm not a big believer in comparative advertising. It is rarely done well and I believe a client's money should be spent on building their brand, not denigrating another."—Agency SVP, Creative Director
- "We love underdogs, however, so a tongue-in-cheek poke at the big guys always gets us cheering, as long as it isn't too mean spirited and the execution is slick and smart."—Agency VP & Creative Director

SURVEY COMPARISONS WITH THE RESEARCH LITERATURE

The two-decade trend in evidence-based practice in many professions—such as medicine, dentistry, nursing, psychology, and education—suggests we could learn a lot by combining the practical and experience-based wisdom of the professional with the empirical research results and findings reported in a discipline's scholarly research journals (Beard, 2016c). This perspective, however, has been largely ignored in advertising. Although the "knowledge gap" is probably not as wide as some have suggested it is, it looks like there could definitely be at least a small one between mostly academic advertising researchers and the professionals who practice advertising, both corporate and agency practitioners. This knowledge gap between academics and professionals could be one reason why there's a big difference between the two groups regarding the value of academic research or even how best to teach advertising (Beard, 2002). It's also been argued that the failure of academics and professionals to identify a foundation of theory and knowledge on which standards of education and practice could be built has been a major barrier to advertising's progress toward professionalism (Stankey, 1990).

You may recall that Chapter 2 presented a model summarizing the empirical research literature on comparative versus noncomparative advertising. The model was based on a summary and synthesis of the research results and findings from Rogers and Williams's (1989) review of the literature (1975 to 1987), Grewal et al.'s meta-analysis (1976 to 1996), and an updated literature review (1997 to 2017). The direct effects of comparative advertising on several of the most important objectives and outcomes were summarized in Chapter 2's model. Some of them are also included in the first column of Table 3.5.

When we add our recent survey findings to Table 3.5's second and third columns, what we end up with is arguably the most comprehensive summary of comparative advertising effects ever combined in one place. As you can see, support for overall conclusions for the direct effects of comparative versus noncomparative advertising on many of the objectives and outcomes is limited by unavailable findings and results for several outcomes in the empirical research literature. As I also mentioned in Chapter 2, in some cases researchers did investigate the effects of comparative advertising on some of these outcomes, but they didn't report the direct effects of a comparative ad versus a noncomparative one without the effects of any moderators or situational factors. This limitation of the empirical research literature explains many of the unavailable categories of research results.

Still, the comparisons in Table 3.5 do support a conclusion that comparative advertising is more effective than noncomparative for achieving initial brand trial and message recall. In contrast, the comparisons show there is strong agreement across the empirical research literature and surveys of ad-

Table 3.5. Survey and Empirical Research Review Comparisons: Advertising Objectives and Outcomes

Advertising Objectives/ Outcomes	*Research Review (Model)*	*Creative Survey (2013)*	*Corporate Survey (2016)*
Competitive brand positioning	NA	+	+
Initial brand trial	+/N	+	+
Attribute recall	NA	+	+
Claim/message believability	–	+	N
Brand preference	–	N	N
Message involvement	NA	+	N
Purchase intention (P_i)	N	+	+
Ad interest	NA	+	+
Message recall	+	+	+
Brand interest	NA	N	N
Brand comprehension	NA	N	N
Attitude-Ad (A_{ad})	–	–	–
Brand-name recall	+/N	–	N
Attitude-Brand (A_{br})	N	–	–
Brand loyalty	NA	–	–
Repeat purchases	NA	–	–
Brand awareness	NA	–	–

* + = Comparative advertising superior, – = Noncomparative advertising superior, N = No difference between comparative and noncomparative advertising, NA = Results not available.

vertising creative directors and corporate professionals that comparative advertising has a negative effect on A_{ad}. For at least four important objectives and outcomes, though—claim/message believability, brand preference, A_{br}, and brand-name recall—support for definitive conclusions remains unfortunately contradictory or neutral.

Survey Comparisons with the Research Literature: Situational Factors

Once again, when we add the findings for our recent surveys of creative directors and corporate advertising professionals (see the last two columns in Table 3.6) to the summary and synthesis of the empirical research literature, we end up with the most comprehensive summary available of when comparative advertising will probably be more or less effective than noncomparative advertising. The cross-study findings in Table 3.6 show there are six situational factors for which there are no contradictions at all across the results we found in the empirical research literature and our two surveys: (a) if the advertised brand has a small market share, (b) if claims are made on salient product benefits, (c) if claims are well substantiated, (d) if ads are more creative, (e) if the advertised brand is of higher quality and, of course, (f) for a brand new to the market.

In addition, the findings support a conclusion that there remain few important points of difference between professionals' beliefs regarding the conditions under which comparative advertising will be more or less effective (that is, the effects of the moderators) and conclusions based on our summary and synthesis of the empirical research literature. In fact, there's only one situational factor with a major contradiction, and that's whether or not comparative advertising is more effective when used for TV commercials compared to print ads. When Rogers and Williams (1989) reviewed the literature, they concluded it wasn't. On the other hand, ad agency creative directors believe it is more effective and their corporate clients aren't sure. A definitive answer to this question would be good to have, especially since research strongly suggests comparative advertising is much more frequently used on TV than in the print media (Beard, 2015; Brown & Jackson, 1977; Gnepa, 1993).

In terms of the knowledge gap between academic researchers and working professionals, Tables 3.5 and 3.6 suggest there is more agreement among the views and beliefs of these two camps than many may have thought. One explanation for this agreement is that academic research on advertising occasionally does make its way into professional practice, possibly by way of textbooks or the efforts of the Advertising Research Foundation or WARC (formerly the World Advertising Research Center) (Beard, 2016c). Another is that there may be some overlap between these two camps of advertising professionals. The findings of a survey conducted several years ago of advertising educators in the United States (Beard, 2002) showed that, at the time, the typical advertising academician had more than 10 years' experience working in advertising. On the other hand, quite a few successful advertising professionals also find their way into the halls of academia, where they teach an occasional course as adjunct professors, present guest lectures, or serve on professional advisory boards.

Another explanation for the agreement between the views of advertising professionals and results published in the academic research literature is that researchers have often succeeded in validly and reliably measuring relationships among real-world phenomena—in this case, comparative advertising and its relative effects versus noncomparative advertising (Beard, 2016c). In the study and practice of the scientific method of investigation, this is called

Table 3.6. Survey and Empirical Research Comparisons: Situational Factors Affecting Comparative Advertising Effectiveness

Comparative advertising is more effective	*Literature Review (Model)*	*Creative Survey (2013)*	*Corporate Survey (2016)*
Effectiveness related to market/advertiser characteristics			
if the advertised brand has a small market share	+	+	+
in more price competitive markets	NA	+	+
if loyalty for the advertised brand is strong	–	–	N
if there is no clear market leader	NA	N	+
if the advertiser has a large advertising budget	NA	–	N
if the advertised brand has a large market share	–	–	N
Effectiveness related to advertisement characteristics			
if claims are made on salient product benefits	+	+	+
if claims are well substantiated	+	+	+
if claims are believable	+	+	+
if ads are more creative	+	+	+
if comparative claims are strong	NA	+	+
over a large number of exposures	NA	+	N
for TV commercials as opposed to print ads	–	+	N
Effectiveness related to the nature of the product advertised			
if compared feature is unique to brand	NA	+	+
if the advertised brand is of higher quality	+	+	+
for a brand new to the market	+	+	+
for consumer durables	NA	+	+
for products priced lower than competing brand	NA	+	+
for industrial products	NA	+	+
for low-priced, frequently purchased consumer products	NA	+	+

Comparative advertising is more effective	*Literature Review (Model)*	*Creative Survey (2013)*	*Corporate Survey (2016)*
for more innovative products	NA	+	+

* + = Comparative advertising superior, – = Noncomparative advertising superior, N = No difference between comparative and noncomparative advertising, NA = Results not available.

external validity. It's a good thing because it means the results and findings of studies can be generalized to other people, settings and the wider world in general. It's also a recognized weakness of the experiment as a research method. Yet another explanation for the consistent beliefs among academics and professionals is suggested by advocates of the evidence-based practice approach. They argue that professionals' beliefs are, in fact, a result of their efforts to integrate theory, experience, and intuition in a real-world context. Undoubtedly, someone who's spent 24 years working in advertising, like many of the respondents to the surveys we reviewed in this chapter, should have some fairly well-informed ideas about what works and why.

A FINAL CONCLUSION

As a final conclusion for this chapter, if there's a survey somewhere of advertising professionals in a country other than the United States, it's doing a good job of keeping itself hidden. If there's not, then several such surveys would make valuable additions to what we've learned in this chapter. A good place to start would be with advertising professionals and corporate decision makers in the handful of countries other than the United States that have shown themselves more willing to accept and use comparative ads, such as Australia, Canada, Portugal, and the United Kingdom.

Chapter Four

The Regulation of Comparative Advertising in the United States

After passing through a period frequently characterized by a swashbuckling, anything goes attitude, when flagrantly dishonest advertising for a variety of worthless (and sometimes even dangerous) products was not uncommon, the practice of advertising early in the 20th century attained a much higher level of professionalism. Those responsible for this progress in the United States had faced a significant uphill battle. At the turn of the century, many businesspeople not only viewed advertising as a waste of money, but undignified and somewhat sleazy as well (Hower, 1949). Perhaps the most famous of advertising's agency pioneers, Lord & Thomas's Albert D. Lasker, reported that as late as 1898, businessmen would try to keep their advertising secret from their bankers because many lenders thought anyone who advertised was probably disreputable. Such a businessperson "put himself in the patent medicine class," admitted Lasker (as cited in Wood, 1958, p. 239). Many office buildings even had signs in their lobbies declaring explicitly: "No peddlers, book agents, and advertising men" (Foster, 1967, p. 126).

By 1915, however, ad agency pioneers such as Lasker, Charles Austin Bates, Earnest Elmo Calkins, Francis Wayland Ayer, and J. Walter Thompson had made great progress toward overcoming their predecessors' associations with unscrupulous business practices and the patent medicine trade (Rowsome, 1970). Advertising had fully emerged as an important economic institution and social force.

As we learned in Chapter 1, the practice of mentioning competitors in advertising wasn't entirely respectable during the early decades of the 20th century. Many advertisers agreed with San Francisco ad agency president Emil Brisacher (1928, p. 161): "Comparisons are always odious—but in advertising space they are costly—they lose sales and they lessen the prestige of the advertiser who makes them." But by the late 1960s and early 1970s, even direct comparisons had evolved from somewhat questionable to totally acceptable in many situations. Consequently, comparative advertisers also drew the attention of the various entities responsible for regulating advertising practices.

Early industry reformers and self-regulation advocates devoted to cleaning up advertising focused right from the start on the old and reviled practice of disparaging competitors and their products, as well as unscrupulous efforts to exploit their brand names and reputations. Advertising historian Daniel Pope (1983) reports that as the progressive "truth in advertising" movement was launched at the 1911 convention of the Associated Advertising Clubs of America (AACA), one of the most widely applauded speeches was delivered by Joseph Appel, advertising manager for John Wanamaker's department stores and president of the AACA's retail advertisers' division.

Appel's "Ten Commandments of Advertising" made clear the position of many of these progressive advocates of a more dignified advertising profession on the issue of disparagement: "Thou shalt not covet, nor imitate, nor run down thy neighbor's business; thou shalt not covet, nor imitate, nor run down thy neighbor's name, nor fame, nor his wares, nor his trade-mark, nor anything that is thy neighbor's'" (as cited in Pope, 1983, p. 204). Appel's speech referenced a problem that would contribute to substantial disagreement over comparative advertising and its regulation during the 1960s and 1970s. This was the belief that any mention of competitors, even indirectly, should be considered synonymous with disparagement.

Media owners and managers were also among the first to take action against questionable advertising, encouraged in part by the efforts of advertisers themselves to attack blatant dishonesty. These efforts gave them, as Pope (1983, p. 212) notes, "the courage they needed to enforce higher standards of advertising acceptability." Across the Atlantic, one British newspaper publisher was refusing medical product advertising as early as 1800, condemning the ads and their "*obscene* and *filthy* boastings of quackery" (as cited in Miracle & Nevett, 1993, p. 27).

In the United States, farm magazine publishers in the mid-1800s started a campaign to expose advertising and advertisers they considered fraudulent. Popular magazine editors, such as Edward Bok of the *Ladies' Home Journal*, declared a similar war on patent medicine marketers and other purveyors of dishonest and offensive advertising (Calkins, 1915). The American Business Press was the first industry organization to establish a self-regulation code in the United States, in 1910, preceding even that of the U.S. Council of Better Business Bureaus (CBBB). Problems with comparative advertising soon drew the regulatory attention of these and other early publishers, such as Curtis Publications, whose own advertising code banned ads "knocking" competitors.

As we've learned in other chapters of this book, one of the main problems attributed to comparative advertising is that it's often perceived as dishonest and misleading (especially by outraged competitors), or can quite easily become so as feuding advertisers continue their attacks and counterattacks with increasingly harsh and dubious claims. A good example? How about this magazine ad headline for Bayer Aspirin: "Makers of Tylenol, Shame on You!" Consequently, comparative ads and campaigns in the United States have frequently been among those running afoul of advertising's primary sources of legal restrictions and other regulations, such as consumer protection statutes, agencies, and attorneys-general at the state level; the Federal Trade Commission (FTC) at the national level; and the ad industry itself, in the form of self-regulation.

The use of comparative advertising has represented a regulatory and legal minefield for most of the past 100 years. This chapter examines the legal and regulatory implications of identifying competitors in advertising and reviews the most important events, organizations and entities, individuals, court cases, motives, and principles involved in the regulatory efforts to respond to the widespread adoption of comparative advertising in the United States during the 20th century. Comparative advertising has been in use most extensively in the United States, whereas even as late as 1996, for example, two-thirds of EU member countries still sharply restricted or outright banned it. The emphasis in this chapter is also on how comparative advertising uniquely impacted media and ad industry self-regulation and government regulation and the relationships among the entities responsible for enforcing their policies and principles.

In addition to concluding with a list of the key issues to consider in order to avoid the many regulatory and legal traps lying in wait for the comparative advertiser, this chapter also provides some context for understanding why the use of comparative advertising was restricted throughout much of the rest of the world, which we'll explore in greater depth in Chapter 6. This is mainly accomplished by looking at the principles that serve as a foundation for the regulatory efforts and activities of the media, business executives and advertising professionals themselves, and the law.

REGULATION BY THE MEDIA

As advertising researcher Avery Abernethy (1993), a frequent contributor to the advertising media self-regulation literature, notes: "Media owners and managers have great power to determine the type of advertising their stations carry because they can review each advertising submission and decide if it is appropriate for their audience" (p. 15). Researcher Eric Zanot (1985, p. 44) further proposes that "Some would go so far as to say that this 'behind-the-scenes' process is the most critical and effective of all the different methods of regulating false and deceptive advertising."

Efforts by the Media to Deal with Comparative Ads

If you asked them about the issue of comparative advertising during the first few decades of the 20th century, one of the things many advertisers would tell you was that they thought the media—in particular, magazine and newspaper publishers—had an obligation to protect them from attacks by competitors (Beard, 2012). One magazine publisher, writing anonymously, described the problems created by comparative advertising with the following complaint:

> Why should one advertiser threaten the publisher with cancellations of his business if the publisher continues to carry the business of another advertiser? And not only threaten cancellations of the product under discussion, mind you, but often threaten cancellations of advertising of products of allied or subsidiary companies. Is there any word slightly more polite than blackmail that means the same thing? ("Prima Donnas at War," 1937, p. 17)

The opposing side of the issue was described by an advertiser: "Recently, when a national advertiser attempted to get in the magazines with copy which was a direct slap at a competing advertiser . . . most of the magazines refused to accept the copy." He went on to criticize such publishers for their "lamentable disregard of the rights of patrons" ("Hazardous Business," 1908, p. 27).

Frank Braucher, vice-president of the Crowell Publishing Company (publisher of widely read *Collier's Weekly*) similarly summarized his comparative advertising problems:

> Advertisers have solemnly pointed out the publisher's responsibility in protecting them against a competitor, later to find the situation reversed. If the publisher could take all the responsibilities that many advertisers think are his, he would have to set up his own Federal Trade Commission, United States Supreme Court, not to mention a full Foods, Drugs and Insecticides Division. (1931, p. 66)

A reading of the trade literature of the early 1930s makes it clear that publishers were in near-unanimous agreement that comparative advertising represented a serious business and regulatory problem, trapping many between two or more feuding patrons, frequently forcing advertising refusals and revisions to their codes (also called "clearance policies"), and, worse yet, threatening advertising revenue (Beard & Nye, 2011). The prevalence of comparative advertising at the time is evident in *Printers' Ink*'s response to a reader request for examples of "fighting copy" or advertising that "makes direct or indirect statements regarding the merit of the advertiser's type of product as compared with other types that compete for the same market." *Printers' Ink* replied:

> A history of advertising would tell more war-stories than ever were swapped at a G.A.R. [Grand Army of the Republic, a U.S. civil war fraternal organization] encampment. In advertising space there have been wars over soap, wars over shoes, wars over automobiles, wars over tires, wars over gasoline, wars over most of the products that manufacturers produce and sell. ("If Advertisers Must Fight . . . ," 1930, p. 40)

The term "comparative advertising," in fact, first appeared in the trade literature at about this time, as opposed to "knocking," "competitive advertising," or "unselling."

Media managers and publishers, often caught in the difficult position of arbitrating comparative advertising wars and facing the threat of lost business from angry combatants, also worried that comparative advertising could contribute to long-term damage to advertising as an industry and institution. This is a concern they shared with some of the advertisers we heard from in Chapter 1. The same anonymous publisher bemoaned the problem in the pages of *Printers' Ink*: "But far more important than either the publisher or the advertiser individually, is the adverse influence these copy discussions have on *all* advertising; the effect they have on undermining women's (and men's) confidence in the whole industry of which the participants are but a part" ("Prima Donnas at War . . . ," 1937, p. 17). The Crowell Publishing Company's Braucher (1931, p. 65) delivered a similar warning:

> The biggest copy problem confronting us today is competitive, knocking copy. . . . The kind of advertising which it seems to me if carried to its logical conclusion will destroy the effectiveness of advertising media. . . . It will destroy something that the advertiser needs, the agent must have and the publisher cannot under his present set-up exist without, namely the believability of advertising.

Trade journal *Advertising & Selling*, in a front-page editorial, specifically pointed to one of the biggest problems for publishers: "Running Buncombe [a period term for blatantly phony advertising claims] a close second as a confidence-sapper is the current wave of advertising that knocks competitors. Publication copy censors are throwing up their hands at the enormity of today's task of reconciling competing claims" ("When You Knock Your Competitor . . . ," 1931, p. 17).

A revealing example from the 1930s, which highlighted a limitation of media censorship, was an advertising war waged between mail-order catalogers Montgomery Ward & Co. and Sears, Roebuck & Co. with tire manufacturer Harvey Firestone. Since attacks published in their catalogs couldn't be censored, both Montgomery Ward and Sears regularly compared their private label tires with those of branded competitors, by name. As president of the only major tire company that didn't manufacture tires for the catalogers, Firestone counterattacked with newspaper ads calling for a "showdown" on the "misleading" claims of the "mail order houses." Unfortunately for Mr. Firestone, despite his ads not directly naming his mail-order foes, many newspapers refused to print them. He had better luck with magazines, although the catalogers pressured those publishers to refuse the ads as well (Beard & Nye, 2011).

Despite the problems comparative advertising caused for publishers during the first few decades of the 20th century, few large-scale solutions were proposed in the trade media, and then only in the 1930s. One was suggested in 1934 by Brooklyn department store owner Major Namm, who was also, according to *Printers' Ink*, a "champion of truth-in-advertising." He argued that the responsibility for cleaning up advertising lay almost entirely with the media. "Individual advertisers cannot police the situation, neither can trade associations," he wrote. "Advertising mediums with the help of the Better Business Bureaus, can do so but only if the same fair practice provisions are applied to all mediums. . ." (p. 36). A few years later, a publisher offered a similar solution. "Someone recently suggested a 'Czar' for publishers. It sounds like a fine idea to me because then, in effect, all the publishers will get together and tell all the advertising Prima Donnas to fight their own copy battles on their own advertising time—not between magazine covers. . ." ("Prima Donnas at War," 1937, p. 20).

Further regulation of comparative advertising, or any advertising, for that matter, was mentioned infrequently in the trade literature during the 1940s and into the early- to mid-1950s. Advertising historians Miracle and Nevett's (1993, p. 19) description of this period in the United States suggests why:

> The print media seemed reluctant to accept additional responsibility for the truth of the advertisements they carried. And advertising agencies, enjoying a period of rapid growth, acted as if there were no real need to regulate advertising. Puffery and exaggeration were all too often seen as the keys to advertising success and few advertisers seemed concerned.

Only a single comparative advertising episode was mentioned in the trade literature during the 1940s and 1950s. It suggests many newspapers continued to reject comparative ads, that a likely motive was fear of lost revenue and that a major issue was "unfairness." Cosmetic company Warner-Hudnut, Inc., for example, had run an ad warning users of home permanent kits not to use ones that lacked a "neutralizer" (Headline: "You'll feel like crying. . .but crying won't help!"). As the author of an article in *Printers' Ink* noted at the time: "The consumers' perplexity about which type of permanent to use is matched by the problem faced by newspapers. They must decide if they want to turn down the campaign, forgo the revenue and possibly antagonize the advertiser and its agency, Kenyon & Eckhardt" (Tolk, 1952, p. 37). The advertising manager of one of those newspapers summarized his objection this way: "The copy, we feel, took an unfair slam at competitive products whose advertising we accept. And we don't think it good advertising practice" (as cited in Tolk, p. 37).

The 1960s and 1970s: A Flood of Comparative Ads

In the 1960s, comparative advertising and the media's self-regulation of it again became frequently discussed problems in the trade press. Many advertisers in the United States, especially those in highly competitive product categories such as automobiles, were growing increasingly competitive in their advertising and, more important, had started calling out their competitors by name. Several cases from this period confirm that advertisers continued to complain to the media when they became the target of a competitor's attack, and the typical charge was unfairness (Beard & Nye, 2011).

The publishers of *Encyclopedia Britannica*, for example, complained when they felt rival *Collier's* had unfairly disparaged them in a magazine ad with the headline: "How can all three [encyclopedias] be most used?" The ad's copy claimed one could simply "watch the students" to answer the question. Although the ad didn't mention competitors by name, three, including *Britannica*, were prominently displayed in the visual. In its complaint, *Britannica* suggested publishers should "review their advertising acceptance policies" (*Collier's Encyclopedia* . . . , 1964, p. 34).

Advertisers' desires to run ads naming competitors and publishers' reluctance to clear them in the mid-1960s was prevalent enough to merit an example unique in its approach to avoiding their censorship. As an *Advertising Age* writer described it: "Comes now a substitute for the substitute phrase, 'high-price spread,' in margarine ads. . . . Throughout the ad, Lever uses the *verboten* word 'butter'—except that the word is blacked out every time it occurs" ("Lever Masks Out . . . ," 1964, p. 176). The ad not only directly targeted Imperial's competitor, butter, but also drew attention to publishers' prevalent censoring at the time of directly comparative ads and their copy.

Magazine and newspaper publishers finally got a break in the 1960s, as advertisers sought to identify competitors in their TV commercials, and the major media regulation problem moved from publishers to broadcasters. One of the most contentious episodes offers significant insight into what TV executives and station managers viewed to be the main competitive principles comparative advertising violated, some of the motives to which advertisers attributed the rejection of their ads, and the direction evolving standards of media clearance policies would go during the 1960s and into the even more turbulent 1970s.

Claiming that any of its models could "run circles around the next car in its class," automaker Renault launched a comparative campaign on the West Coast in 1965 ("Renault's Ad Claims . . . ," 1965, p. 6). The TV spots offered feature-by-feature comparisons between Renault and leading importer Volkswagen. Relying on the National Association of Broadcasters (NAB) Television Code, which barred the disparagement of competitors, some stations refused to run the commercials. The NAB's code administrator, Howard H. Bell—the "Father of Advertising Self-Regulation" (Neff, 2017), who also served as the founding president of the American Advertising Federation (AAF)—went officially on the record, stating that network affiliate stations should reject the spots ("TV Code's Bell Warns . . . ," 1966, p. 8).

The NAB Television Code, originally established as the NAB Radio Code in 1937, had already been revised several times when this event occurred, ostensibly to place increasingly stricter controls on fraudulent advertising. By the 1960s, however, special efforts to protect children; a fairly relentless emphasis on issues of "taste" and "decency"; rigid requirements for the substantiation of claims; restrictions on advertising for wine and beer; and a total ban on broadcast advertising for hard liquor had actually made the NAB code stricter than any other existing advertising codes or regulations in the United States (Beard & Nye, 2011). As Miracle and Nevett (1993, p. 19) point out: the NAB's code "had a powerful influence over advertising for 60 years." In fact, the effectiveness of the code's restrictions on comparative advertising is one likely explanation for why many people thought, and some actually still do, that comparative advertising was illegal in the United States.

The head of Renault's ad agency, Marvin Crantz—himself, according to *Advertising Age*, "an outspoken advocate of ethics in advertising" ("TV Code's Bell Warns . . . ," 1966, p. 8)—defended the directly comparative TV spots. He argued they were neither disparaging nor unfair because the claims were based on specific and valid points of difference. Code administrator Bell disagreed. First, he pointed out that "disparagement" was, indeed, a core problem: "While these comparisons may not be disparaging in the legal sense . . . they represent a disturbing development which will hurt advertising" (as cited in "Cantz, Renault Distributor's Anti-VW Copy . . . ," 1965, p. 1). Second, he linked the problem of unfair disparagement with the nature of the comparisons. Although acknowledging that specific "fact-by-fact comparisons" were acceptable under the code, he added that "the problem arises from generalizations that go beyond facts. Sometimes there are unfair implications which may not be factually wrong, but which put the competition in an embarrassing light, or make him look like a goof" (as cited in "Cantz, Renault Distributor's Anti-VW Copy . . . ," p. 102).

In a speech to the Hollywood Ad Club, Bell implied, as did some of his publishing contemporaries in the 1930s, that his motives were the protection of advertisers from each other and the continued credibility of advertising as an institution. As Bell stated:

> It is the responsibility of the broadcaster to assure that the air waves are not used as vehicles for mudslinging and unwarranted attacks. . . . From the viewpoint of the advertising community, it is harmful because it's the kind of abrasive technique that can wear a hole in the welcome mat that the American public places outside its door for media and advertising. (as cited in "Bell Reiterates . . . ," 1965, p. 1)

Apparent confusion as to what the code actually meant was a problem that brought the NAB into direct conflict with the advertising industry itself (Beard & Nye, 2011). Both the American Association of Advertising Agencies (AAAA) and the Association of National Advertisers (ANA) took the position that "the debate hinged on how the NAB would define 'unfairly disparaging'" ("TV Code's Bell Warns . . . ," 1965, p. 102). As ANA President Peter Allport noted at the time, "Just saying it is unfair seems to be sloppy thinking in a competitive economy" (as cited in "Cantz, Renault Distributor's Anti-VW Copy . . . ," 1965, p. 102). The NAB did amend its code again in late 1965, but it was merely a token gesture of accommodation. As *Advertising Age* reported: "As of September, TV stations belonging to the NAB code will accept ads with specific mention of competitors [but] only if the reference is favorable or neutral" ("Four A's Hits . . . ," 1966, pp. 1, 187).

Discussions in the trade literature in the 1970s about the media's attempts to regulate comparative advertising show that it became almost entirely restricted to the TV networks and their affiliates. The Big Three networks' clearance policies had almost completely prohibited directly comparative ads for years. However, NBC became the first to change its policy when it began accepting "substantiated comparative ads" in 1965 (Danielenko, 1973, p. 56). ABC and CBS followed suit in early 1972, after the FTC asked them to give comparative ads a one-year trial. The FTC (1969) had sent a strong signal just a few years earlier, with its 1969 Policy Statement on Comparative Advertising. Regulators at the FTC had come to believe that directly comparative TV commercials were an effective "means of informing the consumer about who competes with whom and how" (Maurine, 1974, p. 1).

Advertisers in the United States were quick to take advantage of the opportunity to go nationwide with their directly comparative commercials. One of the most vocal advocates in favor of comparative advertising at the time, ad agency Kenyon & Eckhardt executive Stanley Tannenbaum (1976), reported that, according to Gallup & Robinson, the number of comparative spots on primetime television had soared from 1 out of 30 in the 1973–74 season to 1 out of 12, as measured through the end of 1975. He further noted that "NBC-TV believes the incidence rate may be considerably greater today than the one-of-12 ratio" (Tannenbaum, p. 1).

Sources agreed unanimously that the network clearance process was becoming excessively time consuming, despite the networks' efforts to establish clear guidelines for comparative TV commercials, and despite their pleas to advertisers to follow them. And like the NAB code, the network's own clearance policies also discouraged disparagement. For example, NBC's policy stated, "advertisers shall refrain from discrediting, disparaging or unfairly attacking competitors" (as cited in Maurine, 1974, p. 1).

Still, there were signs in early 1973 that the TV networks thought the FTC's trial might be a success. One ABC executive, for example, reported the network had "not received any communications from viewers concerning these ads" (as cited in Danielenko, 1973, p. 66). However, a landmark split decision between the FTC and the National Advertising Review Board (NARB) over a Schick electric shaver campaign sent the networks and the NAB scrambling to establish new comparative advertising guidelines (Beard & Nye, 2011).

Managers of the Schick razor brand had launched a campaign declaring overall performance superiority (the "King of Beards!") over identified competitors Norelco, Remington, and Sunbeam. The FTC investigated and ruled Schick's "shave-reshave" test substantiation was valid. Unfortunately, the ad industry's own self-regulation review body, the NARB, judged the advertising to be misleading (Giges, 1980). As the NAB's code director told *Advertising Age* (by way of a noteworthy mixing of metaphors), "the NARB decision holding the Schick comparison with Norelco, Remington and Sunbeam to be 'false and misleading' had opened a kettle of worms" (as cited in Maurine, 1974, p. 1).

By 1975, the broadcasters had pretty much had enough of their agreement with the FTC to give comparative ads a trial. ABC executive Alfred Schneider told the Television & Radio Advertising Club of Philadelphia that "it may be time to reverse gears on the growing number of name-calling ads and take a new look at the appropriateness of this type of advertising" (as cited in "ABC Censor Raps . . . ," 1975, p. 98). He added that it was causing "great consternation" for the networks and the NAB as "complaints and challenges mount from those companies mentioned adversely in a rival's ad" (p. 98). His counterpart at CBS, director of commercial clearance John E. Hinton, similarly told a AAAA panel that "comparative advertising has become a 'great headache,' and expressed the hope that 'it goes away'" (as cited in "Unsolicited Ad Ideas . . . ," 1975, p. 3).

As the networks and their affiliates struggled against the flood of comparative TV commercials, an event occurred, which we learned about in Chapter 1, that would confirm the FTC's belief that directly comparative advertising would substantially benefit consumers. Pain reliever Datril's successful launch with a campaign comparing its lower price to competitor Tylenol had done exactly what the FTC hoped with its campaign to encourage advertisers to name their competitors and the networks to run the ads. Both NBC and ABC, however, did strengthen their rules regarding price comparisons in comparative ads in 1975 and following the Datril-Tylenol skirmishes in the analgesic wars.

The NAB's TV Code Gets "Cancelled"

Little appeared in the trade literature during the 1980s regarding comparative advertising and the media's efforts to regulate it. One event did occur, however, that indirectly impacted both. The NAB was targeted in 1982 by a U.S. Justice Department anti-trust lawsuit. The suit focused mainly on code provisions that put limits on the number of commercials that stations could broadcast per hour. The NAB settled with the Justice Department by completely suspending enforcement of the code, even though the legality of the comparative advertising rules wasn't questioned. One major consequence is that it deprived independent stations and network affiliates of the only national set of guidelines they could rely on to regulate comparative ads (Beard & Nye, 2011). It also paved the way for a fresh controversy during the next decade.

More Advertiser Complaints in the 1990s

As the 1990s unfolded, television advertisers continued their comparative advertising attacks. As one industry observer notes, "Comparative ads—commercials that attack or mock competing products by name—have grown substantially over the last few years, especially in competitive categories such as telecommunications, beverages and automobiles" (Flint, 1990, p. 53). At the same time, the TV networks had reduced their clearance staffs, leading to a fresh spate of advertiser complaints. Citing Ira Herbert, president of Coca-Cola's North American soft-drink sector, *Advertising Age* summarized the situation: "A dramatic rise in the use of comparative advertising, paired with network staff cuts, has hampered the networks' ability to judge the validity of comparative advertising" (as cited in Winters & Walley, 1990, p. 1). Compounding this problem, according to Herbert, was that false claims were increasingly "slipping by network scrutiny and getting on the air" because they were based on "sophisticated research methods that are difficult to judge" (p. 1).

Other advertisers, such as Ford Motor Co., agreed that network clearance staffs lacked the expertise to evaluate claim substantiation based on sophisticated research, as did Robert Pitofsky, future chairman of the FTC (Winters & Walley, 1990). At least one network also agreed with them. As a CBS executive told trade journal *Broadcasting*: "We find with some of these research issues that even the foremost experts can strongly disagree with each other" (as cited in Flint, 1990, p. 53). Advertiser complaints were numerous enough to cause the networks to consider suggestions they establish an independent panel of experts to review comparative ads. They ultimately rejected the plan, however, mainly due to concerns over the same anti-trust threats that led to the elimination of the NAB TV Code (Beard & Nye, 2011) and which had caused huge problems for advertising industry self-regulators in the mid-1970s. You'll read more about that episode shortly.

Hit-and-Run Comparative Campaigns

This situation in the 1990s—the earlier loss of the NAB code, smaller network clearance staffs, more comparative ads, and more complex substantiation research—led to hit-and-run comparative campaigns. Advertisers complaining to the networks could expect the process to take from between 20 to 90 days to run its course. By then, the damage was done, and offenders could simply stop running the ads. This problem was, in fact, behind many advertiser complaints. For example, despite the fact the three networks eventually forced the Pepsi-Cola Company to drop its claim that Diet Pepsi was "the taste that beats Diet Coke," it was only after reviews of between six weeks and three months.

Before the end of the 20th century, however, and despite cutbacks in clearance personnel and budgets, one comparative advertising episode occurred that showed there was a limit to how long the networks were willing let the lengthy review process continue. It involved a new stage in the analgesic wars described in Chapter 1, with Advil and Tylenol taking shots at each other over product safety. As one industry observer reported at the time: "The battle became so bloody that many television networks even pulled the commercials after the manufactures challenged the validity of the claims being made by their competitors" (Snyder, 1996, p. 89). ABC took the ultimate regulatory step of banning comparative drug ads, and "justified its suppression of the painkiller instinct by invoking, in so many words, the public interest" (Goldman, 1996, p. 25).

Regulation by the Media: Motives, Principles, and Limitations

Although some industry observers suggested comparative advertising could represent a profitable opportunity for the media, it's clear that by the early 1930s, most publishers had concluded that comparative advertising was a serious problem. This belief remained consistent throughout the 20th century and, if anything, became even more overwhelming among broadcasters during the 1960s and 1970s.

As we'll see in the next section, calls for advertising reform tend to occur during periods of rising consumerism and public criticism. This pattern is also evident in the ebb and flow of publishers' and broadcasters' efforts to respond to advertisers' demands to deliver their comparative ads. Articles about problems for the media with comparative advertising, and the necessity of dealing with them, were prevalent during the 1930s, almost disappeared during the 1940s and 1950s, peaked again during the 1960s and 1970s, disappeared in the 1980s, turned up again in the 1990s, and then disappeared in the 2000s. The 1930s and the 1960s–1970s were especially important periods of consumer-driven advertising reform. However, it's also important to point out there is little to no evidence that media audiences ever complained much about comparative ads (Beard & Nye, 2011), despite the fact, as we've discovered in other chapters in this book, people don't seem to like them very much.

Publishers and broadcasters did mention occasionally that consumer protection, audience tastes, and the potential for widespread offense, and the desire to avoid advertising inconsistent with editorial and entertainment media content were among their motives for regulating comparative advertising and the competitive and ethical principles they were trying to uphold. Much like their customers, the advertisers, they also voiced concerns about the challenges comparative advertising created for the integrity of advertising as an industry and institution. These concerns and their implications are summarized well by historians Miracle and Nevett (1993, p. 12), who point out that publishers and broadcasters have always recognized that any exceptions to generally acceptable advertising standards "affected the credibility of the advertising they carried, and thereby their financial success." It seems fairly obvious that publishers and broadcasters were mainly reluctant practitioners of comparative advertising self-regulation during the 20th century, and that their policies and practices were mostly motivated by the complaints, criticisms, and demands of their true customers—advertisers.

It's interesting to note that threats by advertisers to withdraw their own advertising over the comparative ads of their competitors, while frequent during the 1940s and 1950s, were never mentioned during the 1960s and 1970s. One explanation for this is that comparative advertising became almost entirely a broadcast media problem rather than a print one. Since the Big Three commercial television oligopoly controlled the national broadcast advertising market and most network affiliates and independent stations followed the NAB code, advertisers who wanted to reach large TV audiences might complain about competitors' attacks, but they had few other options when it came to spending their national TV dollars (Beard & Nye, 2011).

We also know what publishers and broadcasters during the 20th century believed the main problems with comparative advertising actually were—(a) disparagement, leading to advertiser charges of "unfairness," and (b) the validity of often-conflicting comparative claims. A perfect example of the latter occurred in 2013, when both Toyota and Ford claimed to have the world's "best-selling" car (with both claims reasonably well substantiated). The issue of fairness was at the heart of advertiser beliefs that publishers had an obligation to protect them from being identified in competitors' ads in the 1900s to 1930s. Disparagement and the substantiation of comparative claims were clearly the central focus of controversy and debate among broadcasters during the 1960s and 1970s. The NAB code provisions against "claims dealing unfairly" with competitors and the networks' policies against "derogatory" advertising were the main tools broadcasters relied on to control the advertiser- and FTC-driven flood of comparative advertising.

Finally, it's also important to recognize that the problems of disparagement and the validity of claims became linked in the 1960s, as administrators of the NAB code criticized what they saw as the over-generalization of point-by-point comparative differences into claims of overall superiority, which they considered both unfairly disparaging and misleading. During the 1990s, another period when the use of aggressive comparative advertising was on the rise, the TV networks were forced to respond to advertiser complaints that smaller clearance staffs lacked the expertise to judge the validity of comparative claims based on sophisticated research. Ironically, the networks' struggles to interpret the validity of sophisticated research to support comparative claims may have been encouraged by their own increasingly strict demands for more thorough substantiation.

ADVERTISING INDUSTRY SELF-REGULATION

In the United States, business leaders and influential groups of advertising practitioners, such as New York City's Sphinx Club, openly began discussing the need for advertising reform as early as 1896 (Miracle & Nevett, 1993). As we've already learned, these individuals and many other advocates of "truth in advertising" came together at the 1911 convention of the AACA in Boston. Explanations for this campaign against dishonest advertising were advertisers' concerns at the time about alienating consumers, efforts on behalf of the print media to discourage the sale of ineffective or even dangerous products, as well as restricting fraudulent advertising, and the near-inevitability of future government regulation in the form of a Federal Trade Commission act (which was passed soon after).

Historian Daniel Pope (1983, p. 204), however, argues that the surge of enthusiasm in favor of truth in advertising among advertisers and their agencies mostly came from inside the industry: ". . . consumer discontent at the time remained inchoate and impotent. There was no real threat of externally imposed regulation in those years." In fact, Pope goes even a bit further, concluding that the progressive leaders of advertising reform at the time actually favored constructive government action to ensure advertising's contribution to "fair competition." The real motives behind the reform efforts for advertisers and agencies were likely the ones we've already discussed—the desire for professional stature for advertising and its practitioners and, relatedly, the desire to boost their industry's acceptance among both consumers and businesses by encouraging confidence in advertising itself.

One of the most visible advertising reform efforts also took place during the second decade of the 20th century. The local vigilance committees, originally encouraged by the AACA and its National Vigilance Committee, returned to their communities, which included most of the major cities in the United States, and began monitoring advertising and investigating complaints (Pope, 1983). These committees were on a mission to enforce a model statute banning dishonest advertising, drafted by New York unfair competition attorney H. D. Nims and published in *Printers' Ink* in 1911. With the cooperation of trade associations and publishers—who, as we know, also favored improved advertising standards—the vigilance committees eventually became known nationwide in the United States as the Better Business Bureaus (BBBs).

Pope (1983) reports that by May 1921, the BBBs had investigated 6,815 cases, many involving complaints from consumers and advertisers themselves. The lack of sufficient resources and power among the local BBBs to bring about truly meaningful change in advertising practices, however, led to the founding of the National Better Business Bureau (NBBB) in 1925. However, as Miracle and Nevett (1993) argue, despite its efforts to establish more sweeping truth in advertising codes, the NBBB lacked the power of enforcement and achieved limited success at the national level.

As we learned earlier, there was little discussion of advertising regulation during the war years of the 1940s, as well as immediately after. But by the late 1950s and into the 1960s, growing consumer dissatisfaction with advertisers in the United States once again encouraged a renewed interest in advertising reform. Numerous books critical of powerful corporations and their advertising practices were published, such as C. Wright Mills's (1956) *The Power Elite* and Vance Packard's (1957) *The Hidden Persuaders*. During the 1960s, public discontent with advertising's apparent dishonesty peaked, and problems with the industry's self-regulation process, described as a "system of codes and volunteerism" (Arndorfer et al., 2005), became fairly obvious. President Kennedy responded to the rising levels of consumerism in 1962, declaring that every consumer had four fundamental rights—the right to be informed, the right to safety, the right to choose and the right to be heard. Moreover, he called for additional federal legislation to ensure them. Between 1960 and 1972, the U.S. Congress passed more than 25 key acts directly affecting advertising (Miracle & Nevett, 1993).

Several advertising industry associations tried, and failed, once again in 1960 to establish a system of self-regulation in the United States. Those efforts included a four-part program of self-control established by the AAAA and the Advertising Federation of America (AFA, which soon merged with the Advertising Association of the West to become the AAF). The AFA also sponsored the publication of *The Advertising Truth Book*, authored by attorney Morton J. Simon (1960) and offering guidelines for more honest advertising.

Advertisers, however, confronted two other major challenges early in the 1970s. One was the launch of an FTC campaign targeting deceptive TV advertising, which included threats to employ the penalty of corrective advertising in place of mere cease-and-desist orders (Rossman, 1971). Another was consumer advocate Ralph Nader, who with his band of "Nader's Raiders," had already done serious damage to General Motors and was looking for new corporate prey. The major industry associations, working with the CBBB, responded by finally and successfully establishing the National Advertising Division (NAD) and National Advertising Review Board (NARB) self-regulatory system still in place today (with policies established by the Advertising Self-Regulatory Council). As we'll also see, comparative advertising and its regulation led to an extraordinary challenge to the industry's desire to regulate itself.

The Ad Industry's Efforts to Regulate Comparative Advertising

The earliest industry efforts to regulate comparative advertising were those of the ad clubs' vigilance volunteers. In addition to calling out local merchants over the practice of substituting private-label store brands and generics for nationally advertised products and brands ("The Substitution Menace" described in Chapter 1), the committees also attacked comparative price advertising. Pope (1983) reports that the committees cast the comparative price advertising problem as an ethical issue, and that their efforts to combat it were quite successful. Most of the major New York department stores, for example, had agreed to abandon price comparisons by 1916. However, and similar to advertisers' desires to both employ their own comparative ads but avoid being disparaged by those of their competitors, Pope also argues these efforts were at least somewhat self-serving:

> The line between upholding truth and limiting potentially destructive price competition was blurred. Comparative prices in advertisements might be an invitation to deceit, but they might also help consumers shop for the best bargains. Substitution could entail dishonesty, but it also could mean the efforts of salespeople to persuade buyers that there were cheaper equivalents for advertised products. By defining their commercial goals as ethical ideals, the advocates of truth in advertising channeled the self-regulation movement into

areas where action was not only likely to be "safe" but also profitable. (pp. 218–219)

No specific calls for industry reform regarding comparative advertising appeared in the trade literature until the late 1920s, although there were many signs of growing concerns. When the calls finally did materialize, they focused on the regulatory responsibilities of trade associations of manufacturers, rather than advertising agencies or other existing industry groups. One example was the "sweets" industry's outraged response to one of the most infamous comparative campaigns of that or any other time, and which you read about in Chapter 1—George Washington Hill's "Reach for a Lucky Instead of a Sweet." In response to what they claimed was an unfair attack, 21 companies and trade associations joined forces in 1928 to establish the National Food Products Protective Committee, one of the first with a specific interest in advertising self-regulation (Beard & Klyeuva, 2010).

Other industry associations quickly followed suit, with many establishing codes or guidelines that specifically targeted comparative advertising. Less than a year later, for example, the fertilizer industry founded a group to tackle what they considered unfair trade practices. Among the group's proposed trade practice rules was "Rule 3. Defamation of Competitor or Disparagement of his Goods" (as cited in "Fertilizer Industry Hits Unfair Competition," 1929, p. 28). Many other industry groups during the next two decades also established rules seeking to place restrictions on the old annoyance of disparagement. In fact, among the 60 industry codes established between 1940 and 1953, 49 included rules prohibiting disparagement of competitors or their products ("The Law of Commercial Disparagement," 1953).

Rising Consumerism during the Great Depression

During the Depression, there was visible evidence of a growing public discontent with many business practices, including advertising. This evidence included the magazine *Ballyhoo* (with its satirical ad parodies and ruthless attacks on what its publishers considered exaggerated advertising claims), books such as *Your Money's Worth* and *100,000,000 Guinea Pigs* and the increasing influence of the two nonprofit consumer advocacy groups, National Consumers' League and Consumers Research (McGovern, 2006). Also encouraged by the consumer movement in favor of improved product standards and more factual advertising (Miracle & Nevett, 1993), advertisers faced new regulatory pressures, such as the Copeland Bill. This bill proposed moving much advertising regulation from the FTC to the Food and Drug Administration (FDA). Several such bills failed to pass in Congress, thanks, in part, to staunch resistance from companies and industry groups. However, the Wheeler-Lea Act, which amended the FTC Act, passed in 1938, substantially broadened the FTC's powers by including "false and misleading advertising" among its prohibited "unfair or deceptive acts or practices." In addition, more than a dozen other federal agencies eventually gained jurisdiction over advertising, which they still possess.

Since there were few calls for comparative advertising regulation during the first three decades of the 20th century, there were likewise few recommendations as to what specifically should be regulated. One exception is what was found in the fertilizer industry trade group's "Rule 3" regarding disparagement. AAAA President Joel Benton (1932, p. 53) echoed the industry's desire to limit disparagement in comparative advertising. "In the first place," Benton said in a speech to the National Tire Dealers' Association, "no competing product should be named or referred to by name in any derogatory way." However, Benton also proposed some specifics, declaring that comparative ads should not include false statements about competitors' products, that they should not promote the advertiser's product by attributing faults to an entire industry that were true of only a few members, and that they should not attack a competitor's advertising. Benton supported his call with a warning to the feuding tire dealers: "And unless such concerted effort is made by your industry and by every other in a similar state of demoralization, Government censorship is more than likely to ensue, to the discomfort of us all" (p. 53).

As problems with comparative advertising continued throughout the Depression, another call for reform came from Ralph Starr Butler, author of the first marketing textbook and vice-president of the General Foods Corporation. He warned that its proliferation could "lend emphasis to the contentions of those who want to place advertising in the hands of bureaucratic governmental control and bring about that distinctly undesirable condition" (as cited in "Calls for Showdown on Competitive Copy," 1931, p. 105). Butler called for action from advertisers and agency executives: "It is high time for those who profit from advertising to decide whether the 'knocking' type of advertising is or is not to be the pattern for the future to follow" (p. 105).

Printers' Ink editor C.B. Larrabee (1934, p. 59), however, disagreed with Butler, proposing that it was the responsibility of industry trade associations to reform "that least co-operative of all advertising, the competitive battle." As he pointed out: "Advertising has suffered frequently from competitive battles. The way to handle these is industry's problem. The one group best fitted to handle them this way is the trade association" (p. 59). Although Larrabee proposed no formal relationship between trade associations and the media, he was convinced that publishers would "welcome the active support of any co-operative group in fighting competitive advertising which the publishers realize only too well works to the disadvantage of advertising as a whole" (p. 59).

Disparagement and the Naming of Names

Numerous industry sources establish beyond question that the use of directly comparative advertising and the "naming of names" soared during the 1960s and 1970s, as did *Printers' Ink* in a "Commentary" piece. As the journal reported: "Some admen call it 'disparagement,' others object that this word is neither adequate nor accurate. Whatever it is it's spreading like soot and it seems to have caught the conscience of the advertising industry with its definitions down" ("Naming Competitors in Ads . . . ," 1966, p. 32).

In a speech to the Sales Executive Club of New York, Jack W. Minor, director of marketing, Plymouth-De Soto-Valiant division of Chrysler Corp., captured the views of many who were in favor of identifying competitors by name in advertising at the beginning of the 1960s. He agreed that advertisers should be ethical, and that they "should aid the Federal Trade Commission and other regulatory bodies in the efforts to clean up advertising's house" (as cited in Minor, 1960, p. 1A). However, Minor also warned advertisers they should take care "not to turn that house into a poorhouse by being any less aggressive and less competitive than you have an honest right to be" (p. 1A).

The issue of simply naming names was clearly coming to the forefront of comparative advertising practice, reform, and self-regulation in the 1960s. Comparative advertising and, in particular, disparagement, hadn't escaped the attention of Morton Simon (1960) in *The Advertising Truth Book*. Chapter 11, "Disparagement of Competition and Competitive Products," offers 12 guidelines for creating advertising that is "built upon the virtues, value and benefits of the advertiser's own product, [and] not upon the deficiencies or defects of the competitors'" (p. 17). Borrowing from the Trade Practice Rules of the Nursery Industry, Simon also offered a definition of unfair disparagement:

> It is an unfair trade practice to defame competitors by falsely imputing to them dishonorable conduct, inability to perform contracts, questionable credit standing or by other false representations, or the false disparagement of competitors' products in any respect, or of their business methods, selling prices, values, credit terms, policies, or services. (p. 17)

In 1964, the *Advertising Code of American Business* was established by the AFA, the Advertising Association of the West, and the Association of Better Business Bureaus (ABBB) specifically to deal with "unfair disparagement of competitors and their products" (as cited in "AFA, AAW, ABBB Okay Nine-point Ad Ethics Code," 1964, p. 4). The next year, Kenneth B. Wilson, president of the NBBB, declared that "the controversy over the growing trend toward naming names in ads is intensifying" (as cited in Christopher, 1965, p. 1). He called on "all major forces—advertisers, agencies and media—to take a firm, courageous stand against this trend" (p. 1).

In 1966, it was the AAAA's turn to publicly condemn advertising that "untruthfully or unfairly depicts or disparages competitive products or services" ("Four A's Hits Derogatory Ads," 1966, p. 1). *Advertising Age* reported that the AAAA's condemnation in the form of a policy statement came long after numerous other industry associations had "asked for a curb on advertising that belittles competition in order to protect the believability of all advertising" (p. 1).

Numerous critics in the mid-1960s agreed with the NBBB's Wilson that identifying competitors by name was an "invidious practice" (as cited in Christopher, 1965, p. 1), even if it were merely for the purposes of "Riding the Coattails" (this fairly benign and ancient form of comparative advertising was described in Chapter 1). *Printers' Ink* summarized this view: "Some advertisers, well aware of this tactic, are nevertheless uncertain what should be done about it. It does come under the heading of 'identification,' but it is closer to flattery than belittlement, and it is likely to be unaffected by any rules designed to curb disparagement" ("Naming Competitors in Ads," 1966, p. 34). The AAAA agreed:

> While the board of directors of the American Assn. of Advertising Agencies believes wholeheartedly in competition in advertising, it does not believe in advertising which untruthfully or unfairly depicts or disparages competitive products or services. Nor does it believe in advertising that uses another product's trademark or brand name in an effort to trade on the reputation which the competitive brand has built through advertising and public acceptance. It believes that such use of competitors' brand names, packages, and trademarks without express permission of such competitors should be discouraged. ("Four A's Hits Derogatory Ads," 1966, p. 1)

The AAAA spoke out again on the same issue a few years later in a policy statement that also proposed a new protocol for dealing with comparative advertising. "We especially deplore advertising which makes use of a competitive company's trademark or brand name in an effort to trade on the reputation which that brand has built" (as cited in "4 As Cracking Down on Disparaging Ads," 1969, p. 18). This statement was likely motivated by a U.S. court of appeals decision in 1968, which affirmed a California perfume distributor's right to use competitor Chanel's registered trademark "Chanel No. 5" in ads for his own products. This court decision legitimized this form of name-naming and encouraged the subsequent comparative product "knock-off" marketing phenomenon of the late 1970s and 1980s, which we also talked about in Chapter 1.

Calls for the reform of comparative advertising among advertisers and industry self-regulators continued into the early 1970s, partly in response to public criticisms of advertising in general, but also to a continued aversion to disparagement, the lengthy complaint review process, and the increasing prevalence of lawsuits. Shortly after the NARB reported that "the use of comparative advertising has risen steadily" (as cited in "Study Cites Value of Comparative Ads," 1977, p. 52), thanks to encouragement from the FTC, Jack Roberts, an ad agency Ogilvy & Mather executive, issued a new call for comparative advertising reform. He proposed that the NAB's code authority should establish a comparative advertising category and that the newly established NARB could set up guidelines. These guidelines should also, he proposed, "define, by example, the meaning of 'disparagement' and assist media in the judgmental area of comparative advertising" (as cited in Grant, 1973, p. 61).

The next year, the NAB's new code director, Stockton Helffrich, noting that "Ads are going to become more and more competitive and comparative," similarly suggested that "the NARB should go further and institute a program of review of all network advertising to ferret out the advertising that, while hewing to the letter of the law, misleads, overpromises, and deceives through implication" (as cited in Christopher, 1974, p. 52). A J. Walter Thompson vice-president told an AAAA panel that "the monster" of comparative advertising was "generating major lawsuits between advertisers" (as cited in "Unsolicited Ad Idea Problems," 1975, p. 3). At about the same time, ad agency Ogilvy & Mather's chairman Andrew Kershaw (1976, p. 25) pointed to a problem with both FTC and industry self-regulation that would be mentioned by many others during the rest of the 20th century and into the 21st: "The immediate problem is that there is no adequate, speedy process for examination of complaints, and no adequate speedy retribution for offenders."

Many of those involved with the advertising industry's self-regulatory groups agreed with their media counterparts in the mid-1970s that the supposed consumer benefits of comparative advertising had failed to materialize and, consequently, also failed to justify the possible damage to the advertising industry overall resulting from claims of questionable validity. This view was summed up especially well by William H. Tankersley, president of the CBBB. In a speech to the Economic Club of Chicago, he proposed that not only had six years of comparative advertising on network television produced few consumer benefits, "the plethora of such ads has further damaged the credibility of advertising with equal negative effect on the mores of civilized business behavior" (as cited in "Comparative Ads Graded 'F' by CBBB President," 1977, p. 2). As he further explained: "Allowing advertisers injured by unfair comparisons to respond through 'counter advertising,' as he said one ex-FTC commissioner has suggested, is an example of 'jungle morality, paying lip service to competition, but placing an impossible burden on both consumers and business'" (p. 2). Indeed, Tankersley appeared to be complaining that, by this time, the FTC was actually encouraging comparative advertising wars.

The FTC Lays Down the Law on Comparative Advertising

As we learned earlier, while the networks and the NAB were struggling to establish new comparative advertising guidelines, a split decision between the FTC and the NARB over a Schick shaver ad signaled a major difference between the FTC's policy and the one advertisers wanted. Based on the results of a shave-reshave test comparing its Flexamatic with Norelco, Remington, and Sunbeam shavers, the FTC ruled the substantiation valid. Following its review of the complaint, however, the NARB declared that, since the so-called "King of Beards!" claim was substantiated, it wasn't mere puffery and, in addition to that, Schick hadn't justified the claim of overall superiority implied by the slogan. Puffery typically consists of either grossly exaggerated claims that no reasonable person would believe or claims of comparative superiority that is so vague that they would mainly be understood as the opinion of the advertiser (Lieberstein & Lockberby, 2016).

The NARB's disagreement with the FTC over the Schick commercial was a sign of bigger problems to come. Just a year later, the NARB again showed its intent to maintain an even tougher position against similar comparative claims. In its ruling on a Behold furniture polish commercial, the panel concluded that while the advertiser's substantiation supported a claim of superiority in the removal of an oil-based stain, it did not support a claim of overall superiority. As the NARB explained: "Where the advertising concerns a product with multiple qualities and characteristics significant to the consumer, it is insufficient to establish proof of one characteristic in such a way that the consumer can be led to conclude over-all superiority" (as cited in "NARB Toughens Comparative Ad Rules," 1975, p. 1).

Trouble arrived the next year, when the determined efforts of advertisers, ad agencies and media regulators to manage the flood of directly comparative advertisements collided with the FTC's goal to encourage as many of them as it could (Beard, 2012). What resulted was a full-scale federal investigation and an astonishing challenge to the industry's fairly new, and according to most industry observers, successful system of self-regulation. In an interview with *Advertising Age* editor Stanley E. Cohen (1976a, p. 1), FTC Commissioner Stephen Nye, an anti-trust lawyer and "prime mover" behind the investigation, made his position clear. The commission had reached a conclusion that directly comparative advertising was integral to their mission to "de-regulate" the marketplace, which included any codes or other restrictions that might reduce the ability of smaller advertisers to compete, sustain high barriers to market entry, or result in less informed consumers.

The FTC's campaign targeting advertisers and their industry dealt with far more than just the commission's concerns "with codes which prevent advertisers from making comparative claims naming their competitors" (Nye, as cited in Cohen, 1976a, p. 1). The FTC also proposed striking down professional group and state agency rules that restricted comparative advertising for drugs, funeral services, and eyeglasses. Medical association rules that blocked doctors from advertising also came under attack. But perhaps most disheartening for advertisers, the media, and the industry's regulators, was that the agency mandated the elimination of restrictions on disparagement established by trade associations in industries as varied as liquor, beer, toys, air conditioners, soaps, seat belts, and savings and loan associations. Ironically, it seems likely that many of these rules against disparagement had been in place since the 1920s and 1930s, encouraged by the Progressive Era FTC (Beard & Nye, 2011). The agency was extraordinarily meticulous in its efforts, targeting both the CBBB's rule that "it is not an ethical practice to refer to a competitor by name when reporting comparative test data in advertising" (as cited in Cohen 1976a, p. 69) and the NAB's ban on comparative superiority claims in toy advertising.

Many advertisers and industry observers were shocked and angered by the FTC's apparent attack (Beard & Nye, 2011). One of them was long-time *Advertising Age* editor Sidney Cohen (1976b, p. 4), who saw the betrayal as politically and philosophically motivated: "'Free market competition' is the economists' bible. So 'deregulation' enhanced their status," he fumed. "Deregulate by nullifying professional codes and state laws which restrain advertising by doctors, druggists and opticians. Deregulate by wiping out self-regulation codes which interfere with comparative ads, if such codes exist." Ogilvy & Mather's Andrew Kershaw (1976, p. 25), a major opponent of comparative advertising in the ongoing debate over its effectiveness, similarly viewed the FTC's attack to be a power grab:

> Nye . . . had warned us that it was illegal to prevent comparative advertising. Could it have been in the hope that self-regulation would be destroyed? Could it have been in the hope that the power of the FTC and its chances of challenging the truthfulness of advertising would be enhanced by the more widespread use of comparative advertising?

Many in the industry rallied to defend its self-regulation program in the face of this unprecedented threat. As *Advertising Age* editorialized:

> For those who believe in self regulation, it is fight back now—or forget it. Forget it and go back to the jungle of a few years ago? . . . Past experience shows what happens to standards of truthfulness if we have to depend solely on the ponderous procedures of government. ("Self Regulation on Trial . . . ," 1976, p. 16)

Kershaw similarly complained: "Indeed, our troubles stem from the FTC's failure to understand that it is almost impossible to make a comparative 30 [second] TV commercial whose fairness, truthfulness and capacity to mislead is beyond challenge" (as cited in Consoli, 1976, p. 14).

By the next year, the NARB had reviewed and adjudicated dozens of complaints from advertisers who had been mentioned by name in the directly comparative ads of their competitors. The products involved ranged from tires, toilet bowl cleaners, and snack pack puddings to house paints, drain cleaners, and pantyhose. This turbulent and challenging period for those involved in the efforts to establish enduring principles and policies for the self-regulation of comparative advertising came to an end on August 13, 1979. As a capstone to its investigation, the FTC made it clear once and for all, in a published restatement of its 1969 comparative advertising policy, that industry codes prohibiting disparagement would be "subject to challenge" and that those requiring a higher standard of substantiation were "inappropriate and should be revised" (Federal Trade Commission, 1979).

In the Aftermath of the FTC's 1979 Declaration on Comparative Advertising

Many advertisers and industry observers confirm that the widespread use of comparative advertising continued into the next decade and beyond. Citing David Kerr, director advertising-marketing planning for automaker Renault, *Advertising Age* reported in 1985: "Mr. Kerr said up to the past few years the issue of comparative 'drew a lot of crossfire. Now it's an accepted form'" (Serafin, 1985, p. 76). The decades-old problem of comparative price advertising cropped up yet again in the late 1980s, leading to demands for new regulations. And once again, advertisers asked the CBBB for help. "Major retailers are proposing a new advertising code that would set a national benchmark for comparative price claims. . . . The code is the group's response to attacks leveled against comparative price ad tactics by both state and local ad regulators and by retailers upset with competitors' advertising" (Gordon, 1989, p. 45).

A final call for comparative advertising reform appeared in 2003. As in the mid-1970s, it coincided with a wave of lawsuits. In October 2003, Procter & Gamble's (P&G) Chairman-CEO A.G. Lafley called on other marketer CEOs to refer more disputes to the NAD. P&G had been targeted with lawsuits by four competitors during the previous 12 months. As Lafley told *Advertising Age*: "there are a number of us who are going to be supporting using the NAD and handling advertising claims where advertising claims ought to be handled" (as cited in Neff, 2003, p. 3). An industry attorney confirmed the extent of the problem: "it's not just P&G heading to court. Other cases involving MTD Corp.'s Yard-Man and John Deere & Co., as well as Virgin Atlantic and British Airways signify a growing trend" (Urbach, as cited in Thomaselli, 2003, p. 10). It's interesting to note that the

NAD actually did streamline its process for handling disputes in late 2015 for the same reason. Three of the world's biggest packaged goods manufacturers at the time—P&G, Nestlé, and Unilever—had all sued competitors over alleged false advertising claims, rather than take their complaints to the NAD.

Other than a brief recurrence of questionable and possibly deceptive comparative price claims in the 1980s, little appeared in the trade literature regarding what specifically should be regulated after the turn of the 20th century. The FTC's clear and unassailable policy on industry desires to regulate disparagement or require more rigorous substantiation for comparative claims likely encouraged the substantial use of both direct and implied comparative advertising since the 1980s.

At least one self-regulatory unintended consequence of the FTC's encouragement of directly comparative advertising were increases in complaints filed with the NAD. As one source noted in 1999: "The rise in direct-comparison ads has meant 80% of complaints to the National Advertising Division of the Council of Better Business Bureaus now come from marketers, compared to a majority coming from consumers in the 1970s" (Neff, 1999, p. 26). The director of the NAD reported in 2008 that monthly complaints from advertisers who believed they were victims of misleading comparative ads were up 50% that year (as cited in Vranica, 2008). And by the end of 2009, according to York (2010), there had been 84 competitive challenges opened for the calendar year, up from 63 in 2007 and 52 in 2006.

During the past decade or so, such complaints and challenges to the NAD have focused almost entirely on the validity of comparative claims. A typical example is a NAD case initiated in 2014 by Blue Buffalo pet food maker competitor Hill's Pet Nutrition (a subsidiary of Colgate-Palmolive Co.). While Blue Buffalo agreed to make changes to its side-by-side comparison of various brands' pet food ingredients, the brand also appealed other NAD findings to the NARB (Neff, 2014a). Another good example is a 2016 challenge by Kimberly-Clark Corp. (maker of Huggies) over the Honest Co.'s claims for its diapers and baby wipes. The NAD recommended that Honest Co. discontinue its description of its baby wipes as "super absorbent." The Honest Co. also agreed to stop using the same and similar claims about absorbency on its product packaging. Claims determined to be mere puffery, however, included "ultra thick, "ultra soft," and "unbeatable" (Neff, 2016).

Ad Industry Self-Regulation: Motives, Principles, and Limitations

Advertisers and their agencies early in the 20th century seemed quite enthusiastic about working with the U.S. federal government, as they took their initial steps toward reforming their industry. Moreover, the industry still relies on the FTC to support its system of self-regulation, since NAD and NARB complaint rulings are legally unenforceable.

Yet it appears that industry interest in working with government regulators, at least in regard to comparative advertising, declined during and after the 1930s. Perhaps, as editor Larrabee (1934, p. 8) observed at the time, advertisers were tired of the "mass of detail that has been dumped upon them by the NRA." President Franklin D. Roosevelt's controversial (and, eventually, ruled unconstitutional) NRA (for National Recovery Administration) sought to establish a variety of reforms and codes involving business, which were intended to eliminate "destructive competition." Advertisers at the time may also have been motivated by the threat of the Copeland Bill, which passed the U.S. Senate in May 1935 (Beard, 2012). Ironically, as we've discovered, despite the industry's desire to regulate itself, comparative advertising was directly responsible for a major confrontation with federal regulators.

Many advertisers and their agencies also seemed to accept the inevitability of comparative advertising during the 1930s, and, as we learned in Chapter 1, some began to openly endorse it as a legitimate expression of competition in the marketplace. Their primary motivation for regulation of comparative advertising quickly turned to the problem that occupied their attention until their successors lost their fight with the FTC in the 1970s—disparagement. This preoccupation with disparagement as a principal motive for regulating comparative advertising, as we've also learned, was shared with media regulators and their policies and codes. The obsession with disparagement offers some additional insights into the core question of this book: why have advertisers often relied on a message tactic that research and professional experience confirms they often lacked confidence in and frequently regretted using?

Throughout the 20th century, a majority of advertisers and ad agency professionals mainly favored constructive forms of competitive rivalry, those that would allow them to compete effectively, while not causing damage to their own product or service categories, markets, industries, or even advertising as a social and economic institution. Comparative ads that emphasized valid differences among features and benefits were consistent with these principles. Disparagement in comparative advertising, on the other hand, is the type of excessively competitive business tactic that can lead to "ruinous competition" (Shapiro, 2005) that might not only encourage further criticism from the general public but also ultimately leave all the competitors in a market worse off.

Consequently, while advertisers and their agencies may have wanted to compare their products and services with identifiable competitors, especially when they believed their features and benefits were superior, it's also clear why they wanted to put self-regulatory restrictions on disparagement. This certainly explains why many advertisers expressed regret over abandoning more constructive brand-building image campaigns in favor of mutually damaging comparative advertising wars (Beard, 2010). Daniel Pope's (1983, p. 201) description of advertisers' beliefs about competition early in the 20th century summarizes the core principle quite well: "Support for the idea of competition remained, but it was defined as competition *through* advertising, not rivalry *in* advertisements or attempts to undersell [italics in original]."

Yet another motive for comparative advertising self-regulation was the appropriation or infringement of trademarks, which is almost unavoidable in directly comparative ads that identify competitors by naming or showing them. It seems likely that advertisers' concerns about the appropriation or infringement of their trademarks and brand names is linked to the problem that emerged early in the 20th century, along with the expansion of national brands—"The Substitution Menace," which was described in Chapter 1. The desire to avoid this type of problematic competitive rivalry in advertising is also likely explained by the historical and contemporary beliefs that among the biggest problems with comparative advertising, as we also learned in previous chapters, are that it provides free exposure for competitors and often leads to brand confusion. Also underlying the motive to protect trademarks and brand names is a belief in the principle that it is an unfair business practice for one marketer to exploit another's often lengthy and expensive efforts to build a brand with advertising. In Chapter 6, we'll see how a belief in this principle kept the more widespread use of comparative advertising in check throughout much of the rest of the world for decades.

Another limitation of the ad industry's self-regulation of comparative advertising that clearly established a motive for reform was the cumbersome and time-consuming NAD and NARB review processes. As an especially egregious example, it took over 16 months to produce a decision in response to S.C. Johnson & Sons' complaint that the makers of Behold furniture polish had falsely claimed overall superiority over Lemon Pledge. And if that wasn't bad enough, throughout the 16 months, the Drackett Company, makers of Behold, continued to run the offending commercial.

What explains arguably the single most influential and contentious episode in the history of advertising self-regulation: the dispute over the industry's right to regulate truthful disparagement of competitors and its failure to secure that right from the FTC? This is especially important to understand given the fact that it was the FTC of the 1920s to1940s that encouraged the emerging trade associations to include disparagement in their codes (Beard, 2012) and that the FTC itself was discouraging disparagement as late as the 1950s.

In principle, as we've learned, advertisers and their ad agencies were against what they considered "unfair" disparagement. Yet they wanted to compare their products and services with those of competitors, especially if, as the Renault campaign showed in the 1960s, the comparisons were factual, truthful, and could be substantiated. The survey findings we reviewed in Chapter 3 confirm that all this is still true today. Ultimately, "unfair disparagement" failed as a self-regulatory principle because, and as we'll see in the next section, it doesn't work very well as a legal one. Neither the media nor the advertising industry's self-regulators could enforce restrictions that lacked the support of government regulators, in particular, the FTC. By the 1970s, it became clear that the FTC really cared about only two issues—(a) striking down any media, industry, or advertising self-regulatory codes or policies that might restrict free and open competition in the marketplace or (b) outright deception in advertising. In other words, if an advertiser felt disparaged, the FTC didn't care as long as the disparagement wasn't false or misleading.

Consequently, it's clear that, as advertising researchers Herb Rotfeld and Marla Royne Stafford (2007) propose, laws and government regulations exert the greatest and most direct influence on all the other principles, policies, and entities responsible for advertising and its regulation. In the 1970s, comparative advertising became a vehicle for an FTC campaign against those responsible for advertising self-regulation, inspired by the prevailing political and economic ideology of the time, deregulation. So it's clear that laws and regulations establish limitations on what the ad industry could do to self-regulate comparative advertising and its practice. In the next section, we'll look at the specific ways the law provides a foundation in the United States for both media regulation and industry self-regulation.

LAWS AND REGULATIONS

Boddewyn and Marton (1978, p. 27) note in their classic work on comparative advertising that the creator or user of a comparative ad or campaign in the United States just might "discover that he had committed a common-law tort, violated a state or federal statute, and/or failed to comply with FTC standards." The surveys of advertising professionals we reviewed in Chapter 3 confirm they are very concerned that running a comparative ad could produce legal problems ("Get a good lawyer!" as one creative executive warned). Legal challenges may come from an agency such as the FTC acting on its own in the public interest, complaints from disappointed consumers, or more frequently, much like challenges under media or ad industry self-regulation codes, opposition from targeted and outraged competitors. As advertising law scholar Lee Wilson (2000, p. 23) insightfully notes in her book: "Even if your conscience doesn't keep your ads honest, your competitors will, at great expense to you and at some inconvenience."

In this final section of Chapter 4, we'll be focusing on regulation by the FTC and then legal challenges brought under the federal Lanham Act and state false advertising and anti-dilution statutes. It's important to recognize, also, that all forms of legal regulation of advertising are founded on the legal and constitutional principles of freedom of speech, freedom of trade, support for fair competition, the protection of industrial property, and the prohibition of harm to others (Boddewyn & Marston, 1978). In the next chapter, we'll see how respect and recognition for some of these principles has produced the differing levels of public, industry, and political support we see for comparative advertising around the world.

The law of comparative advertising is complex, including elements of copyright and trademark law, false advertising, disparagement/libel, and outright fraud. While the review here is accurate and up-to-date as of the time of this book's publication, as we'll see shortly, laws do change over time. Moreover, due to space considerations, this chapter highlights only the most important legal issues and their implications. For these reasons, I and this book's publisher want to make clear that the following overview is only for informational purposes. Like the advertising executive I just mentioned, we encourage you to consult "a good lawyer" experienced in advertising law for answers to any questions about a particular comparative ad or campaign. For further reading, advertising law scholar Dean Fueroghne (2017) offers a thorough chapter on comparative advertising in his excellent textbook. Attorneys Marc Lieberstein and Michael Lockberby (2016) have also recently published a comprehensive summary of the law of comparative advertising on behalf of the American Bar Association (included in this book's references and available online).

The Federal Trade Commission

As we saw with industry self-regulation, decisions and recommendations from the NAD or NARB lack legal enforcement. Consequently, advertisers occasionally refuse to abide by the NAD's recommendations or even participate in the self-regulatory process at all. For example, in 2013, MillerCoors LLC rejected Anheuser-Busch LLC's complaint that MillerCoors' comparative claim to have "the world's most refreshing can" lacked substantiation and was false. MillerCoors argued the claim should be considered either puffery or literally truthful and declined to participate in the NAD complaint review process. When something like this happens, the NAD may refer the matter to the FTC, as it did in this case. Fortunately for everyone, this is somewhat rare. In fact, between 2010 and 2013, only 17 of 339 NAD cases were referred to the FTC (Rodriguez, 2013). Still, for the comparative advertiser in the United States, there's always the possibility that an ad or campaign will attract the attention of the FTC, possibly because of a NAD/

NARB referral, another advertiser's complaint, or because the federal agency proactively decided to challenge the advertising.

The U.S. government didn't acknowledge a need to protect consumers from deceptive or dishonest business practices until the passage of the Federal Mail Fraud Statute in 1872. The landmark Sherman Antitrust Act soon followed, in 1890, and had as its primary emphasis the preservation of a competitive marketplace by prohibiting unfair methods of competition. For advertisers, the two most important subsequent laws were the Food and Drug Act (1906) and the Federal Trade Commission Act (1914).

The early FTC's position was that deceptive or misleading advertising claims were unfair methods of competition that gave an advantage to the dishonest advertiser. By the mid-1920s, the FTC was spending much of its time dealing with such advertising. Whether or not the FTC could or should protect consumers, in addition to business competitors from each other, was an issue that began attracting some attention. To deal with it, Section 5 of the Federal Trade Commission Act was amended with the Wheeler-Lea Act of 1938. In addition to providing civil penalties for violations, it declared "unfair or deceptive acts or practices in commerce" to be unlawful (Federal Trade Commission, 1938), which authorized the FTC to protect consumers from false advertising. Section 5 of the FTC Act is the most important one for advertisers, although Sections 12–15 and Section 13(a) also directly or indirectly affect advertising practices.

The FTC will determine whether a claim made in a comparative ad is false or misleading under its policy on deception and using the same elements the agency uses to evaluate any other potentially deceptive or misleading advertising claim. They are summarized as follows:

> An advertisement is deceptive if it contains a misrepresentation or omission that is likely to mislead consumers acting reasonably under the circumstances to their detriment. Although deceptive claims are actionable only if they are material to consumers' decisions to buy or use the product, the Commission need not prove actual injury to consumers. (FTC, as cited in Fair, 2008, p. 1)

This summary statement of the FTC's elements of deception suggests a few important points to remember. First, an ad and its claims may be factually truthful but still deceptive or misleading because something important was left out or the ad creates a misleading overall impression. Second, the law only protects consumers "acting reasonably." As Fueroghne (2017, p. 45) explains: "Under the reasonable man standard, an ad claim does not become false and deceptive merely because it will be misunderstood by an insignificant and nonrepresentative segment of people within the market the ad addresses."

Third, to be actionable, claims have to be "material"; that is, they have to have something to do with why a consumer would choose to make a purchase decision. What's an example of an immaterial claim or representation? Recall the last time you saw a TV commercial for a special "value meal" at McDonald's, Wendy's, Burger King, or Carl's Jr. Remember that tall, icy glass tumbler of Pepsi or Coca-Cola included in the beauty shot of the burger and fries? What are the chances, if you go to one of these restaurants and order one of those meals, that you'll get your beverage in a glass tumbler instead of a paper cup? That's right. They're zero. But since the FTC doesn't believe the false, implied claim that you'll get your drink in a much more appealing glass tumbler instead of a paper cup is a good enough reason for you to choose to buy one of those value meals, it's not a material deception. Finally, the FTC doesn't have to prove anyone was injured or even deceived by an ad, only that the ad or one or more of its claims are likely to be misleading.

If the FTC finds that a comparative claim is false or misleading, the agency has several legal remedies at its disposal. It may negotiate a consent decree, which basically specifies what the advertiser must do immediately and in the future to resolve the matter. For example, in 1998, the FTC settled such a false advertising action with the makers of "Slick 50" (an automotive engine treatment), requiring an end to the false advertising and the provision by the company of $10 million in consumer rebates, discounts, and free products (Coleman, 2017). The FTC can also issue a cease-and-desist order or sue violators in court. If the FTC is convinced a deceptive ad or campaign has had a widespread impact on consumer perceptions or has done significant damage to a specific competitor, in the case of comparative advertising, the agency can order the offender to create and pay for corrective advertising. Although the corrective advertising penalty has only been enforced twice—against Warner-Lambert Co.'s Listerine in 1978 and Novartis Corp.'s Doan's pills in 2000—similar orders requiring warnings and disclaimers on labels, packaging, and in future advertisements have been used quite often.

The Lanham (Trademark) Act of 1946

Since 1946, the U.S. federal statute governing deceptive advertising has been found in what is more broadly the country's trademark law. Signed by President Harry S. Truman, and named after Representative Fritz G. Lanham of Texas, the Lanham Act (15 U.S.C. Section 1125[a]) prohibits a variety of activities involving the infringement of trademarks and service marks and false advertising. If advertisers believe another advertiser's claims are false or misleading, rather than filing a complaint with the FTC or the NAD, they can bring private lawsuits in federal court under Section 43(a) of the Lanham Act. As Wilson (2000, p. 16) points out, Section 43(a), "the scourge of exaggerators and fabricators, was originally meant to provide a means of recourse against several forms of unfair competition, including false advertising." However, it's important to remember that Section 43(a) also protects advertisers from the misleading use of their marks and their infringement. We'll deal with these two types of comparative advertising legal challenges in the next two sections.

Falsity Claims under Section 43(a)

Originally, Section 43(a) provided businesses who felt they had suffered injury because of false representations advertisers had made about their own products or services with a federal cause of action for false or misleading advertising. However, in 1990, the Trademark Law Revision Act expanded Section 43(a) to allow businesses to bring lawsuits for false and misleading representations about their own goods or services made by other businesses in their comparative ads. Wilson (2000, p. 16) helpfully summarizes the implications as follows: "This means that now Section 43(a) prohibits any advertising claim that misrepresents the nature, characteristics, qualities, or origin of another company's or person's goods, services, or commercial activities."

Section 43(a) protects both businesses and consumers against false advertising and the misleading use of trademarks. However, in the past, the most common comparative advertising court actions filed under the Lanham Act were challenges from competitors who compete for business within the same product or service category. This was due, in part, to the courts' sometimes inconsistent rulings that under the law, no one except a direct competitor was considered to be directly injured by a competitor's false or misleading comparative ad. A unanimous U.S. Supreme Court ruling in 2014, however, established important new guidelines for who has legal standing to sue under the Lanham Act (Schultz, 2014). In that case, plaintiff Static Control, a company in business manufacturing microchips that enable other companies to refill spent printer cartridges, had sued Lexmark International. Static Control alleged that Lexmark was misleading consumers into believing they were legally required to return Lexmark's spent cartridges only to them. The Supreme Court ruling established that, to sue for false advertising under the Lanham Act, a company like Static Control didn't have to be in direct competition, only that it had suffered damage or injury caused by false or misleading advertising.

A business may also sue a comparative advertiser for disparagement under the Lanham Act. In addition to dealing with trademark issues, the Trademark Law Revision Act of 1988 amended Section 43(a) to make illegal advertising that falsely disparages "another person's goods, services, or commercial activities" (as cited in Fueroghne, 2017, p. 162). Fueroghne further defines disparagement and the 1988 amendment's consequences as follows:

> Disparagement (often referred to as trade libel or injurious falsehood) is a false and deliberate attack on the advertiser's product. This disparagement tends to diminish the respect, confidence or esteem in the product that is attacked. . . . Section 43(a) previously applied only to false representations pertaining to the "inherent quality or characteristics" of the defendant's "goods." After the 1988 amendment, however, the section applies to false representations pertaining to any commercial activities. (pp. 162–163)

An instructive example of commercial disparagement occurred in 2014, when Nestlé's Purina PetCare Company sued competitor Blue Buffalo Pet Products Inc. under the Lanham Act for disparagement as well as false advertising and unjust enrichment. You may recall from earlier that Blue Buffalo was required to make changes to its advertising, after the company lost a NAD complaint brought by competitor Hill's Pet Nutrition. In its 2014 lawsuit, Purina alleged that Blue Buffalo had falsely claimed its products contained only natural ingredients and no corn, wheat, soy, or animal byproducts (Neff, 2014a). Disparagement entered the picture because Blue Buffalo had also routinely claimed in its advertising that competitors Purina, Royal Canin, Pedigree, and Iams were misleading consumers about the ingredients in their products. For example, in one of Blue Buffalo's commercials, a pet owner was portrayed as shocked when she discovered that "big name pet foods" often contain poultry byproducts. Blue Buffalo's website had also enabled "pet parents" to compare the ingredients in the competitors' dog or cat foods they usually purchased with those made by Blue Buffalo.

If a business believes the claims in a competitor's ads are false, misleading or comparatively (and falsely) disparaging, its owners can file a lawsuit under Section 43(a), alleging that the advertising violates the act. The following are the elements that are usually required to prove a false advertising violation (Fueroghne, 2017; Litowitz & Nicoletti, 2011; Wilson, 2000):

- The ad must contain a false or misleading statement or representation of fact about the defendant's or plaintiff's product or service.
- The advertising must have actually deceived consumers or have the tendency to deceive.
- The deception must be material (that is, relates to an inherent quality or characteristic of the brand) and likely to influence a purchase decision.
- The advertiser's product or service must have entered interstate commerce.
- The advertising must have caused actual injury or damage to the plaintiff or is likely to.

One important trend since the late 2000s is for advertisers to countersue under the Lanham Act in response to lawsuits over comparative ads and campaigns. In 2009, for example, the makers of Coppertone filed not one but two false advertising lawsuits against Neutrogena over sunscreen advertising. Neutrogena immediately countersued, alleging Coppertone's claim of "better coverage" was literally false. The case is especially noteworthy because the U.S. District Court for the District of Delaware ruled that both companies had violated the Lanham Act, criticizing them for their "essentially meaningless" claims and lamenting that "sadly, it is the American consumer who ultimately ends up the real loser in these advertising wars" (as cited in Litowitz & Nicoletti, 2011). Other recent comparative ad wars that wound up in court with dueling lawsuits include a confrontation between Clorox's Fresh Step and Church & Dwight's Super Scoop kitty litters and a comparative "Weiner War" between Sara Lee Corp. and Kraft Foods, contesting "100% pure beef" versus "America's Best Beef Franks" claims.

The winner of a lawsuit for false advertising under the Lanham Act can receive preliminary or permanent injunctive relief (by way of a court order) that halts the competitor's false advertising or claim monetary damages. Claiming damages, however, requires proving there were damages and that consumers were actually deceived. "If only a likelihood of deception can be shown, an injunction is the sole remedy allowed" (Fueroghne, 2017, p. 186). The successful plaintiff in a lawsuit can also recover the defendant's profits from the false advertising, court costs, and legal fees, and even demand that the defendant be required to run corrective advertising (Wilson, 2000). You may recall from Chapter 1 that the latter is what happened to Jartran Inc., after the company lost a Lanham Act lawsuit brought by U-Haul International Inc. back in the 1980s.

Finally, it's worth considering why a national advertiser might choose to sue a competitor over false comparative advertising rather than file a complaint with either the FTC or the NAD, especially since a lawsuit could easily cost upwards of $1 million versus just $25,000 to $100,000 for a NAD complaint (Neff, 2014b). One reason is that injunctive relief under the Lanham Act, which brings the dishonest advertising to a stop, is likely to happen much faster (Boddewyn & Marton, 1978). Another reason is that smaller competitors, like Blue Buffalo, tend to be much more competitively aggressive with their comparative claims and less likely to abide by NAD rulings (Neff). Finally, a successful NAD complaint only leads to recommendations that the false claims be modified or discontinued; the complainant can't claim damages.

The Lanham Act and Trademark Infringement and Dilution

The owners of trademarks or service marks (used to distinguish the services offered by different providers) in the United States have no legal right to prevent others from reproducing these intellectual property assets in comparative advertising. The unauthorized use of a competitor's mark constitutes a "fair use," and is neither a trademark or copyright infringement, as long as it doesn't cause confusion regarding the source, identity, or sponsorship of the comparative advertiser's goods or services (Lieberstein & Lockerby, 2016). In fact, the Lanham Act encourages such informational uses of competitors' marks. This, of course, is consistent with the FTC's preference for direct, versus implied, comparative ads in which the features and benefits of identified competitors' brands are compared and there is little likelihood of confusion.

Dilution, versus infringement, is a claim that an advertiser's unauthorized use of an established mark is causing an erosion of its uniqueness and selling power. Prior to the passage of the Federal Trademark Dilution Act of 1995 and the Federal Trademark Dilution Revision Act of 2006, an unauthorized use of a mark was only actionable under federal law if the use was for a related or competitive product or service and it caused confusion. As summarized by Fueroghne (2017, p. 294):

> Owners of "famous" marks are now able to get injunctions, under federal trademark law, that will stop uses that weaken their marks or willfully trade on the reputation of the mark, even if that use does not cause consumer confusion. The idea of trademark dilution looks to the substantial investment an owner makes in the mark and the commercial value of the mark itself.

The law now protects the owners of trademarks and service marks from two types of dilution. Dilution by "blurring" occurs when the uniqueness and selling power of a mark is steadily eroded by its unauthorized use for several different types of products or services. Dilution by "tarnishment" occurs when an unauthorized use of a mark associates it with poor quality or in some other way creates unwholesome associations with it or damages the reputation of its owner.

Legal scholar Charlotte Romano (2005) offers the following helpful definition of dilution-by-blurring:

> Typically, use of a competitor's mark in advertising is blurring when the consumer, although he knows that the competitor did not produce the advertised good, mentally associates the competitor's mark with the advertiser's products upon viewing the competitor's mark in the context of the comparative advertisement. Since, in the future, the consumer will think not only of the competitor's products but also of the advertiser's good upon viewing the competitor's mark, the mark's distinctiveness has been blurred. (pp. 401–402)

The above definition strongly suggests that such a legal definition could prevent many comparative ads in the United States. However, Romano (2005) adds that Section 43(c)(4)(A) of the Lanham Act also states that the purely descriptive use of another mark in a comparative ad or promotion solely for the purpose of identifying competing goods or services is not actionable under the Act's dilution section. Such a "nominative fair use," as Romano points out, "allows comparative advertising to be exempted from blurring violation to a large extent" (pp. 402–403).

Avoiding Claims that Comparative Ads Create Trademark Confusion

Since the possibility of confusion is the ultimate legal test for trademark infringement (and not dilution), there are some straightforward suggestions for how to avoid claims that a comparative ad creates confusion regarding ownership of another mark or the manufacturer of the product it identifies. They include the following (Fueroghne, 2017; Lieberstein & Lockerby, 2016; Wilson, 2000):

- Clarify that the mark has no connection with the sponsored product or service by identifying its owner in the ad.
- Reproduce registered marks in exactly the same form that the owner uses it (for example, include the ® symbol for registered trademarks).
- Don't display the competitor's mark in a larger font than other text, make it larger than the ad sponsor's mark, or place it in a more prominent position in the ad.
- Use only so much of the mark that is absolutely necessary to identify the comparison product or service.

The plaintiff in a successful lawsuit under Section 43(a) for trademark or service mark infringement can receive injunctive relief and recover the defendant's profits, damages, and the costs of the legal action.

Regulation by Individual States

False advertising has been regulated by some states in the United States for at least as long as there has been federal law. Although prosecutions and convictions were both rare, historian Daniel Pope (1983) reports Massachusetts and New York were enforcing false advertising laws as early as 1902 and 1904, respectively. By the time Frank Presbrey published his advertising history in 1929, the *Printers' Ink* model "truth in advertising" statute you read about earlier had been incorporated without alteration into the laws of 23 states, and later, into the laws of 43 states. Today, many of these state statutes, often referred to as "little FTC acts," are modeled after Section 5 of the Federal Trade Commission Act, the Uniform Deceptive Trade Practices Act, or the Revised Uniform Deceptive Trade Practices Act (Lieberstein & Lockerby, 2016, p. 5).

It's important to recognize that regulators responsible for enforcing state false advertising statutes may be keeping an eye on more than just local advertisers. Swedish automaker Volvo learned that lesson in 1990. During a monster truck rally in Vermont, a Volvo station wagon had survived being crushed, when none of the other makes of cars did. Volvo and its ad agency, Scali, McCabe, Sloves Inc., quickly hired a production crew to shoot a commercial dramatizing how safe Volvos are by re-enacting what happened at the rally in Vermont.

Unfortunately, after several unsuccessful and expensive attempts to replicate the stunt in Texas with a Volvo station wagon placed side-by-side in a row of other cars, the production crew resorted to reinforcing the Volvo's roof with wooden beams and steel and weakening the roof support pillars in the other cars. Something else they had trouble with was remembering to put a disclaimer on the finished commercial that it was a dramatization and not an actual event. Tipped off to the deception, Texas Attorney General Jim Mattox concluded Volvo was actually not "a car you can believe in" and sued Volvo under the state's false advertising law. As part of its legal agreement with Texas, Volvo pulled the ads and paid the state's legal costs. After running ads in national newspapers apologizing to consumers, Volvo then accepted the resignation of Scali, McCabe, Sloves.

Many states also have trademark dilution laws similar to those of the federal government. In the case of trademark dilution, the influence actually worked in the opposite direction, with state laws influencing federal law, most notably, the Federal Trademark Dilution Act of 1995 (Lafeber & Haugen, 2005). Some 37 states have such anti-dilution statutes, some of which are stricter than the parallel federal law (Barigozzi & Peitz, 2007).

The most important reason advertisers should be aware that these state anti-dilution laws exist is that offending competitors don't have to be engaged in interstate commerce to pursue a dilution claim against them. This is illustrated by one of the most well-known dilution court cases, *Deere & Company v. MTD Products*, 41 F.3d 39 (2d Cir. 1994), which was filed under New York's anti-dilution statute (Deere also filed suit under Section 43(a) of the Lanham Act). In this case, competitor MTD had altered John Deere's famous logo by showing its iconic yellow deer fleeing in apparent confusion and fear from a barking dog and an MTD lawn tractor. MTD had submitted the commercial for clearance to ABC, CBS, and NBC, and all three approved it, although ABC reserved the right to re-evaluate it if there was a complaint and CBS demanded a letter of indemnity from the ad agency that created it.

MTD lost the suit on appeal. Even though the U.S. Court of Appeals, Second Circuit ruled that the use was neither a case of blurring nor tarnishment, it did rule that it was a dilution of the mark because New York's anti-dilution statute protects trademark owners from others altering or satirizing the mark merely to sell its own products. The outcome of this case highlights the importance of seeking experienced legal advice when it comes to comparative ads, especially since not only do the remedies for false advertising and trademark infringement and dilution vary widely from state to state in the United States, the actual laws do, too.

SUMMARY AND CONCLUSION

As we've seen in this chapter, business competitors watch each other's advertising closely, and they're quick to complain when they believe rivals might be stretching the facts in their favor. And when the ad in question is a comparative one, competitors will be watching all that much more closely. As we've also learned in this chapter, from media clearance policies and codes to advertising industry regulations to federal and state false advertising and trademark dilution statutes, the would-be comparative advertiser should be more than careful. Small wonder one of the prominent themes we discovered among the comments and advice from advertising professionals we heard from in Chapter 3 was a warning about the likely risk of legal problems.

So in addition to hiring "a good lawyer" to review comparative claims and ads, what do the many codes, regulations, and cases suggest are the most important factors for the comparative advertiser to keep in mind? Boddewyn and Marton (1978, p. 35) offer a helpful list to start with. We'll begin with those and supplement them with what we've learned from another 40 years of comparative advertising practice and regulation in the United States.

- The FTC has strict regulations regarding terms expressing the most commonly used comparative price claims (for example, "regular price," "list price," and "wholesale price").
- Claims of superiority should be provable under circumstances in which the product is typically used.
- A claim of overall superiority shouldn't be made when it's based on a single or limited group of features or benefits (recall the case of Behold furniture polish).
- Comparative claims should be made between products of similar grade or quality (for example, a high-end model should not be compared to a competitor's low-end one).

- All products compared using demonstrations should be used according to their manufacturers' instructions.
- Testing should be conducted under the same conditions most people actually use the product (for example, Sara Lee challenged Kraft's Oscar Mayer hot dog taste test because they tested "naked" boiled hot dogs without condiments and most people never eat them that way).
- All claims should be supported with substantiation before they are used in an advertisement (both the courts and the FTC may deem a claim false simply because the advertiser lacked adequate and pre-existing substantiation).
- Direct evidence that a competitor's comparative ad is false or materially misleading should be in hand before filing a lawsuit or NAD complaint.
- Clearance by the media or success with a NAD complaint doesn't mean there might not still be legal problems ahead.

As a final conclusion for this chapter, we should consider what the various policies, regulations, and laws as they're applied to comparative advertising in the United States suggest about the varying levels of support it has received in other countries. We learned earlier that all forms of legal regulation of advertising are founded on the legal principles of freedom of speech, freedom of trade, support for fair competition, the protection of industrial property, and the prohibition of harm to others. It's in the latter two—protection of industrial property and prohibition of harm to others—that we find a major difference between the United States and elsewhere. As Jean Boddewyn wrote in 1983: "To claim that one's product is as good as a competitive one—even when lauding the latter—is usually considered in non-Anglo-Saxon countries as undesirable 'parasitic' behavior that exploits someone else's property" (p. 3). In Chapter 6, we'll be taking a closer look at how comparative advertising is practiced and regulated around the world.

Chapter Five

The Satirical Attack Ad

Advertisers occasionally use satire to make fun of generic types of people (such as "hapless dad" or "cranky old man"), non-users of their products (for example, the pitiful Ford pickup owner we'll be talking about in a minute), the advertisers themselves, or even, on rare occasions, their own customers. When they make fun of a competitor, though, they not only compare their products or services to the competitor's, they hope to successfully amuse their audiences at the same time. That's a lot trickier to do than merely a straightforward comparison.

Many advertisers have found the use of humor to be a fairly risky proposition all by itself. Despite its widespread use, humor comes with its own unique set of challenges and potential pitfalls. It can wear out quickly (after all, how many times do you enjoy hearing the same joke?). It can overwhelm the advertising message and keep people from processing or later remembering the information they're supposed to. It can also offend people. Visit YouTube and do a quick search for "Skittles" and "umbilical cord." You'll see an ad that was both quickly pulled by the sponsor and a perfect example of what I'm talking about. In fact, the use of humor in advertising is complicated enough to merit two books devoted to just that topic (Beard, 2007; Gulas & Weinberger, 2006).

As we learned in earlier chapters, advertisers also recognize that "going negative" with a comparative ad is especially risky. For one thing, we've already confirmed that the users of the comparison brand aren't going to like it very much, and there's also a good chance they'll transfer their dislike to the comparative advertiser's brand. So, at the very least, if an advertiser's objective is to steal customers and sales from competitors, aggressively attacking their brands doesn't seem like a very good idea. Still, as researchers Alina Sorescu and Betsy Gelb (2000, p. 36) suggest, "negative elements in an ad can contribute to its effectiveness as long as they are either believable, or offset by some positive elements about the sponsor . . . ." The advisability of including some "positive elements" may be one of the best explanations for why it seems as though so many negative, comparative ads include an attempt at humor.

As we've also already learned, a lot of research has been done in response to the increased use of comparative advertising around the world. However, the combination of humor and negativity has received almost no attention. Negative comparative advertising—and, by the same token, satirical attack advertising—differs from mere comparative advertising on the bases of (a) the degree to which the comparison brand is identified, (b) whether the direction of the comparison is differentiative versus associative (that is, the intent is to make the products appear different rather than similar), and (c) the extent to which the people who view the advertising perceive it to be particularly malicious or unfair (James & Hensel, 1991). In fact, Boddewyn and Marton (1978), in their early and important work on comparative advertising, specifically concluded that attack advertising should not be used at all "When the *attack on the competitor is too vicious or self-serving* and makes the audience rally to the underdog or curse all forms of advertising" (p. 100, italics in original).

The use of satire to attack competitors was an important trend in the use of comparative advertising that became especially prevalent during the 1990s and after. Some especially notable examples include the following:

- The Pepsi commercial you read about in Chapter 1, in which rapper M.C. Hammer loses his ability to rap and is only able to croon the 1974 pop song "Feelings" after accidentally drinking a Coke (don't forget Coca-Cola tried to sue).
- A Joe Camel campaign with the theme "Never Boring," intended to portray the Marlboro cowboy as culturally passé (Warner, 1994).
- A 1994 campaign for Royal Crown Co.'s regional soda Kick that declared Mountain Dew was "wimpy" (Laperouse, 1994).
- A 1997 Procter & Gamble campaign for Millstone coffee, portraying Starbucks Coffee Co. as a good place to buy t-shirts and novelties (but not necessarily coffee).
- A 2011 campaign in which Pepsi shows Coca-Cola's iconic Santa Claus and polar bears disloyally preferring Pepsi.
- A 2017 campaign that similarly shows your average milkman tasting and ultimately having to admit to the "Silk Milk Man" that he likes Silk soy milk better than dairy milk ("Dang it, it's so good!").

One of my favorite examples of a satirical attack ad, however, was one included in a campaign for the Chevrolet Silverado in 2009 and featuring former NFL star and TV sports personality Howie Long. After bemusedly observing a pudgy fellow awkwardly climbing out of the bed of his Ford F-150 in the parking lot of a home improvement store, Howie gets the guy's attention—"Hey, buddy. You left your little, uh, man step down" (you can view this spot online at YouTube [AdFreakTwo, 2009]). Clearly, this reference to a feature available on the F-150 but not the Silverado (which I can assure you Ford does not call a "man step") is intended to suggest that only a pansy would have any use for it. The extent to which the spot was perceived as particularly malicious or unfair at the time is suggested by some of the responses posted by viewers on YouTube. Here's a pretty good example, including a pointed reference to the fact Ford didn't participate in the U.S. government's financial rescue of the auto industry: "Hey Howie: My 'Man Step' didn't take a bailout, A$$H*LE." In our previous chapters, responses like this one were referred to as "backlash."

In this chapter, we're going to combine the academic theory and research findings and professional insights on comparative advertising we covered in previous chapters with the available theory and research on disparagement and humor in advertising. The purpose of this chapter is to explore the conditions under which we can expect that a satirical attack ad will likely be more effective (or not) compared to a comparative ad without satire (positive or negative) or a noncomparative ad.

THEORETICALLY, WHAT'S SO FUNNY?

Satire is the use of humor to ridicule or disparage someone for their apparent failings or shortcomings. The causes and effects of humorous disparagement are explained by a group of psychological theories, which have gone by various names, including hostility, superiority, malice, aggression, and derision theory (LaFave, 1972; Cantor & Zillman, 1973). Research and theory-building focusing on disparagement and two other important humor theories, incongruity and its resolution and arousal-safety (or relief theory), can be found in disciplines as diverse as literature, sociology, psychology, and linguistics.

Some say humorous disparagement is the oldest explanation for why people laugh. In fact, one influential humor scholar proposed that ridicule inspired by victory in hand-to-hand combat was actually the first kind of humor people consistently recognized (picture the kilted Scottish warriors in the film *Braveheart* . . . or not) (Rapp, 1951). Several scholars have reviewed the literature exploring this theoretical and literary tradition (Keith-Spiegel, 1972; Monro, 1951; Zillman & Cantor, 1976), which proposes people experience amusement when they are encouraged to feel superior to someone else. Since disparagement involves the social context in which humor takes place, it seems as though it could be a particularly powerful tactic when used in a comparative ad.

Although especially harsh disparagement is still relatively rare in advertising—aside from political advertising, of course—at least mild disparagement does seem to be showing up more and more often in the form of satirical, comparative commercial advertising. Explanations for this trend include the widespread use of humor in advertising in general, the increasingly favorable views of senior advertising creative executives toward the use of humor (Beard, 2007), increases in exceptionally aggressive advertising (including "shockvertising" [Dahl, Frankenberger, & Manchanda, 2003]) and, as we've already talked about, the belief among advertisers and ad agency creatives that tactical humor may help blunt the audience perception that a comparative ad is excessively mean-spirited.

So what makes disparagement or ridicule funny; that is, how does it work? It starts with a disparaging portrayal or victimization of another person, group, or idea. Social and behavioral scientists call this an "arousal stimulus." The chubby Ford F-150 owner and his clumsy use of his man step in the Chevy Silverado TV spot is a perfect example. The result is that people will experience a tension or dissonance caused by a combination of pleasure and anxiety—pleasure from a feeling of superiority ("Thank goodness I'm not that guy!") and anxiety caused by the feeling that it's not very nice to enjoy somebody else's ridicule. With disparagement, the anxiety (or guilt) is not resolved cognitively, as it is in the more widely used incongruity-resolution humor (which we'll look at more closely below), but through a process called *misattribution* (Zillman & Cantor, 1976).

Misattribution allows us to enjoy the disparagement of other people without feeling guilty. It works by encouraging us to attribute our enjoyment to something other than our own moral failings or insensitivity to the feelings of others. Misattribution can occur based on (a) the extent to which the target of the ridicule has been previously ridiculed by others, (b) the fact that the object of the ridicule isn't our responsibility, (c) the perception the victim deserves it, (d) the likelihood nobody will think less of us for enjoying it, and (e) the extent to which we can attribute our amusement to the cleverness of the put-down and not the attack itself (Speck, 1987). A great example that takes advantage of this last type of misattribution appeared as part of the credit card wars between American Express and Visa in the 1990s. American Express hammered home its comparative claim of lower interest charges with this declaration: "Visa. It's everywhere you want to pay more interest charges." Even if you didn't believe Visa was charging higher interest rates and that the claim was, consequently, false and unfair, you might still be amused because it's a pretty clever parody of the slogan "Visa. It's Everywhere You Want to Be."

Humor in the form of satire is generated by disparagement when combined with an incongruity. Incongruity theories propose we're amused when we see or hear something unexpected or incompatible. The simple incongruity theories are called *one-stage incongruity theories*. We *cognitively process* (or think about) an incongruous message or image in a single stage that includes three parts—interruption (what is this?), perceptual contrast (there's something unexpected here!), and playful confusion (what does this mean?). One-stage incongruity humor is actually pretty rare, especially in advertising. It's like a joke without a punchline. What are some examples? When entertainer Steve Martin first started gaining national attention as a standup comedian, he'd often perform with a fake arrow stuck through his head. Why? Nobody but Martin seems to know the answer to that question. But it was funny. My wife's interaction with the iPhone's Siri not long ago also produced a one-stage incongruity. "Siri," she asked, "tell me a joke." Siri's response (in a male voice with an Australian accent): "Two guys walk into a bar. . . . I've forgotten the rest." We both laughed, but it was only because it was unexpected.

Incongruity-resolution theory, on the other hand, proposes that an unexpected or incongruous message or stimulus may not be enough all by itself to be funny (Suls, 1972). These theorists agree with the one-stage theorists that humor generation begins when a single message or image simultaneously presents us with two pieces of information that are normally incompatible. Incongruity-resolution theory, though, also requires the incongruous elements to overlap in meaning in some way, or have two meanings, both of which make sense. People think it's funny when a punchline suddenly (and often surprisingly) switches them from the first meaning to the second, making it possible to resolve the incongruity and the confusion caused by it. There's a good example in Chevy's man step commercial that you may have noticed. Why did Howie refer to the Ford owner's man step as "little"? Ah, ha! Is he (subtly) comparing the F-150's man step to something else his victim has that might also be suffering from a lack of size? That double-meaning certainly helps explain the level of outrage in the backlash toward the ad from so many Ford owners. Theories that explain this type of humor are called *two-stage incongruity-then-resolution theories* because they add a second cognitive processing stage—the resolution of the confusing incongruity.

An incongruity and, thus, satire, are important in a negative comparative ad because disparagement alone can easily backfire and produce the problem we've talked about several times already—backlash. When asked about this problem, some of advertising's top creative professionals in the United States offered the following observations:

- "It is easy to cross the line when using comparative ad methods. Rather than finding ways to demonstrate key differentiation through creativity—going after a competitor can quickly turn off possible customers. Nevertheless, brands still do it. It's not easy to do well."—Agency Associate Creative Director
- "Comparative advertising must be ventured into with the utmost care and research or risk doing damage to the public perception of the advertised brand. Even when the advertising brand's claims and statements are true they must be conveyed in a manner that does not cast a 'cry baby' light onto them. You can't build your brand if your focus is to destroy someone else's."—Agency Creative Director
- "The backlash risk is substantial in comparative advertising."—Agency President and Executive Creative Director

Research findings on comparative commercial advertising and political attack advertising also suggest this is something to watch out for. As one humor theorist pointed out, "Playfulness and wit are needed for disparagement to seem humorous" (Zillman, 1983). Legendary advertising satirist Stan Freberg (1988, p. 272) recognized, and described, the problem better than anyone: "outrage in its natural state is not too salable." As an example, and going back to the parody of the Visa slogan, a parody is based on an incongruity. It's something that pretends to be one thing (in this case, the Visa slogan) when, in fact, it's something else (not the Visa slogan, but a derogatory imitation of it). Without that incongruity, the American Express ad actually wouldn't have any humor. Consequently, it would just be an attack ("Shame on Visa for charging higher interest rates!"), it wouldn't be funny, and it would be much more likely to be perceived as malicious and unfair.

Many other comparative campaigns over the past 20 years or so have also responded directly to their competitors' advertising by parodying slogans, trade characters (Pepsi's use of Coke's polar bears, for example), message strategies, creative themes, and even uniformed employees. Some notable examples include the following:

- a 1996 campaign for automaker Volvo that targeted BMW ("The ultimate driving machine, outdone by a Volvo.")
- GMC truck's 2002 response to Dodge Ram's "Mayor of Truckville" campaign ("If this is the mayor of Truckville, maybe it's time for a recount.")
- a 2007 Microsoft ad that starts with a lookalike for actor John Hodgman, who played the role of "PC" in Apple's successful "Mac vs. PC" comparative campaign ("Hello. I'm a PC. And I've been made into a stereotype.")
- a 2009 billboard featuring a photo of Buick LaCrosse with the headline "Something else for Lexus to relentlessly pursue"

- Verizon's 2009 parody of Apple's "There's an App for That" with its own "There's a Map for That"
- T-Mobile USA's 2011 parody of the "Mac vs. PC" campaign, featuring an attractive young woman repeatedly putting down the iPhone
- a 2007 Pizza Hut commercial, showing Domino's and Papa John's delivery drivers—in uniform, and apparently on the job—eating pizza at the home of a Pizza Hut delivery driver

WHAT DO WE KNOW ABOUT HUMOR IN ADVERTISING?

The effective use of humor in advertising has raised many practical and theoretical questions. As a rationale for their survey of advertising professionals, advertising researchers Thomas Madden and Marc Weinberger (1984, p. 8) pointed out that "knowledge regarding the effectiveness of humor is as equivocal today as it was in the 1950s and 1960s when some advertising executives cautioned against its use." One of those executives, by the way, was advertising legend and Hall of Fame inductee David Ogilvy. Nearly 25 years later, researcher Martin Eisend (2009), author of a meta-analysis of advertising humor effects, also used the term "equivocal" to describe our state of knowledge regarding how humor works in advertising and why. When I reviewed the research literature on advertising humor some years ago, I similarly reported that, although the use of humor became increasingly acceptable to most advertisers during the second half of the 20th century, questions and concerns about its effectiveness were still common (Beard, 2004).

But even though both researchers and advertising professionals often point out the risks associated with humor, advertisers use it a lot. Humor is especially prevalent in the broadcast media, with estimates of its use ranging from 15% to 46% in U.S. TV advertising (Kelly & Solomon, 1975; Li, 1995; Toncar, 2001; Weinberger & Campbell, 1991; Weinberger & Spotts, 1989). Humor is nearly as frequently used in U.S. radio advertising, at 30% (Weinberger & Campbell). Humorous ads may represent as much as 20% of the ads in U.S. trade magazines and as much as 10% in consumer magazines (McCullough & Taylor, 1993). Note, as well, that these are all old sources. It's likely the use of humor in advertising is even greater today than these mostly 20-year-old estimates suggest.

The findings from three comprehensive qualitative reviews of the advertising humor research literature (Beard, 2004; Sternthal & Craig, 1973; Weinberger & Gulas, 1992) and Eisend's (2009) more recent quantitative meta-analysis (which included 47 studies offering sufficient data to calculate effect sizes) have almost overwhelmingly shown that humor attracts attention to advertising. Some studies suggest humor in advertising probably has a negative effect on comprehension, which is usually defined as whether people processed and can recall the information they were supposed to. Others, including Eisend, conclude that humor is positively related to recall, comprehension, cognitive responses, and brand recognition. Reviews of the literature suggest humor's effects on these cognitive outcomes is especially effective for expressive (or feeling) products (ones we typically buy because of the way they make us feel rather than for practical reasons) and low-risk/low-involvement products (routine purchases that don't cost much or that we don't worry about too much). Eisend, contrary to his own expectations, reports that humor has a greater effect on positive attitudes for high involvement and thinking products versus low involvement and feeling products.

Surveys of advertising creative executives show that the majority agree humor is effective at gaining attention, better at gaining attention than non-humor and that it helps gain awareness when used in advertising for new products (Beard, 2007; Madden & Weinberger, 1984). The same surveys show creatives believe humor is (a) not particularly effective at registering complex copy points; (b) no more harmful to comprehension and recall than non-humor; and (c) as effective as non-humor for gaining name registration, retention, and for registering simple copy points. The majority of advertising creatives also believe consumer nondurables, many of which are either expressive and/or low-risk or low-involvement, are the products best suited for humorous advertising.

A review of the most recently published research literature, as well as Eisend's (2009) meta-analysis, show that academic researchers have established nearly beyond a doubt that successful humor enhances liking for not just message sources and ads (that is, A_{ad}), but that the liking is also often transferred to the brand, product, or service (that is, A_{br}). This finding is consistent with what's called the *affect-transfer hypothesis* (Aaker, Stayman, & Hagerty, 1986). The transfer of affect—liking, as well as other emotional responses—from an ad to a brand is based on classical conditioning. Simply put, classical conditioning means taking two things that are already connected (for example, humor and liking) and then adding something else (like the insurance company Aflac). The result is that the more people like an ad, the more they will like the brand that sponsored it. And research also shows that the more people like a brand, the more likely they are to buy it (or at least say they will, which is typically measured as purchase intention [P_i]). Although studies suggest humorous advertising enhances liking for the sources or sponsors and might enhance their credibility, Eisend (2009) concludes humor reduces credibility.

Early studies of humor in advertising generally supported a conclusion that the effects of humor on persuasion probably aren't any greater, on the average, than the effects of a serious or non-humorous ad. The two surveys of advertising executives, Madden and Weinberger's (1984) and mine

(Beard, 2007), both reported that most creatives don't agree humor is effective at getting people to yield to message arguments, increasing P_i or that it can increase persuasion more than non-humor. Conversely, most agree that humor can persuade people to switch brands.

A review of the most recently published literature uncovered several studies supporting the belief that, in many cases, humor distracts people from processing the claims in an ad and, consequently, reduces counter-arguing. As we learned in Chapter 2, comparative ads tend to encourage counter-arguing, so this finding would seem to be another pretty compelling reason to use humor in a comparative ad, satirical or not. Eisend (2009), however, failed to find either a positive or negative relationship between advertising humor and distraction.

Until recently, most researchers had concluded that a humorous ad's direct effect on sales is no greater than a non-humorous one's or that humor is an especially effective way to get consumers to actually purchase a product. Surveys also show that advertising creatives are universally skeptical that humor has a direct effect on sales. However, the results of Eisend's (2009) meta-analysis showed that humor can have a direct and positive effect on P_i.

Finally, everyone agrees humor works better when it's related in some way to the advertised product or service (Beard, 2007; Madden & Weinberger, 1984). Research has also suggested that related humor is more effective (Weinberger & Gulas, 1992; Weinberger, Spotts, Campbell, & Parsons, 1995). There are three kinds of humor relatedness in advertising, but the most important is called *thematic relatedness*, which means the humor is directly related to the brand, its uses, benefits, name, or typical users (Spotts, Weinberger, & Parsons, 1997). There isn't a lot of thematically unrelated humor in advertising—most advertisers appear to be smarter than that. One of the few examples I've personally seen was the use of lip-syncing chimpanzees in a local car dealership campaign.

A review of the recent literature revealed substantial support for a conclusion that humor will probably help encourage people to process at least some of the information in an ad if it's (a) related directly to something about the sponsoring brand, (b) necessary for recognizing and understanding an ad's message, or (c) incidentally used to reinforce message elements. The long-running campaign for Aflac Supplemental Insurance offers a great example. It would be almost impossible to watch one of their commercials without at least hearing the name of the brand and recognizing who the sponsor was—Aflac! The following list summarizes some of these key research findings regarding advertising and humor:

- Humor attracts attention.
- Humorous messages may detrimentally affect comprehension.
- Humor creates awareness (especially for new products).

- Humor is probably most effective for nondurable and low-risk, expressive products.
- Humorous ads increase liking for sources, ads, and brands.
- Humor may enhance source credibility.
- Humorous ads can be persuasive, but the persuasive effect is probably no greater than that of a serious appeal.
- Humor often works by distracting the audience, yielding a reduction in counter-argumentation and an increase in persuasion.
- Humor probably does not directly affect sales more than other types of appeals.
- Related or relevant humor is more effective than unrelated humor.

Audience Responses to Humor

A substantial amount of research on humor in advertising, as well as humor in general, has shown that people vary quite a bit in how they respond to it. Research, for example, has shown that people who have a low need for cognition (NFC) respond to funny ads with stronger A_{ad}, A_{br}, and P_i than high-NFC people (Zhang, 1996). NFC is defined as the enjoyment people get out of thinking or actively processing information. Researchers have concluded NFC is positively correlated with intelligence, education, the need to evaluate, objectivism, and openness to experience. NFC is negatively correlated with dogmatism and the tendency to become bored (Cacioppo, Petty, Feinstein, Blair, & Jarvis, 1996).

I can confirm these relationships with a personal experience. I once gave a presentation about humor in advertising to a local chapter of Mensa International (the high IQ society). The responses to the ads from this obviously high-NFC audience—mostly serious attention rather than laughter (some of the ads were, literally, the funniest ones in the world)—were totally different from any other group to which I'd ever given the same presentation. In fact, I told my wife afterward that even if I hadn't known my audience consisted of Mensa members, I would have noticed there was something uniformly different about them.

If it sounds like high-NFC people are probably a lot brighter than low-NFC people, a lot of researchers who've studied NFC probably wouldn't argue with you. It's interesting to note that, although researchers have concluded that high-NFC individuals respond more to factual information and logical claims in ads, they also concluded that low-NFC people attend more to *peripheral cues* (discussed in greater depth below), among them, of course, humor.

Not surprisingly, people who enjoy humor in general like funny ads more than people who don't enjoy humor. Advertising researcher Thomas Cline and his colleagues (2003) were the first to study in an advertising context the effect of an audience characteristic they called "need for humor" (NFH). They defined NFH as a person's tendency to generate and seek out humor. They found that people who were high NFH actually did respond to funny ads with a stronger A_{ad}. In fact, they found that people who were both high NFH *and* low NFC liked funny ads even more.

There's also a gender difference in preferences for different types of humor, with men favoring aggressive and sexual humor while women seem to like nonsensical and witty humor more. Moreover, my survey of advertising creative professionals also found that they believe funny ads work better with men than women (Beard, 2007). Both that survey and Madden and Weinberger's (1984) showed that advertising agency creatives believe, as well, that people who are younger and better-educated respond more positively to humorous advertising.

Audience Responses to Satire

There's also quite a bit of research specifically on the topic of how people vary in their responses to disparaging humor, although, as I noted earlier, none of it focuses directly on satirical ads. Research suggests appreciation of disparaging humor starts as children reach the end of early childhood, around the age of 7 (Buijzen & Valkenburg, 2004). As they grow older, so does their enjoyment of sarcasm and humor featuring violent and irreverent behavior (Acuff & Reiher, 1997; McGhee, 1979). When children reach adolescence (ages 12–18), they increasingly enjoy sarcastic, ironic, irreverent (Acuff & Reiher; Oppliger & Zillman, 1997), and absurd humor.

It probably also isn't a big surprise, especially if you've ever spent much time around a group of little boys, to learn that boys and girls have different preferences when it comes to disparaging humor. In early childhood, boys like disparaging humor that includes teasing and ridicule (McGhee, 1979) and aggressive, violent humor. They also like humor that includes irreverent behavior (Acuff & Reiher, 1997). Similarly, during middle childhood, boys like hostile humor more than girls do, especially humor that makes fun of other people or displays irreverent behavior toward adults. Even as adults, men prefer aggressive, hostile, and malicious types of humor more than women do (Mundorf et al., 1988; Unger, 1995; Whipple & Courtney, 1980). The following list offers a nice summary of what we can safely expect when it comes to how people typically respond to humorous ads:

- People with a low need for cognition (NFC) tend to respond more positively to most funny ads compared to high-NFC people.
- People who enjoy humor in general (have a high NFH) like funny ads more than people who don't enjoy humor.

- An appreciation for disparaging humor generally doesn't appear until kids reach the age of seven or so.
- There's a big difference in the types of humor men, versus women, tend to enjoy the most. These differences generally hold for boys versus girls, too.

PUTTING IT ALL TOGETHER

We have to be careful when drawing broad generalizations about the use of satirical attack advertising from all this theory and empirical research to specific outcomes in the real world. As we found in Chapter 2, the direct effects of an advertising message tactic, like the use of humor or direct and indirect comparisons, can differ based on the effects of multiple moderators or situational factors and their interactions. Still, some generalizations seem to be well supported by the theory, research findings, and the practices of successful advertising creative and corporate professionals that we've uncovered in this and previous chapters. Summarizing them is a good way to conclude this chapter.

As with other advertising message strategies and tactics, it's a good idea to consider the implications of employing a satirical attack in terms of its possible effects on the three categories of message objectives and outcomes that provide the foundation for advertising's "hierarchy-of-effects" models. These include (a) cognitive (for example, attention, awareness, knowledge, believability), (b) affective (for example, A_{ad} and A_{br}), and (c) conative (for example, P_i) advertising outcomes (Lavidge & Steiner, 1961; Rossiter, Percy, & Donovan; Vaughn, 1980). These, of course, match up with the empirical and theoretical work on comparative advertising we reviewed in Chapter 2 and the professional beliefs and empirical research results we compared in Chapter 3.

In each section that follows, we'll consider how the uses and effects of a satirical attack might be expected to differ from those of a non-satirical comparative ad, a noncomparative ad, or both. These generalizations will also address how some of the other situational factors we considered previously in Chapters 2 and 3 might be taken into account to fine-tune a satirical attack ad in order to maximize its effectiveness or, at least, avoid a major disaster.

Satirical Attack Ads and Cognitive Outcomes

The theory and research we covered on disparagement humor in this chapter and negativity bias in Chapter 2 strongly support the likelihood that because satirical attack ads are both critically negative and humorous, their effects on attention, message awareness, brand-name awareness, and recall should be greater than both non-satirical comparative ads and noncomparative ads. As we learned in Chapter 1's history of comparative advertising, advertisers have long believed that the main advantage of a comparative ad is that it attracts attention. Similarly, Chapter 2 confirmed that quite a bit of research supports the conclusion that comparative ads versus noncomparative ads generate more attention, increase message awareness and recall, may increase brand name recall, and encourage greater message processing. And thanks to the survey findings we reviewed in Chapter 3, we know that both advertising creative professionals and their corporate counterparts generally agree that comparative versus noncomparative advertising has a positive effect on most measures of awareness and recall.

Research on humor in advertising and its effects on credibility are a little mixed but suggest humor could enhance source credibility. On the other hand, and as we learned in Chapter 2, research suggests comparative ads can encourage derogation of the sponsor of the ad and the perception of manipulative intent (Chang, 2007) and, relatedly, discourage source credibility. So it seems likely that the sponsor or source of a satirical attack ad will be more credible compared to a non-satirical comparative ad, but not compared to a noncomparative ad.

In regard to believability, we learned in Chapter 1 that many advertisers over the past century questioned the believability of comparative ads. Much of the research we reviewed in Chapter 2 similarly suggested that the believability of claims in a comparative versus noncomparative ad is probably lower. We learned in Chapter 3, however, that advertising creative professionals aren't sure if comparative ads are more believable, while corporate ad executives agree slightly. Based on this summary of research and survey results and findings, it's not really clear whether satirical attack ads are more believable than non-satirical comparative ads, but they're probably less believable than noncomparative ads.

Both research and theory strongly support a conclusion that humor can distract audiences, leading to a reduction in counter-arguing. In contrast, as we learned in Chapter 2, comparative ads definitely encourage counter-arguing. Consequently, satirical attack ads should encourage less counter-arguing than non-satirical comparative ads but more than noncomparative ads.

Chapter 1's history of comparative advertising showed that advertisers have long recognized the problem of excessive negativity. Empirical research (Sorescu & Gelb, 2000; Jain & Posavac, 2004) has also supported the conclusion shown in Chapter 2's model that increases in negativity, nearly regardless of how it's measured, reduces the effectiveness of a comparative versus noncomparative ad. It's also important to keep Chow and Luk's (2006) research-supported conclusion regarding comparative advertising intensity in mind as well. They succinctly concluded that no advertiser should ever create an intensely comparative ad (or at least place it where consumers could see it). More important, however, is that the research we reviewed in this chapter strongly supports a conclusion that humor likely reduces the perception of mean-spiritedness and bad sportsmanship that often characterizes consumer responses to especially aggressive or intense comparative advertising.

Compared to a noncomparative ad, a satirical attack ad's effects on cognitive outcomes should be different based on whether the sponsor of the ad is a new brand, the market positions of the sponsor and comparison brands, and the user segments being targeted. As we learned in Chapter 3, surveys of both advertising creative and corporate professionals provide substantial support for conclusions that comparative advertising is more effective for brands holding smaller market shares and for new products and brands. An equally well-supported generalization is that a satirical attack ad will, on the average, be less effective for brands with larger market shares as well as brand leaders, compared to a noncomparative ad.

The research results we reviewed in Chapter 2 suggest the users of a third brand, brand switchers and probably users with a low degree of brand loyalty will likely respond more favorably to satirical attack ads than consumers with a commitment to the comparison brand (such as the Ford owner quoted above) (Sorescu & Gelb, 2000; Vijayalakshmi et al., 2015). It's not clear, though, whether or not there are any differences between satirical comparative ads and non-satirical ones.

As we learned in Chapter 2, there hasn't been much research on how the effects of comparative advertising differ based on its use for various types of products. We also discovered in Chapter 3 that both today's creatives and their corporate clients agree comparative advertising is more effective for low-priced, frequently purchased consumer products. In addition, as we discovered earlier in this chapter, humor is believed to work more effectively for the same types of products—that is, low-risk/low-involvement products—as well as for expressive products. Consequently, satirical attack advertising likely works more effectively for these types of products, and it's probably not surprising to learn that among the many low-risk/low-involvement products are those that often seem to rely on satirical attack advertising, for example, beer, fast food, and soft drinks. This, however, also explains the frequent use of satirical attack advertising in the automotive product category (such as our Chevy Silverado example). While they are definitely high-involvement products, most theorists and advertising professionals consider cars and trucks, especially sports cars and luxury imports, to be mainly expressive products.

Finally, and this is true of attempts at any kind of humor in advertising—satirical attack advertising will be more effective if it's thematically related. What would be another good example of unrelated humor in an attack ad (that is, in addition to the car-dealing chimpanzees I mentioned earlier)? A TV spot featuring Domino's Pizza CEO David A. Brandon comes fairly close. After Domino's ran ads claiming their Oven Baked Sandwiches beat Subway's by a 2–1 margin in an independently conducted taste test, Subway's lawyers sent a cease-and-desist letter demanding that Domino's stop running the ads. Domino's reply, in which CEO Brandon "playfully" ("Did You Know That Domino's and Subway Are in a Food Fight?" 2009) torched the letter in a 450-degree pizza oven in a TV spot broadcast during *American Idol* seems about as unrelated to the brand or its features, benefits, or customers as satirical humor could get. In fact, the only thing that saves the humor from being totally unrelated occurs when Mr. Brandon assures us, "Everything's better when it's oven-baked." You can find this commercial on YouTube (Ramon De Leon, 2009).

Here's a nice summary of some generalizations we can make regarding the relationships between satirical attack advertising and cognitive advertising outcomes:

- Satirical attack ads gain more attention, message awareness, brand-name awareness, and recall compared to both non-satirical comparative ads and noncomparative ads.
- Satirical attack ads generate more source or sponsor credibility than non-satirical comparative ads but less than noncomparative ads.
- Satirical attack ads may or may not be more believable than non-satirical comparative ads, but are less believable than noncomparative ads.
- Satirical attack ads generate less counter-arguing and source derogation than non-satirical comparative ads but more counter-arguing and derogation than noncomparative ads.
- Satirical attack ads containing similar levels of negativity will be perceived as less negative than non-satirical comparative ads but more negative than noncomparative ads.
- Satirical attack ads gain even more attention and awareness, compared to non-satirical comparative ads or noncomparative ads, when the sponsor is a new brand or product or is a smaller advertiser attacking a larger competitor.
- Satirical attack ads generate more favorable responses on informativeness and believability among users of the advertised brand, third-brand users, switchers, and those with low brand loyalty compared to comparison brand users.
- Satirical attack ads gain more favorable responses for expressive products and low-risk/low-involvement products compared to other product types.
- Satirical attack ads will be more effective in achieving cognitive outcomes if the humor is thematically related.

Satirical Attack Ads and Affective Outcomes

The effects of satirical attack ads on affective outcomes should be similar to those of other comparative ads, but also vary somewhat. For example, we found in Chapter 2 that comparative ads tend to generate more negative A_{ad} than noncomparative ads. On the other hand, the evidence in favor of more positive A_{br} is pretty mixed, with some studies suggesting positive effects and some neutral. We also learned in Chapter 3 that ad creatives and corporate advertising professionals tend to believe that the effect on A_{br} is negative. On the other hand, we learned in this chapter that humor enhances both A_{ad} and A_{br}. So, the addition of satire should cause comparative ads, on the average, to generate more favorable A_{ad} and A_{br} (thanks, in part, to the affect-transfer hypothesis) compared to non-satirical comparative ads.

As we learned in Chapters 1 and 2, there's good evidence to suggest that comparative ads result in significantly more positive A_{br} when the sponsored brand's market share is less than the comparison brand, when the comparison brand is the market leader and when the sponsored brand is new (Grewal et al., 1997). In addition, as we found in this chapter, it seems almost a certainty that satirical attack advertising by market leaders will almost always be perceived as a "big guy picking on a little guy," resulting in backlash.

In terms of audience characteristics, since low-NFC individuals respond to humor in general with more positive A_{ad} and A_{br} compared to high-NFC individuals, responses to satire should also vary based on this characteristic. Moreover, since high-NFC individuals respond more positively to factual versus emotional appeals and low-NFC individuals are more responsive to peripheral cues, high-NFC people should respond less favorably to satirical attack ads compared to non-humorous ads and non-satirical comparative ads. Similarly, as we learned earlier, people who are high-NFH should also respond more positively to satire. Consequently, low-NFC individuals, high-NFH individuals, as well as younger consumers should all respond to satirical attacks with greater liking, compared to non-satirical ads and noncomparative ads. Males, particularly younger ones, should also respond most positively to satire, especially aggressive satire, especially compared to women.

Thanks mainly to the important study conducted by Sorescu and Gelb (2000), we've gained some helpful insights into how the level of negativity in comparative advertising may affect how people respond to it affectively. Low-negativity satirical attacks ads are probably going to be more effective compared to both high-negativity satirical ads and high-negativity comparative ads overall, especially if advertisers are interested in how much audience members like the ads themselves and their brands. In addition, and similar to the effects of satirical attack ads on the cognitive outcomes of informativeness and believability, users of the advertised brand, third-brand users, and switchers should all respond to satirical attack ads with greater approval and perceptions of fairness, when compared to the users of the brand being attacked.

Finally, and similar to other types of comparative ads in general, satirical attack ads will likely have more positive effects on most affective outcomes when the ads contain evaluative claims rather than factual ones, and when they contain attacks on a competitor's product rather than brand image (Grewal et al., 1997; James & Hensel, 1991; Nye et al., 2008). Here's a good summary of some generalizations we can safely make about the relationships between satirical attack advertising and affective advertising outcomes:

- Satirical attack ads generate more positive A_{ad} and A_{br} than non-satirical comparative ads but more negative A_{ad} and A_{br} than noncomparative ads.
- Satirical attack ads generate more favorable A_{br} when the sponsored brand's market share is less than the comparison brand and when the sponsored brand is new.
- Low-NFC individuals respond to satirical attack ads with more positive A_{ad} and A_{br} compared to both non-satirical comparative ads and noncomparative ads.
- People who have a high NFH respond to satirical attack ads with more positive A_{ad} and A_{br} compared to both non-satirical comparative ads and noncomparative ads.
- Men respond to satirical attack ads with more positive A_{ad} and A_{br} than women do.
- The difference between the positive perceptions of men and women of satirical attack ads increases with the negativity of the attack.
- Older and more highly educated audience members perceive satirical attack ads more negatively than do younger and less educated audience members.
- Satirical attack ads generate more favorable responses on approval and fairness among users of the advertised brand, third-brand users and switchers compared to comparison brand users.
- The effects of satirical attack ads on A_{ad} and A_{br} are greater when the ads contain evaluative messages rather than factual ones.

Satirical Attack Ads and Conative Outcomes

Based on what we learned in Chapter 2, the research support for a positive effect of comparative ads on purchase intention (P_i) are somewhat mixed, and we concluded they should be shown as neutral in the model. Grewal et al. (1997) concluded that comparative ads appear to increase both purchase intention (P_i) and actual purchase more than non-comparative ads. Moreover, recent studies of the effects of comparative advertising on P_i and initial brand trial have reported far more nonsignificant or neutral effects than positive or negative ones. However, and perhaps most important for the present discussion, the surveys of advertising creative and corporate professionals we looked at in Chapter 3 show their beliefs are consistent with Grewal et al.'s results, that is, that comparative advertising encourages P_i.

In terms of the effects of humor in advertising, however, and as we learned in this chapter, research generally suggests that humorous ads likely don't have a stronger effect on conative outcomes such as P_i or initial brand trial than do non-humorous ads. Not only have many studies concluded that humorous ads are no more persuasive than non-humorous ones, surveys of advertising creative professionals show that the only real exception to this rule is the belief that humor might encourage people to try a different brand. So the effects of satirical attack ads on P_i and initial brand trial or actual purchase should be more positive than those of noncomparative ads but no different compared to other types of comparative ads.

These effects should also vary by market positions of the sponsor and comparison brands and the content of satirical attack ads. As we learned in Chapter 2, Grewal et al. (1997) reported that when the comparison brand is a market leader or the sponsored brand's market share is less than the comparison brand's, comparative ads result in significantly greater intention to purchase the sponsored brand than noncomparative ads do. Here's a summary of these generalizations:

- Satirical attack ads increase both P_i and purchase behavior more than noncomparative ads but not more than non-satirical comparative ads.
- Satirical attack ads generate greater P_i and purchase behavior when the comparison brand is the market leader.
- Satirical attack ads generate greater P_i and purchase behavior when the sponsored brand's market share is less than the comparison brand's.

A FINAL THOUGHT

Although there are no studies of the extent to which satire is used in commercial advertising for products and services, comparative or otherwise, the examples mentioned in this chapter as well as casual observation of the media suggest advertisers use it a lot. This chapter's review and synthesis of the advertising humor research literature strongly support a similar conclusion that earlier chapters have suggested about comparative advertising—to achieve certain advertising objectives and outcomes and when certain situational factors apply, having a little fun at a competitor's expense while simultaneously claiming brand superiority can be well worth the attempt.

Tactically, and as the examples mentioned in this chapter show, the satirical possibilities are nearly endless. Perpetually ripe targets for opportunistic ridicule are competitors' inferior features and attributes, ingredients, claims, slogans, brand images, customers, uniformed employees, and spokes characters. In fact, the potential advantages of a satirical attack seem to far outweigh the disadvantages, which, perhaps, also explains why there are so many advertisers today who seek to raise themselves up by putting their competitors down.

Chapter Six

Comparative Advertising around the World

As I mentioned in the introduction to this book, identifying competitors or even making comparisons of any kind were essentially not allowed in most countries in Europe and many other parts of the world until the late 1990s. In fact, naming a competitor in a direct comparative ad was banned in Belgium, Italy, and Luxembourg for years. Identifying another advertiser by name wasn't allowed without the advertiser's permission in Portugal, and it was considered a form of unfair competition in Germany and France unless the competitor was notified about the ad in advance. These requirements may seem quaint, if not downright amusing, to many comparative advertisers in the United States (which, as you know, has been the land of bloody advertising wars since the dawn of the 20th century). Although times have changed, considerable differences remain among many countries, where comparative advertising may be used often, occasionally, or never. Some of the explanations for the differences are legal and regulatory codes, but underlying those are what many industry observers and researchers have concluded are significant cultural differences.

As you no doubt recall at this point, the landmark work on comparative advertising around the world is Boddewyn and Marton's (1978) *Comparison Advertising: A Worldwide Study*. Boddewyn himself updated the research in 1983 to account for what he saw as the rapidly changing regulatory and professional landscape in many countries. Despite their value, these works have been out-of-print for years. Moreover, since the publication of that research, most of the trends they identified have continued, such as the increased use of comparative advertising in many countries and revisions to many previous regulations, directives, policies, and practices.

As we've learned in earlier chapters, the Federal Trade Commission (FTC) in the United States encouraged the Big Three TV networks to revise their clearance policies restricting the use of direct comparative advertising in the early 1970s. Despite the fact that European Union (EU) member states began meaningful discussions about allowing comparative advertising in the late 1970s (Barigozzi & Peitz, 2007; Boddewyn, 1983), it took another 20 years for something similarly significant to happen in Europe. In fact, there was an EU Misleading Advertising Directive in 1978 that included a provision in support of comparative advertising, but the provision was deleted because a single member state opposed it (Kirmani, 1996). Early international support also came from the International Chamber of Commerce, which revised its Advertising Code in 1973 to acknowledge the value of "fair" comparative ads (Boddewyn & Marton, 1978).

The EU finally adopted Directive 97/55/EC in 1997 (European Union, 1997), which went into effect in April 2000 and encouraged the more widespread use of comparative advertising. This directive, which updated a previous directive on misleading advertising (Directive 84/450/EEC) to include comparative advertising, established legal requirements intended to harmonize the laws across the EU. Similar to the FTC's policy statements in the United States in 1969 and 1979, Directive 97/55/EC is one of the most important events in the history and practice of comparative advertising. EU law on misleading and comparative advertising was updated again and codified in 2006 with Directive 2006/114/EC (European Union, 2006).

Resistance among the member states in the EU, as well as elsewhere, centered mostly around three important and central themes in unfair competition law: (a) the potential for consumers to be misled or outright deceived, (b) the disparagement of competitors and their goods or services, and (c) the exploitation of another business's hard work and justly earned consumer goodwill (Ohly & Spence, 2000; Stuyck, 1993). The latter two issues brought direct or explicit comparative advertising into conflict with trademark laws in many countries.

There were at least three especially good reasons for harmonizing the laws regarding comparative advertising across the EU. First, differences in laws among the member states were expected to be an obstacle toward the goal of developing a single market and encouraging the free movement of goods. Second, since many EU consumers would inevitably begin seeing many more cross-border ads for products in unfamiliar sizes, packaging, and levels of quality, it was believed comparative advertising would be a valuable source of objective information to help shoppers make informed purchase decisions. Third, advocates believed comparative advertising would stimulate competition, especially when it was used, as it often was in the United States, to challenge leading brands. As summarized by legal scholars Ansgar Ohly and Michael Spence (2000, p. 57):

> The Directive assumes that markets operate to serve consumers best when traders compete on the basis of the quality and price of their goods or services and consumers assess quality and price on the basis of objective information that is readily available to them.

Now that advertising on the Web, social media, and mobile apps enable almost any advertiser to easily reach a global audience, it's important to understand how laws, regulations, and attitudes regarding comparative advertising differ from countries like the United States that allow truthful comparative ads to others that continue to limit them in various ways. The desire by marketers to build global brands and launch international advertising campaigns also suggests important implications. Some international advertising scholars argue that the use of comparative advertising is growing fast in emerging markets such as India, China, and the Philippines (Kalro, Sivakumaran, & Marathe, 2017; Nagar, 2014).

This chapter reviews the available empirical research on these and related topics and explores some of the core cultural explanations for differences in attitudes toward comparative advertising among business decision makers, consumers, and advertising regulators around the world. The chapter also includes a closer look at a handful of countries that represent the world's largest economies and advertising markets and some of their unique experiences regarding comparative advertising history, law, and practices.

SEGMENTING CULTURES

Two of the most widely applied systems for describing important differences among the various cultures of the world are those of Dutch management researcher Geert Hofstede (1980) and American anthropologist Edward Twitchell Hall (1976). Hofstede originally segmented many countries and cultures along four dimensions: individualism, masculinity, power distance, and uncertainty avoidance. It's the first, however, individualism and its polar opposite, collectivism, that has had the most enduring impact on research attempting to explain differences in international uses of comparative advertising, as well as other advertising strategies and tactics.

Put simply, members of individualistic cultures look to their own interests first, share loose social ties with others and establish their goals with minimal thought given to groups other than their immediate ones, such as their families. Hofestede, Hofstede, and Minkov (2010) propose that this cultural dimension fundamentally captures how interdependent a culture's members perceive themselves to be and the extent to which they define their self-images in terms of "Me" versus "We." As you would expect, people in collectivist cultures are believed to be substantially the opposite, with the interests of the group coming before those of individuals, relationships characterized by a long-term commitment to cohesive in-groups, and high levels of group loyalty and the preferences of others taken into account when establishing goals.

Hall (1976), on the other hand, developed an especially important dimension based on different cultures' tendencies toward "context" (lower versus higher), which has also subsequently been used by researchers in studies of comparative advertising and its uses and effects. Hall offers a more communication-oriented perspective on culture, arguing that different cultures use combinations of non-verbal context versus explicit information to construct meaning in different ways. According to Hall, members of higher-context (HC) cultures share communication transactions that contain very little textual or explicit information, but which rely greatly on contextualized implicit and pre-programmed, often non-verbal information, which is recognized by message receivers and anticipated in particular settings.

In lower-context (LC) cultures, however, messages are direct and explicitly information-rich with people anticipating little in the way of context. So what distinguishes communication transactions across cultures is the ratio between context and information. More important, Hall and Hall (1990) argue that the extent to which context influences the nature of the communication among the members of different cultures is the foundation for most of their subsequent behaviors. Authors Lennie Copeland and Lewis Griggs (1986) offer the following segmentation of HC versus LC cultures:

Higher-Context Cultures

Afghan, African, Arabic, Brazilian, Chinese, Filipino, French Canadian, French, Greek, Hawaiian, Hungarian, Indian, Indonesian, Italian, Irish, Japanese, Korean, Latin American, Nepali, Pakistani, Persian, Portuguese, Russian, Southern United States, Spanish, Thai, Turkish, Vietnamese, South Slavic, West Slavic.

Lower-Context Cultures

Australian, Dutch, English Canadian, English, Finnish, German, Israeli, New Zealand, Scandinavia, Switzerland, United States.

The link between Hofstede's (1980) individualism versus collectivism and comparative advertising is also related to preferred communication styles, with people in individualistic cultures favoring more direct versus indirect ones. A direct communication style involves the explicit expression of the speaker's wants, needs and expectations. Language is interpreted based on its apparent surface meanings. Members of collectivistic cultures, however, favor an indirect style, where the wants, needs, and goals of the speaker lie below the surface. Consequently, it's not surprising to learn that the direct communication style is favored more in individualistic cultures and indirect communication in collectivistic cultures.

Some researchers have confirmed that cultural context and preferences for different communication styles are consistent with how people respond to different advertising appeals and executional tactics (Miracle, Chang, & Taylor, 1992). As an example, "People from high-context cultures often find low-context advertisements pushy and aggressive, whereas those from low-context cultures often find them informative and persuasive" (Rossman, 1994, as cited in Choi & Miracle, 2004, p. 76). Ohly and Spence (2000, p. 3) similarly point out the relationship between culture and attitudes toward different types of ads, even among cultures that share fairly similar values: "Advertising has a function in shaping contemporary culture. The reception of a particular advertisement that might be amusing to an Englishman might be offensively denigrating to a German and vice versa."

Figure 6.1 summarizes three culture clusters. As you can see, and based on a review of the most recent scholarship available on these topics, for this sample of 40 countries and cultures there are no collectivist-LC cultures. The individualism index scores for these countries and cultures (Hofstede, Hofstede, & Minkov, 2010) range from a high of 91 (the United States) to a low of 14 (Indonesia).

It's important to remember that both sets of cultural dimensions aren't perfect and have, despite their influence and value, received some criticism. For example, Hall's (1976) low- versus high-context concept and the research supporting it hasn't made it very clear as to where Arab and African cultures should fall in the continuum, although Copeland and Griggs (1986) propose they are predominantly HC. It's also important to remember that both high versus low context and individualism/collectivism are measured using continuous scales. However, high versus low context is often treated as a dichotomous dimension for convenience, as it is in Figure 6.1.

Individualistic-LC Cultures

The countries that fall into this cluster are as follows, based on their individualism index scores (Hofstede et al., 2010, pp. 95–97) and Copeland and Griggs's (1986) and international management consultancy firm IOR's (2017) context recommendations: Australia (90), Austria (55), Belgium (Nl/Fr, 78/72), Canada (80), Denmark (74), Finland (63), Germany (67), Great Britain (89), Israel (54), the Netherlands (80), New Zealand (79), Norway (69), Sweden (71), Switzerland (Ge/Fr, 69/64) and the United States (91).

According to IOR (2017), for the most part, and for the countries listed above that are included on their Website, preferred communication styles are consistent with what we'd expect for most of these predominantly individual-

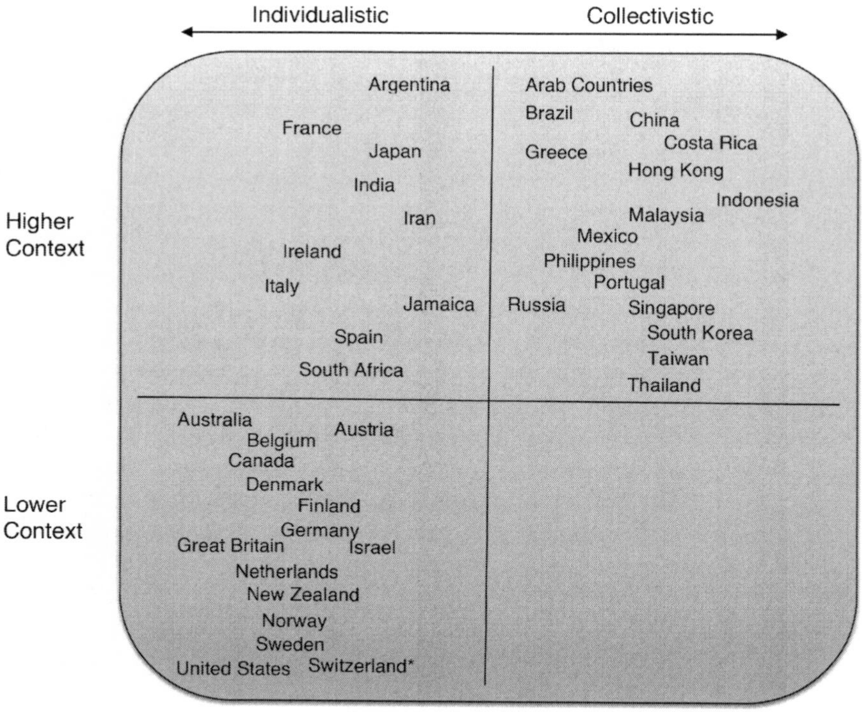

Figure 6.1. The Three Culture Clusters. *Figure provided by author.*

istic countries. One interesting exception is the U.K. (which includes Great Britain), where, according to IOR, people favor a more indirect communication style. One explanation for this discrepancy is that the U.K. also includes Northern Ireland, and according to IOR, Ireland (overall) is a HC culture, where people prefer an indirect communication style.

As you may have noticed, the cluster of Individualistic-LC countries is somewhat dominated by members of what has been called the "Anglosphere," a group of countries that share the same language (English) and similar cultural values. The Anglosphere includes Australia, Canada, Ireland, New Zealand, all four countries comprising the U.K., and the United States. In these countries and cultures, comparative advertising is generally believed to be informational. As de Mooij (2014, p. 317) concludes: "Only the Anglo-Saxon cultures like the hard confrontation as represented by the 'cola wars.'" This cluster also includes four of the five Scandinavian countries (data were unavailable for Iceland).

The available research on the frequency of use of comparative advertising generally supports our expectation that it would be more acceptable in the Individualistic-LC countries and cultures. In 1978, Boddewyn and Marton reported that comparative advertising was essentially illegal in six countries; Austria and Belgium were the only countries from this cluster for which that was the case. Boddewyn similarly reported in 1983 that there was no use of comparative advertising at all in the following nine countries: Argentina, Austria, Belgium, France, Greece, Italy, Japan, the Philippines, and South Korea. Again, Austria and Belgium were the exceptions among the countries and cultures in the Individualistic-LC cluster.

In 1978, Boddewyn and Marton reported comparative advertising was essentially legal with minor restrictions and "used" (p. 120) in the following countries: Australia, Canada, Denmark, Sweden, the U.K., and the United States. In two of the Individualistic-LC countries in 1978, the Netherlands and West Germany, comparative advertising was legal but infrequently used due to significant restrictions. New Zealand was something of an anomaly in 1978, with comparative advertising legal but banned by industry self-regulation policies. Boddewyn and Marton (1978) similarly report that comparative advertising was legal in Switzerland in 1978, but heavily restricted by cultural attitudes and "gentlemen's agreements" among business owners, managers and executives. By 1983, Boddewyn reported there was minor use of comparative advertising in Australia, Finland, the Netherlands, Norway, Switzerland, and West Germany. He also reported its use had become "significant" in four of the countries in this cluster (Canada, Denmark, the U.K., and the United States).

In 1998, researcher Naveen Donthu reported on the frequency of use of comparative advertising and its legal status in 17 countries. Only two had "high" levels of comparative advertising use at that time (Canada and the United States) and one country was listed as "moderate" (Great Britain). By this time, direct or explicit comparative advertising was legal everywhere except Belgium, Hong Kong, and South Korea. Six years later, Shao, Bao, and Gray (2004) summarized the research literature (including Donthu's [1998] work) and proposed estimates of comparative advertising's frequency of use in 37 countries and Puerto Rico. They reported the use of comparative advertising was "high to moderate" in Canada, New Zealand, Puerto Rico, the U.K., and the United States. Puerto Rico's inclusion on this list is also an interesting and somewhat surprising exception. Although a legal territory of the United States, the Puerto Rican culture is both collectivist and HC (IOR, 2017).

The Individualistic-LC cultural influences are evident in the laws and regulations these countries apply to comparative advertising. Boddewyn and Marton (1978, p. 18) helpfully summarized some of the core differences as they existed in 1978 and their implications for trends since then:

> Considered to be essentially parasitical, such advertising is generally prohibited in continental Western Europe. In the United States, United Kingdom, and Canada, it is thought to be actionable only if the implication tends to mislead the buyer. The most frequent and thus most important case is the negatively implied comparison, whereby critical statements tend to diminish competitors in the eyes of the consumer. In West Germany, France, and Belgium, critical comparisons are basically prohibited, and only compelling grounds can justify a departure from this principle, such as self-defense or using such comparisons to illustrate an advantage that cannot be explained in any other way. . . . On the other hand, truly critical comparisons are in principle allowed in Switzerland, the Scandinavian countries, and the Anglo-American countries.

These differences certainly seem to help explain the historically slower acceptance of comparative advertising in several of the Individualistic-LC countries, especially compared to the United States. Perhaps the most important difference, as suggested by Boddewyn and Marton (1978), has to do with how different cultures view negativity in comparative advertising, or what has also been defined in the literature as "disparagement" or "denigration." Whereas comparisons are not considered denigrating among the Anglo-Saxon cultures as long as they are truthful, most of the other Individualistic-LC cultures tend to view even truthful claims in advertising that harm or discredit the commercial reputation of someone else as denigrating, especially if the claims are also viewed as unnecessary. Although it's also worth noting, as we learned in Chapter 4, that even advertisers in the United States would have greatly preferred that the FTC not force them in the 1970s to eliminate industry self-regulation policies that restricted truthful disparagement.

Boddewyn (1983) also found that advertising self-regulatory codes were fairly consistent with cultural values. "Voluntary codes of advertising practice exist in some 35 countries. Their positions regarding comparative advertising range from very positive (e.g., in the United Kingdom) to very negative (e.g., in Italy and Venezuela where comparisons are said to be 'contrary to the principles of truth, morality and lawfulness')" (p. 4).

Comparative Advertising in Germany

Thanks to its status as the world's fourth largest economy (Bajpai, 2017) and fifth largest advertising market (Statista.com, 2017), we know quite a bit about Germany's unique history with comparative advertising. As early as 1931, the highest criminal and civil court in the German Reich (the *Reichsgericht*) ruled that comparative advertising was contrary to honest business practices for two reasons: (a) no business should have to allow itself to be used as a promotional tool by another business and (b) (as stated somewhat cryptically) "nobody could be a judge in his own case" (Ohly & Spence, 2000, p. 35).

In 1978, Boddewyn and Marton reported that the use of comparative advertising in West Germany was "miniscule" (p. 177), in part because the Germans viewed most comparative ads as excessively negative and because the ZAW (the German Advertising Federation) discouraged it based on concerns it could damage the reputation of the advertising industry. However, Boddewyn and Marton also argue comparative advertising's limited use was substantially due to continuing uncertainty over its legality under German law, since West German companies such as Bosch, Volkswagen, and BMW were enthusiastically attacking competitors by name at the same time in Scandinavia, the U.K., and the United States.

Another legal explanation for its limited use in West Germany was that the right to petition courts for injunctive relief in regard to a comparative ad was available not only to other advertisers, but trade associations and consumer groups, even with no evidence whatsoever that they had been directly affected by them. As Boddewyn and Marton (1978) concluded at the time: "This helps explain why the use of comparison advertising has so far been extremely limited in Germany, and frequently invites litigation—since so many private parties can initiate or threaten legal pressures—with the unsuccessful defendant having to bear all court costs" (p. 177). However, they also predicted the use of comparative advertising would grow in the future.

Comparative advertising continued to be regarded as essentially unfair in Germany during the 1990s, with very few exceptions, and advertising law scholar Samia Kirmani argued that, in 1996, Germany still had the strictest laws against comparative advertising in the EU. In fact, the German Unfair Competition Act still banned German advertisers from making price comparisons. However, important legal decisions occurring in 1999 (Ohly & Spence, 2000) and changes in legislation in 2000 encouraged the use of comparative advertising as long as it (a) referred to goods and services used for similar purposes; (b) referenced relevant attributes or prices in an objective manner; (c) didn't cause confusion regarding goods, services, or trademarks; (d) didn't cause unfair damage to a competitor's reputation; (e) didn't disparage a competitor's goods, services, or activities; and (f) didn't promote goods as imitations of those bearing a registered trademark (Schwaiger et al., 2007). These conditions are, for all practical purposes, identical to those included in Directive 2006/114/EC (European Union, 2006).

Comparative Advertising in the U.K.

We also know quite a bit about the U.K.'s unique experiences with comparative advertising regulation and practice, thanks to its rankings as the world's sixth-largest economy (Petroff, 2017) and fourth-largest advertising market (Statista.com, 2017). As we saw in Chapter 1's history, there were some early-20th century examples of comparative advertising in the U.K. However, the influence of the English Trade Marks Act, 1938 (Legislation.gov.uk, 2017a) amounted to an outright ban on comparative advertising because it required advertisers to obtain the permission of a registered trademark's owner before reproducing the mark in an ad (Ohly & Spence, 2000). A ban by the self-regulatory Independent Television Authority of detergent commercials that even seemed to compare the advertised brand with one or more competitors substantially eliminated comparative commercials on TV, when television became an important media option a few decades later.

Boddewyn and Marton (1978) report that comparative advertising was permissible under British law and industry self-regulation by the late 1970s, and that advertisers had used it in a limited way in the U.K. since at least 1968. They mention three important reasons why its use remained limited at the time, which are notably unrelated to advertiser concerns about running into trouble with the law:

> British practitioners retain a gentlemanly aversion against "knocking copy." They are also opposed to the overuse of facts in advertising, stressing instead the evocation of hopes and pleasant moods: "The world is full of facts but short of dreams!" [There was also concern that] Disaffection with the comparative claims of rival parties and politicians could also spread to [commercial] advertising: "They all lie!" (p. 40)

Noting that implied comparative advertising has become so common it "has rarely led to complaint" (p. 27), Ohly and Spence (2000) point out that the Trade Marks Act, 1994 (Legislation.gov.uk, 2017b) "significantly liberalized the law in relation to the use of trade marks in comparative advertising . . . " (p. 19). Arguably another of the single most important historical events in the history of comparative advertising, the act permitted the use of a competitor's trademark with conditions almost identical to those eventually included in Directive 2006/114/EC (European Union, 2006): as long as it was used in an "honest" manner and not in such a way as to take unfair advantage of the mark or cause damage to its distinctive character (Ohly & Spence). As we learned in Chapter 1's history, a similar landmark legal decision occurred in the United States nearly 30 years earlier, when a U.S. court of appeals ruled that a California perfume distributer was not illegally "free-riding" on the "Chanel No. 5" trademark, when using the trademark in its own advertising to identify and describe its "knock-off" brand of perfume.

Finally, and as we also learned in Chapter 1, attitudes and industry policies can still vary significantly from country to country, and even amongst those in the same individualism and context clusters. A TV commercial portraying soda bottles exploding every time someone used Sodastream's home carbonation soft drink system was banned in 2012 by Clearcast, a service that preapproves ads intended to run on commercial channels in the U.K. The reason? Clearcast concluded the spot denigrated the entire bottled water market and all its competitors. The same commercial ran in the United States, but more important, also in Australia, Sweden, and several other countries.

Individualistic-HC Cultures

As you can see in Figure 6.1, there are some moderately Individualistic-HC cultures. Based on their Individualism index scores (Hofstede et al., 2010, pp. 95–97) and recommendations regarding context and preferred communication styles (Copeland & Griggs, 1986; IOR, 2017), they include Argentina (46), France (71), India (48), Iran (41), Ireland (70), Italy (74), Jamaica (39), Japan (46), South Africa (wte, 65), and Spain (51). IOR (2017) reports that the peoples of France, Ireland, India, and Japan all favor indirect communication styles, whereas Argentinians were identified as preferring a moderately direct communication style.

In 1978, Boddewyn and Marton reported that comparative advertising was essentially illegal in three of these Individualistic-HC countries—France, Italy and Spain. When Boddewyn published his update in 1983, it was still illegal in France and Italy. In regard to comparative advertising frequency of use among this cluster of countries and cultures, Boddewyn reported in 1983 that there was no use of comparative advertising at all in Argentina, France, Italy, and Japan. Of these countries that Donthu reported on in 1998, the use of comparative advertising remained "very low" in France, India, Italy, and Japan. An interesting footnote to the international history of comparative advertising is that Italy, which had maintained some of the most restrictive regulations and policies against it, was one of the first among the EU member states to implement Directive 97/55/EC (Calboli, 2002). When Shao et al. (2004) published their review of the literature, they concluded that comparative advertising was still "low to not used" in France, India, Iran, Jamaica, Japan, and Spain.

Thanks to German legal scholar Frauke Henning-Bodewig (2006), we have a fairly recent estimate of comparative advertising use among several of the newest members of the EU, all of which are ranked moderately high on Hofstede et al.'s (2010) Individualism index. Estimates regarding context and preferred communication styles, however, were unavailable, with the exception of Hungary. According to IOR (2017), the Hungarian culture is HC, but its citizens prefer a direct communication style. The Czech Republic (58), Cyprus, Estonia (60), Hungary (80), Latvia (70), and Lithuania (60) (Hofstede et al., pp. 95–97) have all adopted Directive 97/55/EC, so it would be safe to conclude that comparative advertising is legal in all these countries. However, Henning-Bodewig reported that, in 2006, there was little comparative advertising in any of them.

Comparative Advertising in Japan

We also have some available background devoted to comparative advertising in Japan, ranked as the world's third-largest economy (Bajpai, 2017) and third-largest advertising market (Statista.com, 2017). Boddewyn's (p. 29) summary of the explanations for the limited use of explicit comparative advertising in 1983 are consistent with what we would expect for an Individualistic-HC culture:

> Until now, advertisers have voluntarily refrained from using comparative advertisements for fear that denigration would lead to declining confidence in advertising as a whole, but also as a reflection of the Japanese preference for decorum in public competitive behavior. Still, claims of superiority are on the increase as far as soft drinks, disposable diapers, detergents, whiskeys, and cars are concerned, particularly on the part of foreign companies, although the competitor's name is never mentioned.

When Pepsi attempted to run its "Pepsi Challenge" TV commercials in Japan in the 1990s, a local bottler required that the explicit reference to Coke be blocked out. It was also evident the campaign was extremely unpopular among Japanese consumers (Ang & Leong, 1994). Even more recently, the deregulation of comparative advertising was included among several other changes intended to ensure advertising better serves Japanese consumers. As explained by Morimoto (2014, p. 215), who also confirmed quite recently that comparative advertising remains fairly rare in Japan: "Though not a common advertising tactic in Japan, comparative advertising was officially permitted based on the idea that it provides more options for consumers and facilitates competition among advertisers. . . . However, comparative advertising is prohibited for advertising legal services and medical professional services."

Apple's effort to extend its hugely successful "Mac vs. PC" (also known as "Get a Mac") campaign to Japan offers some valuable insights into how subtle the effects of cultural differences can be on the ways consumers respond to comparative ads, even in countries that have relaxed their laws and restrictions. The Japanese versions of the TV commercials replaced young, casual, and hip actor Justin Long ("Mac") and older, nerdy actor John Hodgman ("PC") with a local comedy team called the Rahmens. International advertising textbook authors Katherine Toland Frith and Barbara Mueller (2010, p. 21) explain what happened:

> While Apple did adjust the scripts, nevertheless, the Japanese audiences disliked the ads because in Japanese culture it is rude to brag about one's strengths and to disparage the competition. In addition, the Japanese viewers thought the Mac guy was wearing low-end brand clothing, while they felt the PC guy (who was supposed to look like a nerd) was actually quite well

dressed. In terms of body language, the viewers thought that Mac looked embarrassed while PC looked stylish. So all in all even with Apple's efforts to localize the humor, the commercials were finally withdrawn in Japan.

Comparative Advertising in France

Thanks to its rankings as both the seventh-largest economy (Bajpai, 2017) and seventh-largest advertising market (Statista.com, 2017), quite a bit has been reported about comparative advertising in France. As we've already learned, comparative advertising was generally viewed as a form of unfair competition in that country, and Boddewyn reported it was still illegal there in 1983. In 1986, a major change in French advertising law took place when the *Cour de Cassation* (the highest court in the French judiciary) struck down the prohibition against comparative advertising. However, as international legal scholar Charlotte Romano (2005) reports, while authorized in principle, there were still so many restrictions, virtually any comparative claim remained prohibited by the courts. Moreover, any comparative claims continued to be viewed as synonymous with disparagement.

Early in 1991, a draft law designed to enhance consumer protections in France was approved, which included an article permitting comparative advertising as long as it met certain conditions (Ohly & Spence, 2000). That law went into effect in January of 1992, amending the French civil code to permit comparative advertising as long as it was fair, true, objective, and not misleading (Kirmani, 1996). However, once again, French law worked against the more widespread adoption of comparative advertising. Describing this law's restrictions on comparative advertising as "draconian" (p. 385), Romano (2005) also describes one of its fairly unique limitations:

> The most "unexpected limitation" in the 1992 Act was the requirement for comparative advertisers to disclose, in advance, the comparative advertisement to the competitors named or referred to in the ad, in order to enable them to defend against it. This disclosure requirement was regarded as a major obstacle to the use of comparative advertising. (p. 384)

France's major legal event involving comparative advertising took place on August 23, 2001, when Decree 2001–741 implemented Directive 97/55/EC and relaxed some of the conditions regarding comparative advertising legality. Overall, Romano (2005) proposes that French law—and, consequently, comparative advertising practices—became increasingly similar to those in the United States. French advertising law now allows comparisons between a wider variety of comparable products (for example, earlier law would have forbidden comparisons between butter and margarine), as well as product prices. Both countries also require comparative ads to be truthful, non-misleading, and non-confusing. Moreover, courts in both countries generally agree that a competitor doesn't have to be explicitly identified for an ad to meet the definition of a comparative ad.

There remain, however, important limitations in French comparative advertising law. For example, France's objectivity requirement significantly contradicts what is defined as "puffery" in the United States. French law does not allow vague, general, subjective, or opinionated claims. Romano (2005) argues that the main reason for this difference has to do with how the courts view consumer perceptions of advertising and its claims. In the United States, the FTC, the courts and industry self-regulators all determine the likelihood of deception based on the "Reasonable Man" theory (Fueroghne, 2017). In its requirement that advertisers "objectively compare relevant, decisive, verifiable and representative" features of goods and services (Romano, p. 397), however, French law follows more closely what has been called the "Ignorant Man" standard in the United States. This view that even a handful of the laziest, most unthinking and feeble-minded consumers should be protected from the likelihood of being deceived by advertising was recognized briefly in the United States between approximately 1937 to 1963 (Fueroghne). It still functions, however, as a significant obstacle to comparative advertising in France. As Romano (p. 400) concludes:

> It has the effect of prohibiting a large number of comparative advertisements that are allowed by United States standards, such as general claims of superiority, "like/love" ads, or statements comparing the taste or smell of products. In practice, companies contemplating comparative advertising campaigns in France are deterred from using this advertising format.

Two other legal obstacles in France are limitations on the exploitation of the value of a competitor's trademark and how the courts view disparagement. As Romano (2005) reports, comparative claims that a product is of the same "type" or "kind" of goods as those of trademarked competitors' are illegal and considered trademark infringement in France. This is due, in part, to the fact that French law places significant importance on protecting the reputation and goodwill of a trademark owner, much more so than in the United States. Consequently, there was no "knock-off" brand phenomenon in France. Regarding disparagement, French courts continue to rely on the concept to prohibit a wide variety of comparative claims. The consequences are helpfully summarized by Romano:

> Surprisingly, disparagement is often found even in the absence of either a false or a misleading statement about the competitor's mark or desire to damage his reputation. . . . As a result, advertisers contemplating comparative campaigns in France should avoid criticizing their competitors in order to maximize their chances of saving their advertisements from illegality. (pp. 405–406)

Industry observer and attorney Bryan Cave confirmed in 2013 that the use of comparative advertising was not "widespread" in France but also that the French courts' strict interpretation of disparagement or denigration continued to place obstacles in the way for advertisers. In 2013, Nestlé Nespresso S.A. claimed that competitor Bodum France's catalog and Website ads containing the copy "clearly the best way to brew coffee" and "make taste not waste," positioned next to visuals of used and crumpled coffee capsules, was an act of "denigration" and "parasitism." Nespresso was not mentioned in the ads and there are, in fact, several other companies that manufacture similar coffee machines and capsules. The *Cour de Cassation* overruled a lower court's ruling that the ads were not denigrating and held that they portrayed only a negative feature of a competitor's product and were presented in such a way as to discredit it. Cave concluded that the ruling "calls for the exercise of even more caution and objectivity by advertisers when deciding to issue comparative advertising."

Collectivistic-HC Cultures

In the right upper quadrant of Figure 6.1 we have, based on their Individualism index scores (Hofstede et al., 2010, pp. 95–97) and recommendations regarding context and communication style preferences (Copeland & Griggs, 1986; IOR, 2017), a cluster of the following Collectivistic-HC countries and cultures: Arab countries (38), Brazil (38), China (20), Costa Rica (15), Greece (35), Hong Kong (25), Indonesia (14), Malaysia (26), Mexico (30), the Philippines (32), Portugal (27), Russia (39), Singapore (20), South Korea (18), Taiwan (17), and Thailand (20).

Most Asian and Latin American countries and cultures fall into this cluster. All the individual Middle Eastern and Latin American countries described by IOR (2017) are HC, and their members, on average, prefer an indirect communication style. IOR also identified China, Costa Rica, Hong Kong, Indonesia, Mexico, the Philippines, Russia, Singapore, South Korea, Taiwan, and Thailand as HC countries favoring an indirect communication style. As noted earlier, Copeland and Griggs (1986) included all these countries and cultures on their list of HC cultures, with the exceptions of Costa Rica, Hong Kong, Malaysia, Mexico, the Philippines, Singapore, and Taiwan, which they didn't mention.

Observing that more than two-thirds of the world's population is more or less collectivistic, de Mooij (2014, p. 317) concludes that "This is a no-go area for competitive comparative advertising. In collectivistic cultures, comparison with the competition is not acceptable because it makes the other party lose face. It will backfire: You are the one who loses face, as it is not proper." Usage estimates over the years support de Mooij's conclusions.

In 1978, Boddewyn and Marton reported that comparative advertising was essentially legal, but infrequently used because of major restrictions in Greece. In 1978, it was legal but restricted or totally banned by self-regulation policies in Hong Kong and the Philippines. In 1978, it was legal but restricted by cultural attitudes or gentlemen's agreements in Brazil, Japan, and South Korea. In 1983, Boddewyn reported there was no use of comparative advertising in the Philippines, Greece, and South Korea, but "minor use" in Brazil, Malaysia, and Mexico.

In 1998, Donthu reported estimates of comparative advertising use among the Collectivistic-HC countries and cultures of Brazil, Hong Kong, Mexico, and South Korea. Its use was "very low" in Brazil and Mexico and it was illegal at this time in South Korea and Hong Kong. Based on their estimates in 2004, Shao et al. reported the use of comparative advertising remained low to nonexistent in several of these Collectivist-HC countries: Brazil, China, Greece, Indonesia, Mexico, South Korea, Taiwan, and Thailand. According to law firm Venture North Law Limited, comparative advertising was still severely restricted in Vietnam in 2015. Regulations prohibit direct comparisons based on prices, quality, and efficiency; "puffery" is not allowed, with claims such as "best," "the best," "only," and "number one" requiring substantiation. A comparative ad in Vietnam could also be subject to a legal claim if it were believed to have damaged the reputation of the targeted competitor.

Three other recent estimates of international comparative advertising use are fairly general ones, but they also offer some valuable insights. Researchers Enrique Manzur, Rodrigo Uribe, Pedro Hidalgo, Sergio Olavarrieta, and Pablo Farías (2012) report that comparative advertising, while permitted in most Latin American countries, often generates controversy and litigation, so most advertisers in those countries are reluctant to use it. Researcher Ross Petty (2014, p. 403) observed recently that "it's probably safe to say that the use of comparative advertising remains infrequent to non-existent in most other countries in Asia, Africa, Europe and South America." Finally, among the "Four Economic Asian Tigers," researcher Meghna Singh (2014) reports that comparative advertising is legal but allowed when meeting strict conditions in Singapore, prohibited in Hong Kong and "shunned and seldom used in Taiwan and South Korea."

Comparative Advertising in China

As the world's second-largest economy (Bajpai, 2017) and second-largest advertising market (Statista.com, 2017), some additional background is available on recent revisions to the law of comparative advertising in China. Advertising spending in China, in fact, is soaring, with an increase of 8.7% in 2016 and the expectation of another increase of 7.4% for 2017 (Johnson,

2017). Moreover, China is currently home to four of the world's biggest marketers: Alibaba, Tencent, SAIC Motor, and Yili Group.

What has been reported in regard to the status of comparative advertising in China is a little inconsistent on some points. Schwaiger et al. (2007) note that the Advertising Law of 1995 banned comparative claims in Chinese advertising. Similarly, and as recently as 2014, Singh reported that, while China does not "censor" ads, the country "still allows no Comparative Advertising." However, according to Beijing law firm Xangxin Partners, PC (2009), "there are no explicit legal provisions governing comparative advertising" in Chinese law.

The Chinese courts and standards applied by the legislature approach the regulation of comparative advertising almost entirely as a potential threat to fair competition. Noting that the courts have heard numerous cases alleging unfair competition resulting from the use of comparative ads and campaigns, Xangxin Partners (2010) concludes the following: "Pursuant to legislation and judicial case law, it appears that the key criterion to determine whether comparative advertising is legal is whether the ad damages the lawful rights of other market operators and harms the competition in the market."

A SUMMARY OF THE INTERNATIONAL RESEARCH LITERATURE

As we've learned in this chapter so far, there are still a great many differences in the uses of comparative advertising around the world. Yet there are still only a limited number of studies available to help us understand how the effectiveness of comparative advertising likely differs from country to country. What follows is a summary of the available research that offers some insights into those differences.

The first study of comparative advertising to investigate consumers from a country other than the United States was likely a doctoral dissertation conducted by D.R. Lyi (1988). Efforts to locate a copy of this work were unsuccessful; however, according to Manzur et al. (2012), Lyi reported that comparative ads produced lower levels of source believability among consumers in South Korea.

Researchers Swee-Hoon Ang and Siew-Meng Leong (1994) noting that, at the time, research on comparative advertising had been limited almost entirely to consumers in North America, conducted a study of 148 undergraduate business students from a university in Singapore. Consistent with what we learned earlier, strict policies regarding comparative advertising had kept its use to a minimum there, with even a handful of attempts quickly withdrawn after running into trouble with the administrators of the *Singapore Code of Advertising Practice*.

Ang and Leong (1994) report that the explicit or direct comparative print ads they used in their experiment produced significantly more favorable attitudes toward the brand (A_{br}), attitude toward product usage, likelihood of trial purchase, and information search intentions (a measure of the likelihood that participants would ask for a copy of a free booklet containing more information about the advertised brand), compared to a noncomparative ad. These differences disappeared, however, under a condition called "interference." Some of their research subjects rated the comparative or noncomparative ads they saw immediately after viewing them and others rated them after viewing three additional filler ads. Consequently, their conclusions were that comparative ads could be more effective for some affective and conative outcomes for Singaporeans, but these differences in effectiveness disappear almost as soon as viewers are distracted by other ads. It's also important to point out that they found attitude toward the ad (A_{ad}) was higher for the noncomparative ads in their experiment, versus the comparative ones, regardless of interference, although they didn't report whether the differences were statistically significant.

As we learned in Chapter 2, researcher Naveen Donthu (1998) conducted an early international study of comparative advertising with consumers in Canada, Great Britain, India, and the United States. The rationale for these countries was that, at the time, comparative advertising was frequently used in Canada, occasionally in Great Britain, and never in India (where it was illegal at the time). He included a sample from the United States for overall comparison purposes. Donthu's test TV commercials were explicitly (that is, direct) comparative and they were moderately intense, based on the comparative advertising intensity (CAI) scale we learned about in Chapter 2 (Donthu, 1992). He measured the effects of the direct comparative ads versus noncomparative ads on two measures of recall (aided and unaided) and A_{ad}. The comparative ads were recalled more than the noncomparative ads by all four groups, however, and contrary to his expectations, there were no differences among the groups. However, as we'd expect, there were significant differences among the four groups on A_{ad}. Attitudes were significantly more negative among the participants from India and Great Britain, compared to those from Canada and the United States. It's worth noting, however, that attitudes weren't significantly different between participants from Great Britain and India.

Observing that countries like Japan and Thailand "are collectivist cultures that foster competition by cooperation," Zeynep Gürhan-Canli and Durairaj Maheswaran (2000, p. 5) studied consumers from the United States and Thailand. They hypothesized that consumers in collectivistic cultures like Thailand would favor comparative ads that highlight the attributes shared between competing brands (that is, associational claims), whereas those in individualistic cultures would favor differentiative comparative claims of superiority. They offer the following summary of the reasons why they predicted these cultural differences, which helpfully expands on our previous discussion of the major differences between individualism and collectivism:

> Collectivists are more concerned about past associations and long-term relationships. They are brand loyal and unlikely to buy products from unknown and foreign companies. Information about familiar brands will receive more consideration and be more likely to be believed. Unfamiliar brands are out-group members and won't be easily trusted. Any comparison claims made by unfamiliar products may not receive careful consideration and are not likely to be considered credible. In individualist cultures, familiarity doesn't have any specific advantages. These consumers are more likely to buy a superior quality product no matter who makes it. (p. 10)

As Gürhan-Canli and Maheswaran (2000) predicted, a similarity-based comparison led to more favorable evaluations among their research subjects (undergraduate college students) from Thailand versus the United States. Their Thai subjects also found comparison claims more believable when the advertised brand was familiar rather than unfamiliar. Thai consumers generated more support thoughts when the comparison was based on similarity and not superiority, compared to the U.S. subjects. On the other hand, they found that Thai subjects generated more counterarguments in response to superiority comparisons, while the American subjects generated more counterarguments in response to similarity-based comparisons. They concluded "that more rational appeals like comparative advertising can also be effective if they are executed in culturally compatible ways" (p. 24).

Jeon and Beatty (2002) hypothesized that comparative advertising is more persuasive than noncomparative advertising in both the United States and South Korea. However, their findings for explicit (direct) comparative print ads, implied (indirect) ones and noncomparative ads and responses between United States and Korean student research subjects were somewhat surprising. They report that the Korean subjects had more favorable attitudes toward the direct comparative ads than the U.S. subjects, although they did not rate them as more persuasive than the indirect comparative ads. Interestingly, noncomparative test ads produced lower A_{br} and lower purchase intentions (P_i) in both samples, compared to either of the comparative ads. They concluded that, because the South Korean subjects had likely seen very few direct comparative ads, "the novelty effect seems to be at work here" (p. 911).

Shao et al. (2004) sought the answer to a straightforward question: Could comparative print ads be as effective in other cultures as they often appeared to be in the United States? To answer it, they recruited participants from 36 countries (utilizing a variety of student and non-student sampling sites), with a final sample consisting of 100 subjects representing high-context communication cultures and 96 from low-context ones. They didn't find any differences in A_{ad} or persuasion effects between the two sets of cultures and their evaluations of an indirect comparative ad. However, LC participants rated the direct comparative ad more persuasive than the HC participants did, and they also rated it more persuasive than an indirect comparative ad. Somewhat surprisingly, there wasn't any difference in A_{ad} for the LC participants either between the direct and indirect ads or compared to the HC participants. It's also especially interesting to note that they found no difference in the persuasive effect between direct and indirect comparative ads for the HC participants. They also reported being "perplexed" that HC and LC subjects both rated the direct comparative ad and the indirect comparative ad lower on A_{ad} compared to the noncomparative ad (p. 76).

Researchers Yung Kyun Choi and Gordon Miracle (2004) explored whether South Korean consumers (undergraduate college students) would respond differently to direct and indirect comparative ads compared to consumers from the United States. As they explained: "Comparative advertising is an example of individualistic, low-context communication, which is found to be pushy and aggressive (negative evaluation) or informative (positive evaluation), depending on the culture of the audience" (p. 76). They compared the effectiveness of a direct comparative print ad, an indirect one (a "leading brands" comparison), and a noncomparative ad. Their experimental results showed that study participants from the United States had, as predicted, more favorable A_{ad} and A_{br} toward both the direct and indirect comparative ads, compared to the South Korean participants. There were no significant differences on P_i. When exposed to the noncomparative ad, U.S. subjects also had a more favorable A_{ad} than the Korean subjects, but weren't significantly different on A_{br} and P_i.

Researchers Soojung Kim, Se-Hoon Jeong, and Yoori Hwang (2016) updated these findings some 10 years later with a study of United States and South Korean consumers' responses to comparative ads on Facebook. As they predicted, the Americans responded with more favorable attitudes toward the comparative ads and the South Koreans more favorably toward the non-comparative ads. They concluded that the Korean participants' attitudes were more negative toward the comparative ad messages they viewed because they were perceived to be "less considerate."

Based on a theoretical framework of consumer skepticism toward novel information, Nye, Roth, and Shimp (2008) conducted an extensive and important cross-national study (college students from France, the Netherlands, and the United States) to investigate how novelty of the brand and novelty of the practice of comparative advertising might affect A_{br}. We looked at some of their key results in Chapter 2, but here we'll focus on the ones that revealed differences by country and sample. First, they reported that an indirect comparative ad, versus a direct one, encouraged higher A_{br} for subjects in the United States when the ad was for an established (versus novel) brand. However, whether the advertised brand was established or new had no effect on A_{br} for the subjects from France and the Netherlands, when they viewed either a direct or indirect comparative ad.

Second, Nye et al. (2008) found that comparative print ads containing factual versus evaluative messages generated more favorable A_{br}, but significantly more so for subjects from France and the Netherlands, and especially for established brands rather than new ones. In the United States, where comparative advertising is common, evaluative messages generated more favorable A_{br}. However, also for the U.S. subjects, it didn't make any difference whether evaluative or factual comparative ads were for new or established brands. A third cross-cultural finding of interest focused on combining direct versus indirect comparative ads with factual versus evaluative message content. The combination of a direct format with factual content produced a significantly greater A_{br} for subjects in France and the Netherlands, whereas the direct format with evaluative content was more effective for the subjects in the United States. The other two combinations (the indirect format with evaluative or factual content) didn't produce any significant differences.

Finally, in the United States, where comparative advertising is often used, Nye et al. (2008) reported that brand-loyal subjects responded to comparative ads with evaluative message content (versus factual) with higher A_{br}. Conversely, brand-loyal subjects in France and the Netherlands had more favorable attitudes toward a comparative ad containing factual content rather than evaluative. Overall, they summarized the key results of their study as follows: (a) direct comparative ads with factual message content is most effective in markets where comparative advertising is novel (in this case, France and the Netherlands), (b) indirect comparative ads with evaluative content are more effective where comparative advertising is not novel (in this case, the United States), (c) factual content is more effective than evaluative content when the targeted consumers are loyal to the comparison brand and comparative advertising is novel, and (d) evaluative content is more effective than factual content when the targeted consumers are loyal to the comparison brand and comparative advertising is common (the United States).

Like Choi and Miracle (2004), Nye et al. (2008) found no support for a hypothesis that direct comparative advertising would generate more positive A_{ad} in countries or cultures where comparative advertising is infrequently used (for example, South Korea). This finding, however, differed from that of Jeon and Beatty (2002) who, as we saw just above, reported that their South Korean research subjects had more favorable attitudes toward direct comparative ads, compared to their U.S. subjects.

Schwaiger et al. (2007) studied the effectiveness of comparative versus noncomparative advertising in Germany. Research participants were selected using street recruitment. They used comparative and noncomparative versions of print ads and measured A_{ad}, A_{br}, product involvement, and product experience. Comparative advertising was effective for a telecommunication company called o.tei.o, where the key benefit focused on price, which in the comparative version, was compared with that of a direct competitor by name. Comparison advertising was less effective than a noncomparative ad for automaker BMW, which focused on much more subjective, emotion-laden image attributes. Schwaiger et al. offered the following overall conclusion: "There was virtually no indication of negative attitudes toward comparative advertising in either of the studies. This suggests that, despite the cultural and legal restrictions that have prevented the use of comparative advertising in Germany's past, comparative advertising appeared to operate according to the general tenants of reasoned action . . . " (p. 10).

Researchers Salvador del Barrio-Garcia and Teodoro Luque-Martinez (2003) conducted a study of 720 Spanish consumers, sampled from across the four largest geographical areas of the country. They studied how consumers in Spain would respond to direct, indirect and noncomparative ads. As we learned in Chapter 2, theirs was one of the few to report no difference in attention between comparative and noncomparative ads. In addition, they also reported that Spanish consumers rated the claims in the comparative ads less believable and lower on A_{ad}, but ratings were not significantly different on A_{br} or P_i.

Manzur et al. (2012) studied a sample of 450 Chilean undergraduate college students and also studied three types of print ads for existing brands (Sony and Coca-Cola)—direct comparative, indirect, and noncomparative. Like del Barrio-Garcia and Luque-Martinez (2003), they also found no difference on message recall. They also found that the comparative ads were rated significantly lower on message believability and that the noncomparative ad was more credible than either of the comparative ads. While they predicted that both comparative ads would produce a lower rating on A_{ad}, their prediction that the direct comparative ad would receive the lowest rating was not supported. Their subjects rated the indirect comparative ad lower than the direct comparative ad and the noncomparative ad. There were no significant differences on A_{br} and P_i. Overall, they concluded that their results "are consistent with the idea that comparative advertising tends to be less persuasive for non-U.S. consumers" (p. 288).

As we learned in Chapter 2, researchers Arti Kalro, Bharadhwaj Sivakumaran, and Rahul Marathe (2010, 2013, 2017) have conducted three studies of comparative advertising in India. Their first study was a content analysis of print ads, and they surprisingly reported that direct comparative ads were used more often than indirect ones (although their sample, at 203 ads, was extremely small). In the second study, Kalro et al. (2013) conducted an experiment with 125 Indian college students. They found that direct comparative print ads, versus indirect ones, reduced perceived manipulative intent, and increased A_{ad} and the perceived differences between brands, but only for people who use analytical information processing modes (using reason and semantics) versus imagery ones (using nonverbal, sensory representation of perceptual information).

Kalro et al.'s (2017) third study consisted of four experiments, relying on samples of 362, 246, 265, and 262 Indian college students. The overall results from all four experiments showed that there were no significant differences on A_{ad} and perception of manipulative intent between direct and indirect comparative versions of print ads. However, direct comparative ads did decrease the perception of manipulative intent and increase A_{ad} when multiple brands were targeted (by name) and not just a single market leader. Conversely, indirect comparative ads had these effects when they targeted a "market leader" instead of multiple brands.

SUMMARY AND CONCLUSIONS

Boddewyn and Marton (1978, pp. 20–21) suggested five reasons why the law on truthful comparisons and industry self-regulation policies around the world were, at the time, evolving in the direction of greater permissiveness and broader exceptions in favor of comparative advertising. Three of them were the apparent successes associated with comparative advertising in certain "pilot" countries and cultures (for example, Canada, Scandinavia, and the United States), the 1973 revision to the International Chamber of Commerce's *Advertising Code* and the support of various groups in the EU that ultimately led to Directive 97/55/EC.

However, the two most important explanations for the legal, regulatory, and attitudinal trends in favor of comparative advertising that Boddewyn and Marton highlighted in 1978 (p. 20) are the following (italics in original):

a. *Consumerist pressures* are favoring marketing and advertising techniques conducive to providing more and better information to the consumer.
b. Most *national governments* support this demand, and many also want to foster a type of competition wherein a firm's success rests on real economic superiority. This requires greater "market transparency" about comparative advantages.

As we've seen in this chapter, these latter two explanations are consistent themes throughout our overview of the most recent international history and trends in the uses and regulation of comparative advertising. As Ohly and Spence (2000) pointed out, they clearly explain the support for Directive 97/55/EC among the EU's member states, most of which are Individualistic-LC cultures (with the exceptions of France, Ireland, Italy, and Spain). Yet Morimoto (2014) similarly argued that comparative advertising was recently deregulated in the Individualistic-HC culture of Japan to enhance consumer welfare and facilitate competition. And as law firm Xangxin Partners (2010) reported not long ago, even in China's Collectivistic-HC culture, recent acceptance of comparative advertising is linked almost entirely to the belief that it need not necessarily cause damage to either competition or the legal rights of businesses and marketers.

Something else that seems well worth mentioning about the consistency of these two core comparative advertising themes—more-informed consumers and fair competition—is how consistent they are with widely held beliefs about advertising ethics. Advertising ethics scholars Edward Spence, Brett Van Heekeren, and Michael Boylan (2004) helpfully identify the core commonalities among several of the world's major advertising ethical codes. These commonalities include the following:

- a sense of responsibility to consumers, community concerns, and society
- decency, honesty, and truth
- avoidance of misrepresentation and deception
- a sense of fair competition
- the protection and promotion of the reputation of the advertising industry

Here again, the debate over the value of comparative advertising from country to country often reflected political, social, cultural, and professional beliefs regarding nearly all these ethical principles. Criticisms of comparative advertising throughout the world over the past approximately 100 years tended to emphasize the threats it might represent to advertising honesty, truth, efforts to avoid misrepresentation and deception, the encouragement of fair competition, and the maintenance of a favorable reputation for advertising as an industry and institution. On the other hand, support for comparative advertising tended to emphasize its ethicality as a contributor to the communication of truthful information about products and services that helps consumers make effective purchasing decisions and, relatedly, its contributions to free and fair competition. Consequently, the global and cross-cultural trends we've discovered in favor of comparative advertising reflect a growing belief that it can represent, for the most part, an ethical advertising practice.

However, there are other explanations for trends we discovered in this chapter, as well as the differences in attitudes toward comparative advertising that remain today. First, cultural differences clearly explain a great deal. We see these differences strongly reflected in our review of the research available on frequency of usage of comparative advertising and changes to laws and regulations among the various countries and cultures included in the three culture clusters. They are also evident among the empirical findings regarding how consumers in various countries and cultures respond to direct and indirect (implied) comparative ads when compared to each other and noncomparative ads.

Some studies do offer some evidence that contradicts our expectation that the members of HC cultures would likely and consistently, regardless of the measure of response, respond more negatively toward comparative ads (Ang & Leong, 1994; Jeon & Beatty, 2002; Kalro et al., 2017; Manzur et al., 2012; Shao et al., 2004), especially compared to consumers in the mostly Individualistic-LC cultures where comparative advertising is much more frequently used and has been for a much longer period of time. For the literature as a whole, however, researchers reported a lower A_{ad}, when comparing HC cultures to LC ones, or when comparing comparative versus noncomparative ads in HC cultures only.

The international research findings summarized in this chapter also suggest, as we'd expect, that members of HC cultures will likely respond more favorably to less negative, confrontational, or unfair comparative ads, such as those emphasizing similarity-based rather than superiority-based comparisons (Gürhan-Canli & Maheswaran, 2000) or those emphasizing factual versus evaluative messages (Nye et al., 2008). Apple's experience with the "Mac vs. PC" campaign in Japan should offer an enlightening lesson for any would-be comparative advertiser.

Another important explanation for the varied acceptance of comparative advertising around the world is a major issue that also consistently reflected professional and legal concerns among advertisers and regulators in the world's most aggressive domain for comparative advertising, the United States, and that's the issue of disparagement. While obviously problematic among HC cultures, it was a major obstacle in the EU and still exists as a justification for banning a comparative ad under the most recent directive (2006/114/EC). Perhaps the best explanation for the difference between the United States and much of the rest of the world has to do with the fact that U.S. laws and courts offer less protection to the owners of trademarks, favoring the goal of ensuring the benefits to consumers created by competition and the avoidance of any dishonest or unfair business practices that might inhibit it. The view that comparative advertising represents a tactic that enables smaller competitors to exploit the reputations and brand equity of larger, well-established competitors—originally resisted but now totally accepted in the United States—is also a consistent and related theme of resistance among many of the world's LC and HC cultures.

We didn't go extensively into the specific policies, statutes, or regulations involving either self-regulation or the law in various countries. That would be too large and complex a task for a single chapter in a book. In fact, there's an entire book about just the legal and regulatory implications of Directive 97/55/EC (Ohly & Spence, 2000). A valuable contribution to the literature would be an overview and comparison of the laws and self-regulation policies in the half-dozen or so countries where comparative advertising is most frequently used. As we discovered in this chapter, there can be significant differences in how the courts and industry self-regulators evaluate the same comparative ads even among countries and cultures in the same individualism-context clusters. A more ambitious scholar or research team could make an even greater contribution by replicating Boddewyn and Marton's (1978) 40-year-old worldwide study. The value of such an ambitious undertaking is especially obvious when we consider how little we still know about comparative advertising and its uses in many countries around the world.

Finally, it's worth taking note of what the limitations are in all this writing and research that we've reviewed for this chapter. For example, we seem to know quite a bit about how comparative advertising works in print ads but not much about TV commercials. Considering that we learned in Chapter 1 that comparative advertising is used much more often in TV advertising than print, this is obviously a serious limitation. Just as important, you may have noticed that we know a lot about how college students respond to comparative ads, but hardly anyone else. The use of student samples in psychology and consumer behavior research has been a subject of spirited debate for at least four decades. This apparent limitation in published experimental research has been disparagingly referred to as "the science of the sophomore" (Gordon, Slade, & Schmitt, 1986) or the "college-sophomore problem" (Cooper, McCord, & Socha, 2011). On one hand, it's generally agreed that student samples are not very representative of other populations, so there are problems with generalizing from experiments that rely on them to other populations of consumers. This is a threat to what's called "external validity" in experimental research.

On the other hand, many researchers agree that the use of student samples is acceptable for research with goals of building theory and testing hypotheses. Student samples tend to be quite homogeneous; that is, they're very similar in regard to age, education, and other social and psychological characteristics. Among other methodological advantages, this means that when we look across the results of a series of experiments and generalize the results from one to the next, we can have much more confidence that whatever differences we see were actually caused by differences in experimental treatments—in our case, for example, comparative versus noncomparative ads or evaluative versus factual comparisons—and not differences in the characteristics of the samples. This is the experimental issue of "reproducibility" and its epistemological cousin, "replicability." Some have suggested that the increase in reproducibility and our ability to generalize the results of one experiment to the next especially justifies the use of college student samples in exactly the type of cross-cultural research we just looked at. However, it's also important to acknowledge that the confidence we can have even in generalizing from one student sample to another has recently been called into question (Peterson & Merunka, 2014).

Chapter Seven

Comparative Campaigns in the Real World

As we learned in Chapter 1, many of the 20th century's most influential business executives, advertising professionals, and industry opinion leaders participated in the ongoing debate over when, or even if, comparative advertising is a good idea. Most comparative advertisers were absolutely convinced their ads would, at the very least, attract a lot of attention, generate a lot of recall, and, maybe, encourage initial trial for a new brand. Despite its widespread use, though, we also learned that many were also frequently concerned that a comparative campaign could easily backfire, leading to consumer confusion, lack of believability, the potential for backlash, and even negative attitudes toward all the competitors in a product or service category. In fact, one of Chapter 1's most striking historical insights was just how many marketers and advertisers over the years wound up regretting the decision to launch a comparative campaign in the first place.

Chapter 2's summary of theory and empirical research and Chapter 3's overview of professional beliefs regarding comparative advertising also offered a great deal of insight into the potential for success or failure. For instance, both strongly suggest that comparative advertising on behalf of underdog competitors, substantiated claims (the more visual the better), and comparative ads targeting non-users of the competitor's product or service or brand switchers are more likely to be successful. On the other hand, while both historical research and surveys show advertisers believe maintaining a positive tone (versus excessively negative or mean-spirited attacks) is important, academic researchers are really just beginning to study how negative a comparative ad can or should be. Other equally important questions also remain. Finally, Chapter 4's overview of comparative advertising law and industry self-regulatory policies and practices confirmed the many dangers lying in wait for even the most sophisticated advertisers and agencies in the United States and elsewhere.

Academic research and quantitative methods, such as the many studies summarized in Chapter 2, can do a great job of measuring and predicting what we think might be causal relationships between a phenomenon like comparative advertising and its outcomes in the marketplace. But there are at least a couple of serious limitations. The first is that most of the research takes place in a very artificial setting—for example, research participants, typically undergraduate college students, are often exposed to fake ads for phony brands in theater-like settings or even classrooms (there's a reason why they're called "laboratory experiments").

Another problem is that it's difficult to simultaneously account for the many situational factors we've learned can impact the effectiveness of a comparative campaign and the influence they can have on each other—such as the type of comparative advertising (that is, direct versus implied), how negative the ads are in tone, whether they substantiate their claims or the market standings of the comparative advertiser and the comparison brand. That's why this final chapter contributes to the overall purpose of this book by relying on three qualitative case studies to try and confirm some of our earlier conclusions regarding the effectiveness of comparative campaigns in a real-world context, while also looking for other factors, or combinations of them, that might help explain their success.

WHAT'S A CASE STUDY?

A case study is pretty much what it sounds like. When you want to answer questions about how a complicated phenomenon works in the real world, you look for an example (or *case*) and then gather as much information about it as you can (Yin, 2003). If some of the data consist of numbers, there's certainly nothing wrong with analyzing those data quantitatively. Many case studies, though, are qualitative in nature. That mainly means we rely on the subjective interpretations of the researcher conducting the case study to analyze the data, report the research findings, and then explain what they probably mean (Baxter & Jack, 2008).

That may make it sound as though a qualitative case study isn't very "scientific" or empirical. The method and process may sound a little more rigorous; however, when you take into account what an "analytic generalization" is. In analytic generalization, what we do is make an inference (or a generalization) about a theory based on the data we collect and observe about a particular case or cases. In fact, as one expert on the cast study method argues, this *replication logic* is exactly the same thing that experimental researchers do when they generalize from one experiment to the next in the process of generating more and more evidence in support of a theory (Yin, 2003). In addition, if the analysis of multiple cases supports the same theory—while not supporting an equally plausible, alternative theory—we can argue that this represents replication as well. The research findings and conclusions summarized earlier in Chapter 2's model and their comparisons with the beliefs of advertising professionals in Chapter 3's Tables 3.5 and 3.6 provide most of the theory, or propositions, that will guide our multiple case study data collection and analyses.

The case study method offers another important advantage over the laboratory experiment. The "deep data" and "thick description" of qualitative case studies, rooted as they are in real-world contexts, can help bridge the gap among theory, empirical research findings, and professional beliefs and practices. If that sounds familiar, it should. It's one of the goals we've been pursuing throughout this book. This particular advantage of the case study method is also why many professional disciplines such as business, medicine, and law have relied on it for both research and teaching for a long time.

So what do we use for "real world" data? Fortunately, advertising is a huge business accounting for billions of dollars a year in expenditures in the United States alone, and comparative campaigns are considered quite newsworthy by the many business journalists and trade journals that serve the advertising and marketing world. The result is that we have both trade journal articles and company communications, such as news releases, to work with. Finally, thanks to the Web, we have fairly convenient access to actual ads from many comparative campaigns.

To achieve the purposes of this chapter, what we needed were comparative campaigns that could be considered at least somewhat successful. After careful consideration of dozens of major comparative campaigns that advertisers and their agencies ran during the past several years, three fairly quickly became candidates for more serious consideration. They were then selected for study because they met the following criteria: (a) they consisted of sustained comparative campaigns, (b) there was evidence they were effective (for example, increases in awareness, attitude toward the brand [A_{br}], purchase intention [P_i], sales, or market share), (c) they mostly avoided negative advertising outcomes (for example, awareness for competitors, consumer confusion, perceptions of excessive negativity, or consumer backlash), and (d) they avoided or survived legal or industry self-regulatory challenges.

CASE ONE: SAMSUNG GALAXY SMARTPHONE

When South Korea's Samsung Electronics Co., Ltd. launched the Galaxy S3 smartphone in the United States in June 2012, the company challenged the world's most valuable technology brand with advertising that disparaged not only Apple's iPhone, but the often-obsessive passion of the iconic brand's loyal customers as well. Samsung continued to position the Galaxy as a superior alternative with two more campaign phases in 2013 and 2014 using comparative ads created by LA-based ad agency 72andSunny for the Galaxy S4 and S5 updates. The three phases of the campaign were unified under the common theme and tagline "The Next Big Thing is Already Here." It's also important to note that, at the time, Samsung and Apple were still embroiled in a multi-year and multi-country series of lawsuits over smartphone and tablet patent infringements. This was also well before the Samsung Note 7 disaster. Samsung's cellphone prospects were still flying high during the launches of the Galaxy S7 and S7 Edge when the Note 7—which was supposed to take advantage of that momentum and throw yet another roadblock in front of Apple's progress—suddenly developed an unfortunate tendency to burst into flames (Tibken, 2016).

The Advertising

With the first commercials for the S3, Samsung took advantage of the iPhone 5's September 2012 launch by poking fun at Apple fans for camping out in long lines to buy a phone that had been only marginally updated with features the S3 already had, such as a larger screen and 4G. In one of the commercials, mockingly titled "Fan Boys," a fan waiting in one of the customary and lengthy iPhone upgrade launch lines expresses "mind-blowing" amazement over the revelation that "the headphone jack is going to be on the bottom!" You can view this widely viewed and ridiculed (by loyal iPhone users) commercial on YouTube (epochfilmsprodco, 2012).

For the S4 in 2013, commercials continued the factual comparisons with the iPhone by dazzling its owners with the S4's features. In a spot titled "Grad Pool Party," an S4 user demonstrates its near-field communication feature by sharing photos with a mere tap of the phone with a friend's. When the older woman next to her suggests doing the same thing with her iPhone, the S4 user points out that iPhones "can't do that." The woman's husband then asks, "So some smartphones are smarter than other smartphones?" A YouTube.com search using the search term "Samsung Grad Pool Party" will retrieve this spot for you.

Next, with advertising for the S5 in mid-2014, Samsung launched another satirical dig, this time targeted directly at the iPhone's inferior battery life. The spot titled "Wall Huggers" depicts hapless iPhone users crowding around inconveniently located airport power outlets to recharge, while S5 owners freely wander about, eat in restaurants, or even replace their batteries on the fly. This spot is also available on YouTube (Eberuson, 2014).

One industry observer noted that, with the satirical twist of the initial "Long Lines" campaign, Samsung had successfully repositioned the iPhone as old-fashioned and passé (that is, "your father's Oldsmophone"). As Gary Stibel, a principal of marketing consulting firm New England Consulting Group, further observed: "This is great advertising, available to all but practiced by few: compelling message, memorably delivered to a critical target, at a decisive time that is having a disproportionate influence" (Stibel & Ruf, 2012). As late as 2017, mobile and consumer electronics industry observer Zach Epstein (2017) was still commenting on the long-term success of the campaign:

> Samsung built its massive smartphone empire almost entirely on the back of an extensive, big-budget marketing campaign that portrayed iPhone users as mindless idiots who follow the crowd and don't think for themselves. The phrase "Apple sheep" gets thrown around all the time by hardcore Android fans. Even Merriam-Webster got in on the action earlier this year when it used Apple fans as an example to illustrate the definition of the word "sheeple."

Throughout the campaign, it's apparent that Samsung was attempting to persuade younger, tech-savvy buyers that the Galaxy was technologically superior to the iPhone with a relentless emphasis on its features. As one industry observer revealingly noted, Samsung's intent was not to steal users from among iPhone loyalists but to, instead, exploit the technology's widespread adoption by targeting young consumers searching for their first smartphones (McDermott, 2013). In addition, by mid-2013, Samsung had also co-opted Apple's long-time strategy of offering an easy-to-use, integrated family of products and services. The company established Samsung "Experience Shops" in more than 1,400 Best Buy retail outlets to demonstrate how its own line of smartphones, tablets, and laptops all work together.

Other observers, as you'd expect, warned that the campaign was risky and could produce many of the negative consequences linked to comparative advertising. John Ruf, also a partner with the New England Consultant Group, does a great job summarizing several that should sound quite familiar at this point: the initial S3 campaign "Positions the iPhone 5 as the gold standard. Expands awareness of the new iPhone 5 launch. Reinforces the passion of iPhone owners waiting in line. [And] Worse, . . . could spark an ad war that Samsung might be sorry it even started" (Stibel & Ruf, 2012). In response to the "Wall Huggers" spot, industry observer Rene Ritchie (2014) similarly pointed out that, instead of a commercial highlighting the comparative superiority of the S5, she saw "An airport full of people, the vast, vast majority of whom are iPhone users and who value their iPhones so much they can't stop using them, even if they have to stay plugged in, hugging the walls, just to keep on using them. That's a pretty spectacular endorsement for a competitor."

Effectiveness

Thanks to the "Next Big Thing . . ." campaign, which began running in June of 2012, Samsung's comparative advertising actually surpassed that of the iPhone in online views the first week the S3 went on sale in September. According to data collected for the Viral Video Chart, an *Advertising Age* service that tracks brand-driven social media ad campaigns, in the two weeks following the September 12 iPhone launch, the S3 campaign earned 15.7 million views versus only 10.6 million for the new iPhone campaign (as cited in Russell, 2012). In addition, from 2011 to 2012, Samsung increased its share of fourth quarter smartphone sales from 21% to 30% and Apple's share decreased from 41% to 39% (McDermott, 2013). While it's true that Samsung's share of smartphone shipments (not sales) plummeted to 24.9% during the second quarter of 2014, industry observers also pointed out that it wasn't because of a surge in iPhone sales. Apple's share of smartphone shipments fell from 18.8% to 11.7% during the same period (Asay, 2015).

Following the S5 release in April of 2014, Qriously, a mobile ad platform, began tracking user sentiments toward both the Galaxy and iPhone. The firm reported that, from mid-March through early June, more iPhone users were likely to switch to the Galaxy S5 than Samsung users to an iPhone (as cited in Rahner, 2015). However, it's also important to note that such consumer sentiments varied considerably from month to month throughout 2014.

Of course, there was (and probably still is) an incredible backlash of negative attitudes toward the campaign from iPhone users. Samsung continued the attacks in 2014 with commercials targeting not only the iPhone's slower charging speeds and Apple's delay in producing a larger screen, but even Apple's livestream fiasco for the iPhone 6 launch in September of that year (thousands of people trying to watch the carefully orchestrated, high-tech extravaganza ran into stuttering video and blackouts). In response to the new wave of commercials, industry observer David Ruddock (2014) probably captured the bruised sentiments of many iPhone users as well as anyone: ". . . in its latest slew of iAds, Samsung basically throws any semblance of taste and humor out the window to make fun of Apple mostly for the sake of doing it."

CASE TWO: CAMPBELL'S SELECT HARVEST SOUPS

New Jersey-based Campbell Soup Company chose to launch its lighter, healthier, and higher-priced Campbell's Select Harvest line of soups in mid-2008 with directly comparative advertising targeting General Mills' Progresso. Progresso was an obvious target. The brand's sales were soaring, thanks to an endorsement from Weight Watchers International, the introduction of nine new varieties, and its own diet-related advertising (York, 2009a). The

Select Harvest campaign was not unprecedented. Ten years earlier, underdog Progresso, then a Pillsbury Co. brand, had attacked Campbell's line of condensed soups as an inferior-tasting product more suited for children than adults with its own comparative campaign (Pollack, 1998).

General Mills and Progresso agency Saatchi & Saatchi, New York, initially ignored the Select Harvest campaign, targeting, instead, men with a "light and filling" message strategy. But by early 2009, Progresso's brand managers had had enough and they unleashed a counterattack. The conflict soon degenerated into what observers labeled the "Soup War," with conflicting claims regarding the dubious but generally regarded as safe ingredient monosodium glutamate (MSG). By August of 2009, Campbell abandoned the comparative campaign to focus more fully on Select Harvest's more healthful ingredients (York, 2009b). Citing Campbell Soup Company management, industry observers reported that the change in message tactics was due to a shift away from establishing brand awareness and differentiating Select Harvest among younger consumers who tended to brown bag their lunches to attracting new or lapsed category users by explaining what Select Harvest was rather than what it wasn't (Scott-Thomas, 2009).

The Advertising

The original TV commercial created by agency BBDO, New York featured a blindfolded young woman seated in front of cans of Progresso and Select Harvest chicken noodle soups. Asked to describe the two, she observed that Progresso tasted like "hydrolyzed vegetable protein and MSG." In the Select Harvest soup, however, the now-smiling soup taster tasted "Chicken. One hundred percent natural. White meat!" The commercial ended with a direct attack: "Unlike Progresso soups, new Campbell Select Harvest soups never contain artificial flavor or MSG. Just real ingredients. Real taste." This commercial, unfortunately, was unavailable anywhere on the Web at the time of this writing, which is probably a revealing reminder of how effectively U.S. copyright law can be enforced.

Although General Mills quickly announced they were already reformulating Progresso to remove MSG, Campbell extended the campaign with a full-page attack in *The New York Times* on September 24, 2008. Picture cans of Progresso and Select Harvest chicken noodle soup side by side. Above both are nearly identical headlines, except the Progresso headline is "MADE WITH **MSG**" and the Select Harvest's is "MADE WITH **TLC**." The comparative emphasis on Select Harvest's non-artificial ingredients and lack of MSG is about as negative as comparative attack ads get. The copy goes on to invite consumers to compare the soups by reading the labels. Copy also offered an opportunity to receive a coupon for a free sample, which included the following MSG-related and directly comparative copy: "If you buy Progresso soups, you might want to know what you're actually eating" (Wong, 2008).

New products expert and industry observer Lynn Dornblaser offered praise for the campaign: "You have to give Campbell credit for taking advantage of the good, clean ingredients statement that they have on their soups. . . . It's a very smart move to take that and [contrast] it to the MSG comparison" (as cited in Wong, 2008). Another observer similarly reported that his own research had shown consumers were looking for foods with lower sodium, no MSG, and ingredients they may have in their pantry (Lempert, as cited in York, 2009a).

In addition to claiming victory in a taste test in the Progresso retaliatory strike, General Mills ran a newspaper ad drawing consumers' attention to the fact that more than 90 varieties of Campbell condensed soups also contained MSG. Campbell, in turn, counterattacked with an ad listing the company's soups not containing MSG, which was some five times longer than the list of Progresso soups that didn't. And while Campbell and its ad agency were busy crafting that ad, Campbell's lawyers were equally busy crafting a complaint to the National Advertising Division (NAD) of the Better Business Bureau, the U.S. advertising industry's self-regulatory body. Campbell won this battle as well, when its complaint that the Progresso MSG ad was misleading was upheld, and the NAD recommended General Mills discontinue the advertising. Some seven years later, Campbell succeeded again with the NAD, after complaining that General Mills inaccurately implied Progresso soups were made with ingredients locally sourced from rural New Jersey. The case wasn't a total loss for General Mills, however. The NAD did affirm that there was a "reasonable basis" for the claim that Progresso's hometown is, in fact, Vineland, New Jersey.

Effectiveness

In May of 2009, Campbell reported sales of its ready-to-serve soups had increased 4% over the previous nine months, and CEO Douglas Conant credited Select Harvest's launch and the comparative campaign (as cited in York, 2009a). Select Harvest's brand awareness at the time also stood at 35%, consistent with the goal to build brand awareness. In addition, industry Website *Mediapost* named the company Food Marketer of the Year, in no small part due to their "feisty head-on assault on General Mill's Progresso" (Lukovitz, 2009). Secondary campaign buzz was also substantial, with consumers posting many comments about the campaign on Campbell's online community forum (Wong, 2008). As another industry observer noted: "The ad battle resulted in a free-media free-for-all, with coverage in the national dailies, Sunday talk shows, and even a spoof on the Colbert Report" (York, 2009a).

However, some industry analysts pointed to the familiar threat that the original campaign and ensuing soup war could damage the entire product category. As we learned in Chapter 1, comparative advertisers worried about this potential problem throughout the 20th century, and notable examples from the past include the baking powder wars of the 1910s and the analgesic wars of the 1970s. Overall U.S. soup sales did, in fact, decline 4% in 2010 (Lubin, 2011), and the Select Harvest and Progresso brands had both suffered sales declines of 12% and 8% respectively by October 31 of the same year. As one observer noted regarding the soup war: "They were going head-to-head big time. . . . It was actually turning off consumers" (Schultz, 2010). However, it's also important to note that Campbell ad spending "collapsed" following the soup war (Lubin), and sales for the company's concentrated line of soups declined as well.

CASE THREE: DIGIORNO FROZEN PIZZA

Before launching a direct assault on delivery competitors such as Pizza Hut, Papa John's, and Domino's in August of 2008, managers of DiGiorno, the leading U.S. premium frozen pizza brand, had two obstacles to overcome: (a) consumer perceptions of the inferiority of frozen versus delivery pizza and (b) the actual inferiority of their frozen pizza. Within its own premium frozen pizza category, DiGiorno's main competitor was the Schwan Food Company's Freschetta.

Following significant crust improvements—confirmed when DiGiorno's Rising Crust Four Cheese pizza was named one of the top three frozen pizzas (Consumer Reports, 2010)—the Kraft USA brand launched "DiGiornonomics." Among the across-class, implied comparative campaign's tactics emphasizing a price-value proposition over delivery pizza were advertising, sales promotions, event sponsorships, and social media.

The year 2009 brought a flood of new DiGiorno products, also intended to capitalize on a recession-driven, eat-at-home trend, and targeting fast food brands in addition to pizza makers. The brand went after sandwich-leader Subway with a line of DiGiorno Melts in mid-2009 and added "Ultimate Toppings" pizzas, after research revealed consumers perceived a big toppings difference between frozen and delivery (York, 2009b). The campaign was still running in 2017, under the continuing tagline "It's Not Delivery. It's DiGiorno." Coincidentally, the frozen pizza industry was predicted to grow at approximately 4.5% through 2014 and the biggest trend was expected to be "premium frozen pizza that delivers pizzeria taste" (Dudlicek, 2010).

The Advertising

At the outset of the campaign in 2008, "DiGiornonomics" positioned the brand as offering restaurant-quality taste at about half the price of delivery pizza. One of the first 15-second spots offered a side-by-side product and price comparison between DiGiorno and a "delivery" pizza, with dollar values rolling across a simulated gasoline pump display. "One of these pizzas won't leave your wallet on empty," the voiceover confirms. In the second spot, a delivery guy and his expensive delivery pizza both disappear in a puff of smoke as a voiceover and superimposed copy deliver the comparative message: "Delivery pizza minus the delivery price equals DiGiorno." Although a search of the Web failed to locate copies of these commercials, there is an impressive number of videos available on YouTube that parody the campaign and "It's Not Delivery. It's DiGiorno." tagline.

DiGiorno and ad agency DraftFcb continued the campaign in 2009 with the launch of the Crispy Flatbread Pizza line. In a 30-second spot, another pizza delivery guy repeatedly crashes a game-night party, asking for pieces of the host's DiGiorno pizza. "You know we don't deliver anything like this," he tells the increasingly annoyed party host. This commercial is available on YouTube (wcgabe, 2009). Integrated with the online and TV advertising were accompanying contextual-search ads designed to intercept Yelp and Citysearch users looking for "pizza delivery" (York, 2009b).

Later in the campaign, advertising and promotions included a heavy emphasis on sports-related themes, since delivery pizza is a staple at game-day parties. In 2010, a "You Bettis Believe!" contest offered winners a party with retired U.S. professional football star Jerome Bettis. In 2011, DiGiorno celebrated the Super Bowl by sponsoring pre-game "High Five" rallies in competitor hometowns Pittsburgh and Green Bay and offering $5-off pizza coupons (PR Newswire, 2011a). Also in 2011, brand managers executed another tactic for comparing DiGiorno with delivery pizza by becoming the "Official Pizza of the Chicago Bulls and Blackhawks" and opening a pizzeria in the teams' home venue and selling pizza at concession stands throughout the arena (PR Newswire, 2011b). The football-themed promotions also continued. For example, in 2016 DiGiorno partnered with Green Bay Packers linebacker Clay Matthews to promote their pizza instead of delivery for football parties (#MakeTheRightCall).

Effectiveness

By November of 2009, DiGiorno had posted eight consecutive quarters of sales gains, thanks in part to "going after big brands such as Domino's and Pizza Hut" (York, 2009c). In addition, and despite—or perhaps due to—a recession extending from late 2007 to mid-2009, DiGiorno sales increased more than 20% during the last two quarters of the same period. As an *Advertising Age* reporter noted at the time: "The brand has played an important role in Kraft's turnaround strategy, and has benefited from increased media spending" (York, 2009d). In spite of its success, Kraft sold the DiGiorno brand in 2010, along with the rest of its frozen pizza business, to food manufacturer Nestlé USA. Another indication of the success of the campaign was a commercial parody. In 2009, Dannon, a subsidiary of Groupe Dannon, launched its "Dannonomics" campaign (Wong, 2009), which also emphasized cost savings.

WHAT CAN WE CONCLUDE FROM OUR CASES?

The findings of our multiple-case study strongly suggest that all three campaigns were effective at gaining attention and creating awareness, as predicted by so many of the empirical research findings and professional beliefs we've reviewed in earlier chapters. Some researchers originally argued that comparative ads generate a lot of attention because they're novel or unusual, but that they would grow less effective as their novelty wore off (Jackson, Brown, & Harmon, 1979). However, head-to-head, directly comparative TV commercials are still relatively infrequent (even in the United States, at about 5% of all commercials [Beard, 2016b]), which offers one explanation for why at least two of the three campaigns generated so much attention and were so memorable.

There's also some support for a conclusion that the campaigns were effective at positioning the brands. As we learned in Chapter 3, advertising professionals strongly agree that comparative advertising is very effective for positioning a brand relative to competitors. In fact, implied comparative campaigns claiming superiority over all competitors or the category overall, such as the DiGiorno campaign, are believed to be especially effective at brand positioning (Miniard et al., 2006). In the case of Select Harvest soups, it seems pretty clear that the campaign was effective for achieving another important outcome for a new product—initial brand trial.

However, although advertisers have long believed that comparative ads often generate a great deal of attention and recall, they've also warned that it can be the wrong kind of attention. Explanations for this concern include comparative campaigns that (a) fail to directly speak to consumers, (b) focus on competitors' advertising instead, or (c) fail to emphasize salient benefits or, in many cases, any benefits at all (Beard, 2013a). Although Campbell began responding to Progresso's advertising as the soup war raged on, neither Samsung nor DiGiorno appeared to fall into the trap of failing to focus on features and benefits. This may help explain the effectiveness of these comparative campaigns, as well as the fact that the original Samsung campaign ran through 2015, and DiGiorno was still going strong in 2017. In fact, Samsung returned with an update of its "Fan Boys" spot in late 2017 (titled "Growing Up"), this one also relentlessly focusing on features and timed to arrive right after the iPhone X launch. If you haven't seen the spot, Samsung has posted it on YouTube (Samsung Mobile USA, 2017). More important, however, is that our case study findings strongly suggest all three campaigns led to increases in sales and market share, at least in the short term.

The case analyses provided us with little direct evidence that the campaigns affected attitude toward the ad (A_{ad}), A_{br}, or brand loyalty, with the possible exception of Select Harvest. As we learned in Chapter 1, advertisers have long been concerned that, as comparative advertising wars grow increasingly ugly and begin airing an industry's or product category's "dirty laundry" (in this case, the use of MSG), a war could lead to damage for both sides. The findings of the Campbell case study show that, although effective in the short term at attracting attention, creating brand awareness, and encouraging trial, the soup war that ensued may have contributed to a decline in the ready-to-eat soup category not long after.

As we've discussed throughout this book, surveys of advertising professionals, theory development and empirical research support several conclusions regarding the many situational factors that can help explain comparative campaign effectiveness. As the model in Chapter 2 shows, comparative advertising is believed to be more effective for new products or small-share brands when making comparisons with well-known, often higher-priced competitors. Historically, these tactics were referred to as "Riding the Coattails" (ads that include associative claims of parity but not superiority) or "Twisting the Tiger's Tail" (ads that include differentiative claims of superiority). In all three cases, advertisers were going up against what could be considered leading, well-established brands, Select Harvest was a new product launch and DiGiorno was attacking much higher-priced competitors.

Researchers have recently offered empirical and theoretical explanations for the effectiveness of these tactics. For instance, and based on the Elaboration Likelihood Model (discussed in Chapter 2) and congruity theory, research has shown that consumers are more likely to elaborate on the claims in comparative ads because the mere mention of a more familiar comparison brand causes greater perceptions of relevance, which in turn prompts greater elaboration. Moreover, the more dissimilar or incongruent the sponsored and comparison brands are perceived to be (such as comparing frozen pizza to delivery), the greater will be the elaboration (Priester et al., 2004).

Similarly, and in regard to the DiGiorno implied comparative campaign specifically, based on assimilation theory, recent studies of "across-class" comparative ads like these suggest that creating associations with a leader in a more prestigious class but within the same product category (a tactic we learned is often employed in comparative car advertising) can increase the perceived value for the comparative advertiser's brand. Perhaps even more important, the development of such associations with a leader in a more prestigious class can also result in differentiation from competitors within the comparative advertiser's same product class (Van Auken & Adams, 1999). In other words, while DiGiorno's comparative campaign may not have done a lot to persuade people their frozen pizza really is better or at least as good as Papa John's or Pizza Hut's, it probably did help encourage consumers to perceive DiGiorno as superior to the brand's arch frozen competitor, Freschetta.

Regarding the substantiation of claims made in comparative ads, both the history we reviewed in Chapter 1 and the survey responses reported in Chapter 3 show that advertising professionals widely favor substantiating claims regarding salient product benefits with side-by-side demonstrations, the more visual the better. Moreover, empirical research has shown that comparative ads are more effective when their claims are well substantiated (Grewal et al., 1997), and the findings of a content analysis of U.S. TV commercials showed that comparative ads included claim substantiation (such as the results of tests or surveys or an endorsement by an independent source) significantly more often than noncomparative commercials did (Beard, 2016b).

The findings of our multiple-case study show that all three campaigns were consistent with these comparative tactics. Most of the ads in the campaigns relied on side-by-side comparisons and the comparative claims were substantiated with references to product features (Samsung), specific ingredients (Select Harvest) and lower prices (DiGiorno). The more frequent use of substantiation in comparative TV commercials is consistent with research findings showing that the inclusion of credibility enhancers encourages favorable A_{br} and greater P_i (Grewal et al., 1997). Research has also shown that factual information (that is, information that is objective in nature) will likely encourage fewer counterarguments and more support arguments (Edell & Staelin, 1983) and more favorable brand attitudes and increased purchase intentions.

One important belief confirmed by historical research and surveys of advertising professionals regarding creativity in comparative advertising, and linked to the avoidance of negative A_{ad} and A_{br}, is the importance of maintaining a positive tone and avoiding excessive negativity. As we learned in Chapter 2, researchers have found that low-negativity comparative ads and those having fewer derogatory references to competitors are perceived more favorably by consumers, as are comparative ads of moderate intensity (Jain & Posavac, 2004; Sorescu & Gelb, 2000). Although Samsung and DiGiorno appeared to avoid the perception of excessive negativity in their campaigns, partly by relying on satirical humor (although iPhone fans clearly didn't think so), the findings show that the Select Harvest campaign began with an aggressively negative comparative claim and became increasingly intense as the soup war carried on. This finding likely explains why, although effective in creating awareness and initial brand trial in the short term, Campbell soon abandoned the campaign in favor of more positive noncomparative advertising. Marketers and advertisers have often recommended this approach (Beard, 2013a).

Finally, and regarding the Samsung Galaxy campaign, it's important to acknowledge the fact that they actually disparaged Apple's loyal, and especially emotionally committed, users—a tactic we learned in Chapter 1 that many marketers and advertisers have long believed is a major mistake. However, the findings show that Samsung set out strategically to avoid the iPhone's customer base and that the brand's market share increased substantially while Apple's decreased very little. This finding strongly suggests that the widely held professional belief that it's always a mistake to offend a competitor's customers and loyal users may not necessarily be true, at least when the brand is facing a growing market and a non-zero-sum fight for increased sales.

FINAL CONCLUSIONS

First, and in regard to this final chapter, the findings of our multiple-case study should be interpreted in light of the most commonly recognized limitation of the qualitative case study method—the findings are generalizable only to the cases we studied. However, it's important to point out that we never intended to generalize them to any population of comparative advertising campaigns. Based on Yin's (2003) explanation of the difference between analytic generalization and statistical generalization, the findings are generalizable back to the theory and empirical research generalizations presented in Chapter 2's model and the survey findings summarized in Chapter 3, and that was our goal. In this respect, the findings reveal a good fit between those generalizations and the data and vice-versa. The findings are also limited somewhat in regard to the measurement of the effectiveness of the campaigns, which consist mainly of reports in industry trade journals. It also wasn't possible to link the campaigns with long-term outcomes. On the other hand, it seems well worth pointing out that extensions of the Samsung and DiGiorno campaigns were still running at the time of this book's publication.

For a second set of conclusions, we'll return one more time to this book's core question: Why have advertisers often relied on a message tactic that research and professional experience confirms they often lacked confidence in and many frequently regretted using? Historically, we've learned that perhaps the earliest reason advertisers resorted to mentioning one or more competitors was to differentiate their products or services. Whether we're talking about comparisons between manufactured clay lamps in 3rd-century-

BC Carthage, the problem of intellectual property theft in the 16th century, the Substitution Menace in the early 20th century, or the development of a sophisticated brand positioning strategy in the 21st, at least one of the goals behind comparisons with the goods and services of competitors in promotional messages remains basically unchanged. The same can be said for achieving the objective and outcome of attention. As the old AIDA advertising formula so clearly reminds us, an advertisement can't accomplish anything else unless it first attracts attention.

The empirical research literature we reviewed in Chapter 2 supports these historical conclusions. While Chapter 2's review and model clearly show that comparative advertising can be expected to have direct effects on many advertising objectives and outcomes (and not all of them positive), research has consistently established that the effects on cognitive outcomes—such as attention, awareness, and recall—are likely going to be positive. In more practical terms, there's an excellent probability that the information in a comparative ad, especially a direct one, will be seen, processed, and remembered. This also helps explain why, as we learned in Chapter 6, comparative advertising is becoming more acceptable to advertisers, advertising regulators, and consumers in many countries around the world.

Chapter 2 suggested another reason why advertisers have so often resorted to making comparisons and Chapter 3 confirmed it. There's a great deal of agreement between academic researchers and advertising professionals as to the situational factors that can help or hinder the success of a comparative ad or campaign. Target the brand leader, especially if the advertising is for a new or challenger brand. Emphasize important features, salient benefits, or superior quality (if it exists). Substantiate the claims and make them believable. If customers are loyal to the brand, don't distract them by mentioning or tearing down a competitive one. The competitor's customers are not going to respond favorably. Target younger, male consumers with comparative ads, but definitely not older, female ones.

But perhaps the most important conclusion regarding comparative advertising was confirmed by every chapter in this book in one way or another—product and service advertisers should leave the excessive negativity, including especially sharp satirical humor, to their political contemporaries. Politicians don't have to worry so much about building their brands or securing favorable long-term brand attitudes. If there's anything the U.S. presidential election of 2016 revealed, it's that unlike in the commercial world of products and services, where A_{br} almost always leads to P_i, two politicians can be nominated and one of them actually win the office of president of the United States with brand attitude ratings that would be a disaster for any product or service. Consumers may occasionally choose what they consider to be the lesser of two evils when it comes to a product or service, but not very often.

Bibliography

4 As cracking down on disparaging ads. (1969, March 22). *Editor & Publisher, 102*, 18.
Aaker, D. A., Stayman, D. M., & Hagerty, M. R. (1986). Warmth in advertising: Measurement, impact, and sequence effects. *Journal of Consumer Research, 12*(4), 365–381.
ABC censor raps trend to naming rivals in ads. (1975, March 31). *Advertising Age, 46*(13), 98.
Abernethy, A. M. (1993). Advertising clearance practices of radio stations: A model of advertising self-regulation. *Journal of Advertising, 22*(3), 15–26.
Abernethy, A. M., & Butler, D. D. (1992). Advertising information: Services versus products. *Journal of Retailing, 68*(4), 398–419.
Acuff, D. S., & Reiher, R. H. (1997). *What kids buy and why: The psychology of marketing to kids*. New York, NY: Free Press.
Ad Age. (1999). *The top 100 advertising campaigns of the 20th century*. Retrieved from http://adage.com/article/special-report-the-advertising-century/ad-age-advertising-century-top-100-advertising-campaigns/140150/
AdFreakTwo. (2009, January 13). *Chevy Silverado | "Man Step"* (Video file). Retrieved from https://www.youtube.com/watch?v=jGI8IRXRqpo
Ad industry veterans honored with cola war memorial. (1997, April 9). Retrieved from http://www.theonion.com/article/ad-industry-veterans-honored-with-cola-war-memoria-863
adwomen.org. (2012, May 31). *avis-targeted-hertz-with-the-famous-we-try-harder-slogan-in-the-1960s*. Retrieved from http://www.adwomen.org/2012/05/we-try-harder-technology-vs-ideals/avis-targeted-hertz-with-the-famous-we-try-harder-slogan-in-the-1960s/
AFA, AAW, ABBB okay nine-point ad ethics code. (1964, December 15). *Advertising Age, 35*, 4.
Al-Olayan, F. S., & Karande, K. (2000). A content analysis of magazine advertisements from the United States and the Arab world. *Journal of Advertising, 29*(3), 69–82.
Ang, S., & Leong, S. (1994). Comparative advertising: Superiority despite interference? *Asia Pacific Journal of Management, 11*(1), 33–46.
Arndorfer, J. B., Atkinson, C., Bloom, J., Cardona, M., Endicott, R. C., Goldsborough, R. G., & Thompson, S. (2005, March 28). The biggest moments in the last 75 years of advertising history. *Advertising Age, 76*(13), 12–20.
Arvidsson, A. (2003). *Marketing modernity: Italian advertising from fascism to postmodernity*. London, UK: Routledge.
Asay, M. (2014, October 14). *Why Apple fan boys might want to hold the Samsung schadenfreude: With Samsung falling, it's easy to forget that Android, not any particular vendor, is what matters*. Retrieved from http://www.techrepublic.com/article/why-apple-fan-boys-might-want-to-hold-the-samsung-schadenfreude/

Atazoth. (2016, February 7). *2016 Nissan TITAN XD shoulder of giants commercial* (Video file). Retrieved from https://www.youtube.com/watch?v=sBsf6y-g9nM

Barigozzi, F., & Peitz, M. (2007). Comparative advertising and competition policy. In J.P. Choi (Ed.), *Recent Developments in Antitrust* (pp. 215–265). Cambridge, MA: The MIT Press.

Bajpai, P. (2017). *The world's top 10 economies*. Retrieved from https://www.investopedia.com/articles/investing/022415/worlds-top-10-economies.asp

Barbara Poplits. (2014, February 13). *Pepsi Super Bowl XXVIII ad Chimps Lab 1994510* (Video file). Retrieved from https://www.youtube.com/watch?v=-bm0wZOXXW0

Barone, M. J., & Jewell, R. D. (2012). How category advertising norms and consumer counter-conformity influence comparative advertising effectiveness. *Journal of Consumer Psychology, 22*(4), 496–506.

Barry, T. E. (1993). Twenty years of comparative advertising in the United States. *International Journal of Advertising, 12*(4), 325–350.

Barry, T. E., & Tremblay, R. L. (1975). Comparative advertising: Perspectives and issues. *Journal of Advertising, 4*(4), 15–20.

Barone, M., & Miniard, P. (1999). How and when factual ad claims mislead consumers: Examining the deceptive consequences of copy x copy interactions for partial comparative advertisements. *Journal of Marketing Research, 36*(1), 58–74.

Barone, M. J., Palan, K. M., & Miniard, P. W. (2004). Brand usage and gender as moderators of the potential deception associated with partial comparative advertising. *Journal of Advertising, 33*(1), 19–28.

Battle of the basements. (1935, October 24). *Printers' Ink, 173*(81–2), 81–85.

Baxter, P., & Jack, S. (2008). Qualitative case study methodology: Study design and implementation for novice researchers. *The Qualitative Report, 13*(4), 544–559.

Beard, F. K. (2017). Archiving the archives. Paper presented at the 18th Biennial Conference on Historical Analysis & Research in Marketing, Liverpool, U.K.

Beard, F. K. (2016a). A history of advertising and sales promotion. In D. G. Brian Jones & M. Tadajewski (Eds.), *The Routledge companion to marketing history* (pp. 203–224). New York, NY: Routledge.

Beard, F. K. (2016b). Comparative television advertising in the U.S.: A thirty-year update. *Journal of Current Issues & Research in Advertising, 37*(2), 183–195.

Beard, F. K. (2016c). Professionals' views of comparative advertising and the scholarly research literature: A review and synthesis. *Journal of Marketing Communications, 22*(3), 271–83.

Beard, F. K. (2015). The effectiveness of comparative versus noncomparative advertising for prominent nonprofessional service brands. *Journal of Advertising Research, 55*(3), 296–306.

Beard, F. K. (2013a). A history of comparative advertising in the United States. *Journalism & Communication Monographs, 15*(3), 114–216.

Beard, F. K. (2013b). Practitioner views of comparative advertising: How practices have changed in two decades. *Journal of Advertising, 53*(3), 313–23.

Beard, F. K. (2012). The U.S. advertising industry's self-regulation of comparative advertising. *Journal of Historical Research in Marketing, 4*(3), 369–386.

Beard, F. K. (2011). Competition and combative advertising: An historical analysis. *Journal of Macromarketing, 31*(4), 386–401.

Beard, F. K. (2010). Comparative advertising wars: An historical analysis of their causes and consequences. *Journal of Macromarketing, 30*(3), 270–286.

Beard, F. K. (2008). Negative comparative advertising: When marketers attack. In P. J. Kitchen (Ed.), *Marketing metaphors and metamorphosis* (pp. 42–56). Houndmills, Basingstoke, Hampshire, UK: Palgrave Macmillan.

Beard, F. K. (2007). *Humor in the advertising business: Theory, practice, and wit*. Lanham, MD: Rowman & Littlefield Publishers, Inc.

Beard, F. K. (2004). Hard-sell killers and soft-sell poets: Modern advertising's enduring message strategy debate. *Journalism History, 30*(3), 141–149.

Beard, F. K. (2004). Humor in advertising: A review of the research literature, 1993–2003. In T.C. Melewar (Ed.), *Proceedings of the 9th International Conference on Corporate and Marketing Communications (CMC)*, pp. 42–56.

Beard, F. K. (2002). Peer evaluation and readership of influential contributions to the advertising literature. *Journal of Advertising, 31*(4), 65–76.

Beard, F. K. (1996). Marketing client role ambiguity as a source of dissatisfaction in client-ad agency relationships. *Journal of Advertising Research, 36*(5), 1–12.

Beard, F. K., & Klyeuva, A. (2010). George Washington Hill and the "Reach for a Lucky" campaign. *Journal of Historical Research in Marketing, 2*(2), 148–165.

Beard, F. K., & Nye, C. (2011). A history of the media industry's self-regulation of comparative advertising. *Journalism History, 37*(2), 113–121.

The Bedford Group (2017). *Client/agency relationship sustainability.* Retrieved from http://bedfordgroupconsulting.com/marketing-insights/agency-relationship-sustainability/

Bell reiterates his warning on derogatory ads. (1965, November 8). *Advertising Age, 36*, 1.

Benton, J. (1932, December 15). When competitive advertising need not be destructive. *Printers' Ink, 161*, 53–55.

Berg, M., & Clifford, H. (2007). Selling consumption in the eighteenth century: Advertising and the trade card in Britain and France. *Cultural and Social History, 4*(2), 145–170.

Bernstein, S. (1989, March 20). Comparative thinking. *Advertising Age*, 16.

Boddewyn, J. J. (1983). Comparison advertising: Regulation and self-regulation in 55 countries. New York, NY: International Advertising Association.

Boddewyn, J. J., & Marton, K. (1978). *Comparison advertising: A worldwide study.* New York, NY: Hastings House.

Bodleian Library. (2015). *Advertisement for the Sarum Ordinal or Pye.* Retrieved from https://genius.bodleian.ox.ac.uk/exhibits/browse/advertisement-for-the-sarum-ordinal-or-pye/

Bovée, C. L., & Arens, W. F. (1992). *Contemporary advertising* (4th ed.). Homewood, IL: Irwin.

Brabbs, C. (2001). *Two-thirds find comparative ads "unacceptable."* Retrieved from https://www.campaignlive.co.uk/article/two-thirds-find-comparative-ads-unacceptable/77312.

Braucher, F. (1931, May 7). Calls on advertising to battle the competitive copy scourge. *Printers' Ink, 155*, 65–66.

Brisacher, E. (1928, Jan. 5). Are you riding on the advertising merry-go-round? *Printers' Ink, 2*, 161–167.

Broad-gauge advertising. (1906). *Printers' Ink, 65*(6), 30.

Brown, S. W., & Jackson, D. W. (1977). Comparative television advertising: Examining its nature and frequency. *Journal of Advertising, 6*(4), 15–18.

Buijzen, M., & Valkenburg, P. M. (2004). Developing a typology of humor in audiovisual media. *Media Psychology, 6*(2), 146–167.

Cacioppo, J. T., Petty, R. E., Feinstein, J. A., & Jarvis, W. B. G. (1996). Dispositional differences in cognitive motivation: The life and times of individuals varying in need for cognition. *Psychological Bulletin, 119*(2), 197–253.

Calboli, I. (2002). Recent developments in the law of comparative advertising in Italy—Towards an effective enforcement of the principles of Directive 97/55/EC under the new regime? *International Review of the Industrial Property and Copyright Law, 33*(4), 415–438.

Calkins, E. E. (1915). *The business of advertising.* New York, NY: D. Appleton and Company.

Calls for showdown on competitive copy. (1931, October 29). *Printers' Ink, 57*, 105.

Campbell, M. C. (1995). When attention-getting advertising tactics elicit consumer inferences of manipulative intent: The importance of balancing benefits and investments. *Journal of Consumer Psychology, 4*(3), 225–254.

Cantor, J. R., & Zillman, D. (1973). Resentment toward victimized protagonists and severity of misfortunes they suffer as factors in humor appreciation. *Journal of Experimental Research in Personality, 6*(4), 321–329.

Cantz, Renault distributor's anti-VW copy…. (1965, September 13). *Advertising Age*, 1, 102.

Cave, B. (2013). *Another blow for comparative advertising in France.* Retrieved from https://www.bryancave.com/images/content/1/8/v2/1881/Bryan-Cave-Bulletin-Antitrust-and-Competition-Another-Blow-for-C.pdf

Chakravarti, A., & Jinhong, J. (2006). The impact of standards competition on consumers: Effectiveness of product information and advertising formats. *Journal of Marketing Research, 43*(2), 224–236.

Chaiken, S., Liberman, A., & Eagly, A.H. (1989). Heuristic and systematic information processing within and beyond the persuasion context. In J. S. Uleman & J. A. Bargh (Eds.), *Unintended thought: Limits of awareness, intention and control* (pp. 212–252). New York, NY: Guilford.

Chakravarti, A., & Xie, J. (2006). The impact of standards competition on consumers: Effectiveness of product information and advertising formats. *Journal of Marketing Research, 43*(2), 224–236.

Chang, C. (2007). The relative effectiveness of comparative and noncomparative advertising: Evidence for gender differences in information-processing strategies. *Journal of Advertising, 36*(1), 21–35.

Chang, R., & Parekh, R. (2009). *Verizon vs. AT&T: Blistering battle raging over map coverage fight is good news for shops, media as wireless giants square off.* Retrieved from http://adage.com/article/news/verizon-t-blistering-battle-raging-map/140748/

Chattopadhyay, A. (1998). When does comparative advertising influence brand attitude? The role of delay and market position. *Psychology & Marketing, 15*(5), 461–475.

Chen, Y., Joshi, Y. V., Raju, J. S., & Zhang, Z. J. (2009). A theory of combative advertising. *Marketing Science, 28*(1), 1–19.

Chevins, A. C. (1975). A case for comparative advertising. *Journal of Advertising, 4*(2), 31–36.

Choi, Y. K., & Miracle, G. E. (2004). The effectiveness of comparative advertising in Korea and the United States: A cross-cultural and individual-level analysis. *Journal of Advertising, 33*(4), 75–87.

Chow, W. C., & Luk, C. (2006). Effects of comparative advertising in high- and low-cognitive elaboration conditions. *Journal of Advertising, 35*(2), 55–67.

Christopher, M. (1974). NBC spells out new formal guides for comparative ads. *Advertising Age, 45*(4), 1.

Christopher, M. (1965). National better business bureau hits ads naming competitor as "invidious"; not so fast, says ANA. *Advertising Age, 36*(1), 1.

Church, R. (2000). Advertising consumer goods in nineteenth-century Britain: reinterpretations. *The Economic History Review, 53*(4), 621–645.

Cline, T. W., Altsech, M. B., & Kellaris, J. J. (2003). When does humor enhance or inhibit ad responses? The moderating role of the need for humor. *Journal of Advertising, 32*(3), 31–45.

Cline, T. W., & Kellaris, J. J. (1999). The joint impact of humor and argument strength in a print advertising context: A case for weaker arguments. *Psychology & Marketing, 16*(1), 69–86.

Ciarlo, D. (2011). *Advertising empire: Race and visual culture in imperial Germany.* Cambridge, MA: Harvard University Press.

Cohen, S. E. (1976a). Truth in ads self-regulation in no danger-FTC's Nye. *Advertising Age, 47*(9), 1, 69.

Cohen, S. E. (1976b). What triggered FTC investigation of ad industry self-regulation actions? *Advertising Age, 47*(8), 4.

Coleman, R. D. (2017). *Prudential standing: Who is "any person" under the Lanham Act?* Retrieved from http://www.likelihoodofconfusion.com/legal-publications-ron-coleman/prudential-standing-who-any-person-under-the-lanham-act/

Collier's encyclopedia ad showing competitor's volumes draws protests. (1964, November 23). *Advertising Age, 35*, 34.

Comparative ads graded "F" by CBBB president. (1977, October 17). *Advertising Age, 48*(42), 2.

Competitive claims. (1936, September 17). *Printers' Ink, 176*, 7–9.

Consoli, J. (1976, May 22). Comparative print ads more credible: Kershaw. *Editor & Publisher, 109*(21), 14.

Consumer Reports (2010). *DiGiorno rising crust four cheese named a CR best buy in Consumer Reports' tests of frozen pizzas.* Retrieved from https://www.consumerreports.org/media-room/press-releases/2010/12/digiorno-rising-crust-four-cheese-named-a-cr-best-buy-in-tests-of-frozen-pizzas/

Cooper, C., McCord, D., & Socha, A. (2011). Evaluating the college sophomore problem: The case of personality and politics. *The Journal of Psychology, 145*(1), 23–37.

Copeland, L., & Griggs, L. (1986). *Going international: How to make friends and deal effectively in the global marketplace.* New York, NY: Penguin.

Creamer, B. (n.d.). *Electronic word of mouth presents a window of opportunity for businesses.* Retrieved from www.buzztalkmonitor.com/blog/bid/233669/Electronic-Word-Of-Mouth-presents-a-window-of-opportunity-for-businesses

Creamer, M. (2007). *Caught in the clutter crossfire: Your brand.* Retrieved from http://adage.com/article/news/caught-clutter-crossfire-brand/115873/

Cutler, B. D., & Javalgi, R. G. (1993). Analysis of print ad features: Services versus products. *Journal of Advertising Research, 33*(2), 62–70.

Dahl, D. W., Frankenberger, K. D., & Manchanda, R. V. (2003). Does it pay to shock? Reactions to shocking and nonshocking advertising content among university students. *Journal of Advertising Research, 43*(3), 268–280.

Danielenko, R. (1973, September). Ads that cite the competition: A new trend. *Product Management*, 56–57.

del Barrio-García, S., & Luque-Martínez, T. (2003). Modelling consumer response to differing levels of comparative advertising. *European Journal of Marketing, 37*(1/2), 256–274.

de Mooij, M. (2013). *Global marketing and advertising: Understanding cultural paradoxes* (4th ed.). Thousand Oaks, CA: Sage Publications.

Desai, K. K., & Ratneshwar, S. (2003). Consumer perceptions of product variants positioned on atypical attributes. *Journal of the Academy of Marketing Science, 31*(1), 22–35.

Diamond, S. A. (1978, October 23). Beware of naming the competitor. *Advertising Age, 49*(43), 66.

Diamond, S. A. (1975). The historical development of trademarks. *The Trademark Reporter, 65*(4), 265–290.

Digges, I. W. (1953, March 6). In Europe they sue over competitive media claims; Belgian case of *Reader's Digest. Printers' Ink, 242*(1), 38.

Donthu, N. (1998). A cross-country investigation of recall of and attitude toward comparative advertising. *Journal of Advertising, 27*(2), 111–122.

Donthu, N. (1992). Comparative advertising intensity. *Journal of Advertising Research, 32*(6), 53–58.

Dröge, C. (1989). Shaping the route to attitude change: Central versus peripheral processing through comparative versus noncomparative advertising. *Journal of Marketing Research, 26*(2), 193–204.

Dudlicek, J. (2010). Thin is in. *Progressive Grocer, 89*(9), 49–51.

Eberuson. (2014, July 3). *Samsung Galaxy S5 - Wall Huggers (The Next Big Thing is Already Here) Legendado Pt-Br* (Video file). Retrieved from https://www.youtube.com/watch?v=SlelbGtPEdU

Eckhardt, G. M., & Bengtsson, A. (2010). A brief history of branding in China. *Journal of Macromarketing, 30*(3), 210–221.

Edell, J. A., & Staelin, R. (1983). The information processing of pictures in print advertisements. *Journal of Consumer Research, 10*(1), 45–61.

Eisend, M. (2009). A meta-analysis of humor in advertising. *Journal of the Academy of Marketing Science, 37*(2), 191–203.

Emmrich, S. (1982, May 3). Giving each other the business. *Advertising Age, 53*(19), M1, M5-M6.

Enrico, R., & Kornbluth, J. (1986). *The other guy blinked: How Pepsi won the cola wars.* New York, NY: Bantam Dell Pub Group.

epochfilmsprodco. (2012, November 7). *Samsung "Fanboys" directed by Michael Downing* (Video file). Retrieved from https://www.youtube.com/watch?v=oXu3LHqMOuo

Epstein, Z. (2017). *Apple fanboys reveal their most controversial opinions on Apple products.* Retrieved from http://bgr.com/2017/07/21/apple-news-today-controversial-apple-fanboy-opinions/

European Union. (2006). Directive 2006/114/EC of the European Parliament and of the Council. *Official Journal of the European Union*, 21–27. Retrieved from http://eur-lex.europa.eu/LexUriServ/LexUriServ.do?uri=OJ:L:2006:376:0021:0027:EN:PDF

European Union. (1997). *Directive 97/55/EC of European Parliament and of the council of 6 October 1997 amending Directive 84/450/EEC concerning misleading advertising so as to include comparative advertising.* Retrieved from http://www.wipo.int/wipolex/en/details.jsp?id=1439

Fair, L. (2008). *Federal Trade Commission advertising enforcement.* Retrieved from https://www.ftc.gov/sites/default/files/attachments/training-materials/enforcement.pdf

Federal Trade Commission. (1979). *Statement of policy regarding comparative advertising.* Retrieved from https://www.ftc.gov/public-statements/1979/08/statement-policy-regarding-comparative-advertising

Federal Trade Commission. (1969). *16 CFR 14.15 - In regard to comparative advertising.* Retrieved from https://www.law.cornell.edu/cfr/text/16/14.15

Federal Trade Commission. (1938). *The Wheeler-Lea Act.* Retrieved from https://www.ftc.gov/public-statements/1938/05/wheeler-lea-act

Fertilizer industry hits unfair competition. (1929, February 7). *Printers' Ink, 146*(6), 28.

Firestone, S. H. (1983). Why advertising a service is different. In L. Berry, G. L. Shostak, U. Lynn, & D. Gregory (Eds.), *Emerging Perspectives on Services Marketing* (pp. 86–89). Chicago, IL: American Marketing Association.

Fisher, A. B. (1988, May). Mark Laracy's obsession. *Inc., 10*(5), 70–82.

Fitzgerald, K. (1993, September 29). Telecommunications turn ad-driven hot button. *Advertising Age*, *64*(41), 12.

Flint, J. (1990, October 29). Network handling of comparative ads causing concern. *Broadcasting, 119*(18), 53.

Foster, G. A. (1967). *Advertising: Ancient marketplace to television.* New York, NY: Criterion Books.

Four A's hits derogatory ads. (1966, February 21). *Advertising Age*, *37*(21), 1, 187.

Fox, S. R. (1984). *The mirror makers: A history of American advertising and its creators.* Champaign, IL: University of Illinois Press.

Freberg, S. (1988.) *It only hurts when I laugh.* New York, NY: Times Books.

Frederick, J. G. (1925). Introduction: The story of advertising writing. In Frederick, J. G. (Ed.) *Masters of Advertising Copy*. New York, NY: Frank-Maurice Inc.

Frith, K.T., & Mueller, B. (2010). *Advertising and societies: Global issues* (2nd ed.). New York, NY: Peter Lang.

Fueroghne, D. K. (2017). *Law & advertising* (3rd ed.). Lanham, MD: Rowman & Littlefield.

Garcia, S. (1994, August 1). Why Maxima moved into the lap of luxury. *Adweek Western Edition*, *44*(31), 2.

Garramone, G. M. (1984). Voter responses to negative political ads. *Journalism Quarterly*, *61*(2), 250–259.

Giges, N. (1980, September 29). Comparative ads: Battles that wrote dos and don'ts. *Advertising Age, 51*(42), 59.

Giges, N. (1975, July 28). J&J readies effort to protect Tylenol-new Datril spot airs. *Advertising Age, 28 , 46*(30), 1–61.

Glim, A. (1947, December 19). Competitive or positive. *Printers' Ink, 221*, 74.

Glim, A. (1945, February 16). Reading from left to right. *Printers' Ink, 210*, 25.

Gnepa, T. J. (1993). Comparative advertising in magazines: Nature, frequency, and a test of the "underdog" hypothesis. *Journal of Advertising Research*, *33*(5), 70–76.

Goldman, D. (1996, April 15). The pain in our head. *Adweek Eastern Edition, 37*(16), 25.

Goode, K. M. (1928, November 14). Lucky Strike advertising tosses bombs among the bonbons. *Advertising & Selling*, *12*(1), 19–20.

Gordon, M. E., Slade, L. A., & Schmitt, N. (1986). The "science of the sophomore" revisited: From conjecture to empiricism. *Academy of Management Review, 11*(1), 191–207.

Gordon, R. L. (1989, September 25). Retailers ponder price-ad guides. *Advertising Age, 60*(41), 45.

Gotlieb, J. B., & Sarel, D. (1991). Comparative advertising effectiveness: The role of involvement and source credibility. *Journal of Advertising, 20*(1), 38–45.

Grant, D. (1973, November 19). Be hard on comparison ads—Roberts to Four A's. *Advertising Age, 44*(47), 1.

Greenberg, A. S. (1951). The ancient lineage of trade-marks. *Journal of the Patent Office Society, 33*(12), 876–887.

Grewal, D., Kavanoor, S., Fern, E. F., Costley, C., & Barnes, J. (1997). Comparative versus noncomparative advertising: A meta-analysis. *Journal of Marketing, 61*(4), 1–15.

Grey, J. S. (1902, July 23). The tobacco war in England. *Printers' Ink, 40*(4), 16.

Groucho. (1934, July 12). Groucho says: Build or destroy, there's no middle ground. *Printers' Ink, 168,* 57.

Gulas, C. S., & Weinberger, M. (2006). *Humor in advertising: A comprehensive analysis*. New York, NY: M.E. Sharpe, Inc.

Gürhan-Canli, Z., & Maheswaran, D. (2000). *Comparative advertising in the global marketplace: The effects of cultural orientation on communication*. Working Paper Number 328. Ann Arbor, MI: William Davidson Institute. Retrieved from http://hdl.handle.net/2027.42/39712

Hall, E. (1976). *Beyond culture*. Garden City, NY: Anchor Press.

Hall, E., & Hall, M. R. (1990). *Understanding cultural differences.* Yarmouth, ME.: Intercultural Press.

Harmon, R. R., Razzouk, N. Y., & Stern, B. L. (1983). The information content of comparative magazine advertisements. *Journal of Advertising, 12*(4), 10–19.

Hazardous business. (1908, September 9). *Printers' Ink, 64*(11), 27.

Henning-Bodewig, F. (2006). *Unfair competition law: European Union and member states* (Vol. 18). London, UK: Kluwer Law International.

Hess, H. W. (1922). History and present status of the "truth-in-advertising" movement: As carried on by the vigilance committee of the associated advertising clubs of the world. *The Annals of the American Academy of Political and Social Science, 101*(1), 211–220.

Hill, F. T. (1910, June 9). Attacks upon competitors shown to be poor policy. *Printers' Ink, 71*, 23.

Hindley C. (1884). *A history of the cries of London* (2nd ed.). London, UK: Charles Hindley [The Younger].

Hisrich, R. D. (1983). Executive advertisers' views of comparison advertising. *Sloan Management Review, 25*(1), 39–50.

historyofadvertising. (2018). *The art of advertising.* Retrieved from http://historyofadvertising.tumblr.com/page/2

Hitchcock, H. M. (1927, December 15). The 'knocking' industrial advertisement. *Printers' Ink, 141*(11), 149–52.

Hofstede, G. (1980). *Culture's consequences: International differences in work-related values*. Beverly Hills, CA: Sage Publications.

Hofstede, G., Hofstede, G. J., & Minkov, M. (2010). *Cultures and organizations: Software of the mind* (3rd ed.). New York, NY: McGraw-Hill.

Hollander, S. C., Rassuli, K. M., Jones, D. B., & Dix, L. F. (2005). Periodization in marketing history. *Journal of Macromarketing, 25*(1), 32–41.

Hopkins, C. C. (1930, April 30). How far can I go with George Hill. *Printers' Ink*, 20.

Hotchkiss, G. B. (1938). *Milestones of marketing; a brief history of the evolution of market distribution*. New York, NY: The Macmillan Company.

Howard, S. (2008). The advertising industry and alcohol in interwar France. *The Historical Journal, 51*(2), 421–455.

Hower, R. M. (1949). *The history of an advertising agency: N. W. Ayer & Son at work, 1869–1949.* (Rev. ed., Harvard studies in business history, 5). Cambridge, MA: Harvard University Press.

How the "big four" cigarette advertisers stand in the 1929 sales battle. (1929, September 28). *Sales Management, 19*(13), 563, 592–593.

Hughes, L. M. (1928, December 22). American tobacco describes Lucky Strikes "sweets" campaign. *Sales Management and Advertisers' Weekly, 16*(13), 736–737.

Hwang, J. S. (2002). How to manage the intensity of comparison in comparative advertising over time. *International Journal of Advertising, 21*(4), 481–503.

If advertisers must fight; why don't they protect themselves against looking ridiculous? (1930, July 6). *Printers' Ink, 164*, 40–41.

IOR. (n.d.). *IOR cultural insights*. Retrieved from http://www.iorworld.com/cultural-insights-pages-472.php

Is it really worthwhile…. (1902, May 31). *Printers' Ink, 39*(4), 36.

Jaben, J. (1992, August 31). Mud wrestling. Microsoft's ads highlight new prominence of negative marketing in business. *Business Marketing*, 28–32.

Jackson, D. W., Brown, S. W., & Harmon, R. R. (1979). Comparative magazine advertisements. *Journal of Advertising Research, 19*(6), 21–26.

Jain, S. P., Agrawal, N., & Maheswaran, D. (2006). When more may be less: The effects of regulatory focus on responses to different comparative frames. *Journal of Consumer Research, 33*(1), 91–98.

Jain, S. P., Buchanan, B., & Maheswaran, D. (2000). Comparative versus noncomparative advertising: The moderating impact of prepurchase attribute verifiability. *Journal of Consumer Psychology, 9*(4), 201–211.

Jain, S. P., Lindsey, C., Agrawal, N., & Maheswaran, D. (2007). For better or for worse? Valenced comparative frames and regulatory focus. *Journal of Consumer Research, 34*(1), 57–65.

Jain, S. P., Mathur, P., & Maheswaran, D. (2009). The influence of consumers' lay theories of approach/avoidance motivation. *Journal of Marketing Research, 46*(1), 56–65.

Jain, S. P., & Posavac, S. S. (2004). Valenced comparisons. *Journal of Marketing Research, 41*(1), 46–58.

James, K. E., & Hensel, P. J. (1991). Negative advertising: The malicious strain of comparative advertising. *Journal of Advertising, 20*(2), 53–69.

Jeon, J. O., & Beatty, S. E. (2002). Comparative advertising effectiveness in different national cultures. *Journal of Business Research, 55*(11), 907–913.

Johnson, B. (2017). *World largest advertisers: Spending is growing (and surging) in China.* Retrieved from http://adage.com/article/cmo-strategy/world-s-largest-advertisers-2017/311484/?utm_source=daily_email&utm_medium=newsletter&utm_campaign=adage&ttl=1513079618&utm_visit=205705

Kalro, A. D., Sivakumaran, B., & Marathe, R. R. (2017). The ad format-strategy effect on comparative advertising effectiveness. *European Journal of Marketing, 51* (1), 99–122.

Kalro, A. D., Sivakumaran, B., & Marathe, R. R. (2013). Direct or indirect comparative ads: The moderating role of information processing modes. *Journal of Consumer Behaviour, 12*(2), 133–147.

Kalro, A. D., Sivakumaran, B., & Marathe, R. R. (2010). Comparative advertising in India: A content analysis of English print advertisements. *Journal of International Consumer Marketing, 22*(4), 377–394.

Keith-Spiegel, P. (1972). Early conception of humor: Varieties and issues. In J. H. Goldstein, H. J. Eyesenck, & P. E. McGhee (Eds.), *The psychology of humor* (pp. 3–39). New York, NY: Academic Press.

Kelley, H. (1973). Processes of causal attribution. *American Psychologist, 28*(February), 107–128.

Kelly, J., & Solomon, P. (1975). Humor in television advertising. *Journal of Advertising, 4*(3), 31–35.

Kershaw, A. G. (1976, July 5). For and against comparative advertising—against. *Advertising Age, 47*(27), 25.

Kerwin, A. M. (2007, June 4). Water cooler. *Advertising Age, 78*(23), 49.

Kim, S., Jeong, S., & Hwang, Y. (2016). Why are there cross-national differences in response to comparative advertising?: Some mediators. *Journal of Marketing Communications* (Published online February 2, 2016).

Kirmani, S. M. (1996). Cross-border comparative advertising in the European Union. *Boston College International and Comparative Law Review, 19*(1), 201–215.

Kittler, M., Rygl, D., & Mackinnon, A. (2011). Beyond culture or beyond control? Reviewing the use of Hall's high-/low-context concept. *International Journal of Cross Cultural Management, 11*(1), 63–82.

Klaassen, A. (2009, November 19). *AT&T's Verizon lawsuit gives 'Map for That' ad new life.* Retrieved from http://adage.com/article/the-viral-video-chart/verizon-lawsuit-map-ad-life/140602/

Koprowski, G. (1995, February 20). Theories of negativity. *Brandweek, 36*(8), 20.

Kraft, J. H. (1927, January 13). Kraft cheese shows how to tame the substitution menace. *Printers' Ink, 138*(2), 41–50.

Kreisman, R., & Christy, M. (1982, September 13). Burger King's "challenge" set for heavy drive. *Advertising Age, 13*(1), 1, 74.

Kremers, B. (n.d.). *Electronic word of mouth presents a window of opportunity for businesses.* Retrieved from www.buzztalkmonitor.com/blog/bid/233669/Electronic-Word-Of-Mouth-presents-a-window-of-opportunity-for-businesses

LaFave, L. (1972). Humor judgments as a function of reference group and identification classes. In J. H. Goldstein, H. J. Eyesenck, & P. E. McGhee (Eds.), *The psychology of humor* (pp. 195–210). New York, NY: Academic Press.

Lafeber, M. M., & Haugen, K. L. C. (2005). *The dilution dilemma—Litigating dilution claims and the Trademark Dilution Revision Act of 2005.* Retrieved from https://apps.americanbar.org/litigation/committees/intellectual/roundtables/1105_outline.pdf

Laird, P. W. (1998). *Advertising progress: American business and the rise of consumer marketing.* Baltimore, MD: Johns Hopkins University Press.

Lamb, C., Pride, W., & Pletcher, B. (1978). A taxonomy for comparative advertising research. *Journal of Advertising, 7*(1), 43–47.

Laperouse, T. (1994, July 11). Kick off and funning; Soft drink is hard core vs. Mountain Dew. *Adweek, 16*(28). 4.

Larrabee, C. B. (1934, February 22). Too hot to handle. *Printers' Ink, 166*, 57–59.

Larrabee, C. B. (1923, November 22). When a competitor too closely copies your sales and advertising methods. *Printers' Ink, 125*(1), 112, 117.

Lavidge, R., & Steiner, G. (1961). A model for predictive measurements of advertising effectiveness. *Journal of Marketing, 25*(6), 59–62.

The law of commercial disparagement: Business defamation's impotent ally. (1953). *The Yale Law Journal, 63*(1), 65–104.

Leach, W. (1994). *Land of desire: Merchants, power, and the rise of American culture*. New York, NY: Vintage.

Leach, W. B. (1924, June 26). Is it ethical to point out weaknesses of competitors? *Printers' Ink, 127*, 137–138.

Legislation.gov.uk (2017a). *Trade Marks Act, 1938*. Retrieved from www.legislation.gov.uk/ukpga/1938/22/pdfs/ukpga_19380022_en.pdf

Legislation.gov.uk (2017b). *Trade Marks Act, 1994.* Retrieved from http://www.legislation.gov.uk/ukpga/1994/26/contents

Lever masks out taboo term; avoids (use of words) high price spread. (1964, May 4). *Advertising Age, 35*, 176.

Levy, R. (1987). Big resurgence in comparative ads. *Dun's Business Month, 129*(2), 56–8.

Lewis, H. (1992). The future of 'force-communication': Power communication. *Direct Marketing, 54*(9), 32.

Li, S. Y. (1995). *The use of humor in television advertising: A content analysis of humorous ads across humor types versus product types* (Unpublished master's thesis). Texas Tech University, Lubbock, TX.

Liebertein, M., & Lockerby, M. J. (2016). *Mine is better than yours! The risks and rewards of conducting comparative advertising.* Miami Beach, FL: American Bar Association. Retrieved from https://www.americanbar.org/content/dam/aba/images/franchising/annual16/course-materials-16/w4-pp-mine-is-better.pdf

Litowitz, R., & Nicoletti, D. (2011). *Why you should consider keeping your case out of the courtroom*. Retrieved from http://adage.com/article/guest-columnists/keeping-case-courtroom/149216/

The little schoolmaster's classroom. (1928, December 13). *Printers' Ink*, 208.

Louis , J. C., & Yazijian, H. Z. (1980). *The Cola Wars: The story of the global battle between the Coca-Cola Company and PepsiCo, Inc*. New York, NY: Everest House.

Lubin, G. (2011, July 6). *Campbell's soup is still reeling from the 2008 MSG attack ads.* Retrieved from http://www.businessinsider.com/campbells-soup-wars-citi-2011–7

Luckman, C. (1939, March 9). Pepsodent's 7 points. *Printers' Ink, 186*, 15–18.

Lucky Strike and the candy industry mobilize for battle. (1928, November 22). *Printers' Ink, 145*(10), 10, 12.

Lukovitz, K. (2009). *Food marketer of the year: Campbell Soup*. Retrieved from https://www.mediapost.com/publications/article/97552/food-marketer-of-the-year-campbell-soup.html

Lyi, D. R. (1988). *An experimental study on the effectiveness of comparison advertising* (Unpublished doctoral dissertation). Hanyang University, Seoul, Korea.

MacManus, T. F. (1927). *The sword-arm of business*. New York, NY: The Devin-Adair Company.

Madden, T., & Weinberger, M. G. (1984). Humor in advertising: A practitioner view. *Journal of Advertising, 24*(4), 23–29.

Manning, K. C., Miniard, P. W., Barone, M. J., & Rose, R. L. (2001). Understanding the mental representations created by comparative advertising. *Journal of Advertising, 30*(2), 27–39.

Manzur, E., Uribe, R., Hidalgo, P., Olavarrieta, S., & Farías, P. (2012). Comparative advertising effectiveness in Latin America: Evidence from Chile. *International Marketing Review, 29*(3), 277–298.

Marchand, R. (1985), *Advertising the American dream: Making way for modernity, 1920–1940*. Berkeley, CA: University of California Press.

Markman, A. B., & Loewenstein, J. (2010). Structural comparison and consumer choice. *Journal of Consumer Psychology, 20*(2), 126–137.

Maurine, C. (1974, January 28). NBC spells out new formal guides for comparative ads. *Advertising Age , 45*(4), 1.

McClain, A. (1983, June 6). When it comes to commercials, Iacocca wins out. *Advertising Age, 54*(24), M1.

McCullough, L. S., & Taylor, R. K. (1993). Humor in American, British, and German ads. *Industrial Marketing Management, 22*(1), 17–28.

McDermott, J. (2013). *Samsung's new Galaxy S4 ad strategy is same as the old strategy: Hammer Apple*. Retrieved from http://adage.com/article/digital/samsung-hammers-apple-s-iphone-galaxy-s4-spot/241307/

McDonough, J., & Egolf, K. (2003). *The advertising age encyclopedia of advertising*. New York, NY: Fitzroy Dearborn.

McGarry, W. A. (1931, September 3). Advertise to prospects—not to competitors. *Printers' Ink, 156*, 25–26.

McGhee, P. E. (1979). *Humor: Its origin and development*. San Francisco, CA: Freeman.

McGovern, C. F. (2006). *Sold American: Consumption and citizenship, 1890–1945*. Wilmington, NC: University of North Carolina Press.

Meyers, F. (1966, May 23). Rivals find Volkswagen is hard little car to belittle. *Advertising Age, 37*, 4.

Meyers, W. (1984). *The image-makers: Power and persuasion on Madison Avenue*. New York, NY: Times Books.

Mills, C. W. (1956). *The power elite*. New York, NY: Oxford University Press.

Miniard, P. W., Barone, M. J., Rose, R. L., & Manning, K. C. (2006). A further assessment of indirect comparative advertising claims of superiority over all competitors. *Journal of Advertising, 35*(4), 53–64.

Miniard, P. W., Rose, R. L., Manning, K. C, & Barone, M. J. (1998). Tracking the effects of comparative and noncomparative advertising with relative and nonrelative measures: A

further examination of the framing correspondence hypothesis. *Journal of Business Research, 41*(2), 137–143.
Minor, J. W. (1960, February 29). Competitive ads not unethical. *Advertising Age, 31*, 1A.
Miracle, G. E., Chang, K. Y., & Taylor, C. R. (1992). Culture and advertising executions: A comparison of selected characteristics of Korean and US television commercials. *International Marketing Review, 9*(4), 5–17.
Miracle, G. E., & Nevett, T. (1988). A comparative history of advertising self-regulation in the UK and the USA. *European Journal of Marketing, 22*(4), 7–23.
Monro, D. H. (1951). *Argument of laughter*. Carlton Victoria, Australia: Melbourne University Press.
Moore, K., & Reid, S. (2008). The birth of brand: 4000 years of branding. *Business History, 50*(4), 419–432.
Morimoto, M. (2014). Japan. In M. A. Shaver & S. An (Eds.), *The global advertising regulation handbook* (pp. 206–220). Armonk, NY: M.E. Sharpe.
Mortimer, K. (2008). Identifying the components of effective service advertisements. *Journal of Services Marketing, 22*(2), 104–113.
Muehling, D. D., Stem, D. E., & Raven, P. (1989). Comparative advertising: Views from advertisers, agencies, media, and policy makers. *Journal of Advertising Research, 29*(5), 38–48.
Muehling, D. D., Stoltman, J. J., & Grossbart, S. (1990). The impact of comparative advertising on levels of message involvement. *Journal of Advertising, 19*(4), 41–50.
Mums the word on competitive copy in Greece, Mum finds. (1968, August 26). *Advertising Age, 39*, 230.
Mundorf, N., Bhatia, A., Zillmann, D., Lester, P., & Robertson, S. (1988). Gender differences in humor appreciation. *Humor-International Journal of Humor Research, 1*(3), 231–244.
Muthukrishnan, A., Warlop, L., & Alba, J. (2001). The piecemeal approach to comparative advertising. *Marketing Letters, 12*(1), 63–73.
Myers, J. (2014). *Advertising vs. below-the-line shopper marketing: The economics.* Retrieved from https://www.mediavillage.com/article/advertising-vs-below-the-line-shopper-marketing-the-economics/
Nagar, K. (2014). Consumers' evaluation of ad-brand congruity in comparative advertising. *Journal of International Consumer Marketing, 27*, 253–276.
Naming competitors in ads: Forthright, fair, foolish? (1966, January 28). *Printers' Ink, 292*, 32–34.
Namm, B. H. (1934, June 21). Major Namm looks at auto ads. *Advertising & Selling, 23*(36), 36.
NARB toughens comparative ad rules. (1975, December 1). *Advertising Age, 46*(48), 76.
Neff, J. (2017). *Howard Bell, father of advertising self-regulation, dies at 91.* Retrieved from http://adage.com/article/cmo-strategy/howard-bell-father-ad-regulation-dies-91/310303/?utm_source=daily_email&utm_medium=newsletter&utm_campaign=adage&ttl=1504780692&utm_visit=205705
Neff, J. (2016). *Honest Co. drops ad claims including implications that rivals are unsafe, amid challenge.* Retrieved from http://adage.com/article/cmo-strategy/honest-drops-ad-claims-including-implication-rival-brands-unsafe-amid-challenge-kimberly-clark/306892/
Neff, J. (2014a). *Nestle sues Blue Buffalo claiming false advertising, disparagement.* Retrieved from http://adage.com/article/cmo-strategy/nestle-sues-blue-buffalo-claiming-false-advertising/293060/
Neff, J. (2014b). *Losing market share, big three CPGs shift battle to court.* Retrieved from http://adage.com/article/news/losing-market-share-big-cpgs-shift-battle-court/296020/
Neff, J. (2003, October 20). P&G pushes NAD, not courts for disputes. *Advertising Age, 74*(42), 3.
Neff, J. (1999, November 1). Household brands counterpunch. *Advertising Age, 70*(45), 26.
Nye, C. W., Roth, M. S., & Shimp, T. A. (2008). Comparative advertising in markets where brands and comparative advertising are novel. *Journal of International Business Studies, 39*(5), 851–863.
Ogilvy, D. (1985). *Ogilvy on advertising.* New York, NY: Vintage Books.

Ohly, A., & Spence, M. (2000). *The law of comparative advertising: Directive 97/55/EC in the United Kingdom and Germany*. Oxford and Portland, OR: Hart Publishing.

Oliver, T. (1986). *The real Coke, the real story*. New York, NY: Random House.

Oppliger, P. A., & Zillmann, D. (1997). Disgust in humor: Its appeal to adolescents. *Humor-International Journal of Humor Research, 10*(4), 421–438.

Packard, V. (1957). *The hidden persuaders*. New York, NY: David McKay Co., Inc.

Pepsi dares to compare – Everywhere. (1994, March). *Beverage World, 113*(1562), 18.

Peterson, R. A., & Merunka, D. R. (2014). Convenience samples of college students and research reproducibility. *Journal of Business Research, 67*(5), 1035–1041.

Petroff, A. (2017). *Britain crashes out of world's top 5 economies*. Retrieved from http://money.cnn.com/2017/11/22/news/economy/uk-france-biggest-economies-in-the-world/index.html

Petty, R. D. (2014). International advertising law and regulation: A research review and agenda—the devil is in the details. In H. Cheng (Ed.), *The handbook of international advertising research* (pp. 395–413). West Sussex, UK: John Wiley & Sons, Ltd.

Petty, R. E., & Cacioppo, J. T. (1986). *The elaboration likelihood model of persuasion*. New York, NY: Springer Verlag.

Petty, R. E., Cacioppo, J. T., & Schumann, D. (1983). Central and peripheral routes to advertising effectiveness: The moderating role of involvement. *Journal of Consumer Research, 10*(2), 135–146.

Pickett, K. S. (1910, May 31). How shall competition be met? *Printers' Ink, 73*(12), 28–30.

Pillai, K. G., & Goldsmith, R. E. (2008). How brand attribute typicality and consumer commitment moderate the influence of comparative advertising. *Journal of Business Research, 61*(9), 933–941.

Pilon, A. (2012, May 9). *Comparative advertising survey: Some ads can be too negative*. Retrieved from https://aytm.com/blog/daily-survey-results/comparative-advertising-survey/

Pollack, J. (1998). *Progresso soup gets direct vs. Campbell's in new ads tv, print timed to coincide with ready-to-serve varieties slated for sampling, too*. Retrieved from http://adage.com/article/news/progresso-soup-direct-campbell-s-ads-tv-print-timed-coincide-ready-serve-varieties-slated-sampling/64067/

Pope, D. (1983). *The making of modern advertising*. New York, NY: Basic Books.

Presbrey, F. (1929). *The history and development of advertising*. Garden City, NY: Doubleday.

Priester, J. R., Godek, J., Nayakankuppum, D. J., & Park, K. (2004). Brand congruity and comparative advertising: When and why comparative advertisements lead to greater elaboration. *Journal of Consumer Psychology, 14*(1–2), 115–123.

Prima donnas at war. (1937, July 8). *Printers' Ink, 180*, 17.

PRNewswire. (2011a). *DiGiorno pizza gives fans new reasons to high five this championship season*. Retrieved from https://www.prnewswire.com/news-releases/digiorno-pizza-gives-fans-new-reasons-to-high-five-this-championship-season-114924614.html

PRNewswire. (2011b). *United Center visitors score big as DiGiorno becomes the new official pizza of Chicago Blackhawks, Bulls, and United Center*. Retrieved from https://www.prnewswire.com/news-releases/united-center-visitors-score-big-as-digiorno-becomes-the-new-official-pizza-of-chicago-blackhawks-bulls-and-united-center-134754018.html

PRNewswire. (2009). *Did you know that Domino's and Subway are in a food fight?* Retrieved from http://www.prnewswire.com

Putrevu, S., & Lord, K. R. (1994). Comparative and noncomparative advertising: Attitudinal effects under cognitive and affective involvement conditions. *Journal of Advertising, 23*(2), 77–91.

Rahner, M. (2014). *iPhone vs. Samsung Galaxy sales and user adoption*. Retrieved from http://mobilefomo.com/2014/06/iphone-vs-samsung/

Ramon De Leon. (2009, January 22). *Domino's Pizza Bakes the Letter from Subway!* (Video file). Retrieved from https://www.youtube.com/watch?v=NnADo4h6vSo

Rapp, A. (1951). *The origins of wit and humor*. New York, NY: Dutton.

Renault's ad claims true, Adman tells TV stations that turned down commercials. (1965, September 6). *Advertising Age*, 6.

Ritchie, R. (2014). *Samsung's latest ad shows just how irresistible the iPhone truly is.* Retrieved from https://www.imore.com/samsungs-latest-ad-shows-just-how-irresistible-iphone-really

Robinson, S. (1994). One message, twelve markets. *The Journal of European Business, 5*(3), 16.

Rodiguez, J. C. (2013). *NAD refers AB challenge to MillerCoors advertising to FTC*. Retrieved from https://www.law360.com/articles/464572/nad-refers-ab-challenge-to-millercoors-advertising-to-ftc

Rogers, J. C., & Williams, T. G. (1989). Comparative advertising effectiveness: Practitioners' perceptions versus academic research findings. *Journal of Advertising Research, 29*(5), 22–37.

Rokicki, J. (1987). Advertising in the Roman Empire. *Whole Earth Review*, Spring, 36–40.

Romano, C. J. (2005). Comparative advertising in the United States and in France. *Northwestern Journal of International Law & Business, 25*(2), 371–414.

Rose, R. L., Miniard, P. W., Barone, M. J., Manning, K. C., & Till, B. D. (1993). When persuasion goes undetected: The case of comparative advertising. *Journal of Marketing Research, 30*(3) 315–330.

Ross, F. J. (1924, July 10). Where is your strongest competition? *Printers' Ink, 128*(8), 10, 12, 14.

Rossiter, J. R, Percy, L., & Donovan, R. J. (1991). A better advertising planning grid. *Journal of Advertising Research, 31*(5), 11–21.

Rossman, M. (1971, May 23). Industry tries self-regulation to offset FTC. *Los Angeles Times*, D12—D13.

Rotfeld, H. J., & Stafford, M. R. (2007). Toward a pragmatic understanding of the advertising and public policy literature. *Journal of Current Issues & Research in Advertising, 29*(1), 67–80.

Rowsome, F. (1970). *They laughed when I sat down: An informal history of advertising in words and pictures*. New York, NY: McGraw-Hill.

Rivers, H. W. (1929). *Ancient advertising and publicity*. Chicago, IL: Kroch's.

Ruddock, D. (2014). *Dear Samsung: Your ads making fun of apple are nauseatingly bad, please stop*. Retrieved from http://www.androidpolice.com/2014/09/11/dear-samsung-your-ads-making-fun-of-apple-are-nauseatingly-bad-please-stop-videos-if-it-wasnt-obvious/

Russell, M. (2012). *How Samsung upstaged Apple during the launch of iPhone 5: Aggressive marketing has kept Korean handset maker top of mind.* Retrieved from http://adage.com/article/the-viral-video-chart/samsung-upstaged-apple-launch-iphone-5/237426/

Russell, T. (1929, February 14). England frowns on militant cigarette advertising. *Printers' Ink, 146*(7), 10–12.

Russell, T. H. (1910), *Advertising methods and mediums*. Chicago, IL: Whitman Publishing Co.

Sampson, H. (1874). *A history of advertising from the earliest times: illustrated by anecdotes, curious specimens, and biographical notes*. London, UK: Chatto and Windus, Piccadilly.

Samsung Mobile USA. (2017, November 5). *Samsung Galaxy: Growing Up* (Video file). Retrieved from https://www.youtube.com/watch?v=R59TevgzN3k

Schultz, E. J. (2014). *Supreme Court decision could mean more ad lawsuits*. Retrieved from http://adage.com/article/news/supreme-court-decision-ad-lawsuits/292355/

Schultz, E. J. (2010). *Soup players put spotlight back on taste, new products: Category sales depressed during last year's bruising ad war*. Retrieved from http://adage.com/article/news/soup-players-put-spotlight-back-taste-products/147265/

Schwaiger, M., Rennhak, C., Taylor, C. R., & Cannon, H. M. (2007). Can comparative advertising be effective in Germany? A tale of two campaigns. *Journal of Advertising Research, 47*(1), 2–13.

Schwarzkopf, S. (2011). The subsiding sizzle of advertising history: Methodological and theoretical challenges in the post advertising age. *Journal of Historical Research in Marketing, 3*(4), 528–548.

Scott-Thomas, C. (2009). *Campbell's drops 'soup wars' advertising strategy*. Retrieved from https://www.foodnavigator-usa.com/Article/2009/08/18/Campbell-s-drops-Soup-Wars-advertising-strategy

Self regulation on trial; fight back or forget it. (1976, March 1). *Advertising Age*, 16.

Serafin, R. (1985, October 1). The gloves come off in auto marketing. *Advertising Age, 56*(82), 76.

Shao, A. T., Bao, Y., & Gray, E. (2004). Comparative advertising effectiveness: A cross-cultural study. *Journal of Current Issues & Research in Advertising, 26*(2), 67–80.

Shapiro, N. (2005). Competition and aggregate demand. *Journal of Post Keynesian Economics, 27*(3), 541–549.

Shiv, B., Britton, J. A. E., & Payne, J. W. (2004). Does elaboration increase or decrease the effectiveness of negatively versus positively framed messages? *Journal of Consumer Research, 3*(1), 199–208.

Shields, M. (2009, October 25). Did sour grapes prompt Verizon's apple attack? *Brandweek, 50*(38), 78.

Simon, M. J. (1960). *The advertising truth book*. New York, NY: Advertising Federation of America.

Simon, M. J. (1951, September). Competitive advertising. *Advertising Agency, 44*(1), 81.

Singh, M. (2014). Comparative advertising effectiveness with legal and cross culture framework. *International Journal for Research in Management and Pharmacy, 3*(3). Retrieved from http://www.raijmr.com/wp-content/uploads/2017/11/IJRMP_2014_vol03_issue_03_07.pdf

Sloan, P. (1987, March 2). Toiletries & beauty aids: Knock-offs deliver blows to fragrance market. *Advertising Age, 58*(9), S14.

SmartAdvertising. (2009, January 8). *Pepsi MC Hammer* (Video file). Retrieved from https://www.youtube.com/watch?v=MrsCIK9s2wI

Snyder, K. (1996, April 8). Analgesics makers stage new war of words. *Drug Topics, 140*(7), 89.

SodaStream. (2013, January 30). *Game Day 2013 Commercial: The Unaired SodaStream Ad* (Video file). Retrieved from https://www.youtube.com/watch?v=68al-o2XSpE

Sorescu, A. B., & Gelb, B. D. (2000). Negative comparative advertising: Evidence favoring fine-tuning. *Journal of Advertising, 29*(4), 25–40.

Speck, P. S. (1987). *On humor and humor in advertising* (Unpublished doctoral dissertation). Texas Tech University, Lubbock, TX.

Spence, E., Van Heekeren, B., & Boylan, M. (2004). *Advertising ethics*. Upper Saddle River, NJ: Prentice Hall.

Spotts, H. E., Weinberger, M. G., & Parsons, A. L. (1997). Assessing the use and impact of humor on advertising effectiveness: A contingency approach. *Journal of Advertising, 26*(3), 17–32.

Stankey, M. J. (1990). Ethics, professionalism, and advertising. In R. Hovland & G. B. Wilcox (Eds.), *Advertising in society* (pp. 419–436). Lincolnwood, IL: NTC.

Statista.com (2017). *Advertising expenditure in the world's largest ad markets in 2016*. Retrieved from https://www.statista.com/statistics/273736/advertising-expenditure-in-the-worlds-largest-ad-markets/

Stephen, H. L. (1948, May 31). Vincent Riggio learned selling while pounding the pavements. *Printers' Ink, 225*(8), 37–39, 59, 64, 66, 70, 72, 74.

Stern, T. (2006). On each wall and corner poast": Playbills, title-pages, and advertising in early modern London. *English Literary Renaissance, 36*(1), 57–89.

Sternthal, B., & Craig, C. (1973). Humor in advertising. *Journal of Marketing, 37*(4), 12–18.

Stewart, D. W. & Furse, D. H. (1986). *Effective TV advertising: A study of 1000 commercials*. Lanham, MD: Lexington Books.

Stibel, G., & Ruff, G. (2012, October 12). *Flipsides: Samsung's iPhone-mocking ads are brilliant; no, they're risky*. Retrieved from http://adage.com/article/cmo-strategy/flipsides-samsung-s-iphone-mocking-ads-brilliant-risky/237606/

Stone, J. (1951, July). What is competitive advertising today? *Advertising Agency, 44*, 77.

Strom, S. (2016). *Chobani ads shift a battle out of the yogurt aisle and into the courts*. Retrieved from https://www.nytimes.com/2016/01/11/business/media/chobani-ads-shift-a-battle-out-of-the-yogurt-aisle-and-into-the-courts.html

Study cites value of comparative ads but warns effect hinges on honesty. (1977, August 29) *Broadcasting, 93*(9), 52.

Stuyck, J. (1993). Regulating comparative advertising in the European community. In W. F. V. Raaij & G. J. Bamossy (Eds,), *European advances in consumer research volume 1* (pp. 565–568), Provo, UT: Association for Consumer Research.

Suls, J. M. (1972). A two-stage model for the appreciation of jokes and cartoons: An information-processing analysis. In J. H. Goldstein & P. E. McGhee (Eds.), *The psychology of humor: Theoretical perspectives and empirical issues* (pp. 81–100). New York, NY: Academic Press.

Swinyard, W. (1981). The Interaction between comparative advertising and copy claim variation. *Journal of Marketing Research, 18*(2), 175–186.

Talk success in your advertising. (1903, May 13). *Printers' Ink, 43*(11), 27.

Tannenbaum, S. I. (1976, July 5). For and against comparative advertising – for. *Advertising Age, 47*(27), 25.

Thomaselli, R. (2003, October 27). Industry wrestles with comparative ads. *Advertising Age, 74*(43), 10.

Thompson, D., & Hamilton, R. (2006). The effects of information processing mode on consumers' responses to comparative advertising. *Journal of Consumer Research, 32*(4), 530–540.

Tibken, S. (2016). *Ignore that burning Galaxy Note 7 over there*. Retrieved from https://www.cnet.com/news/samsung-at-ces-ignore-that-burning-galaxy-note-7-over-there/

Tolk, B. (1952, August 15). Battle of the home permanent waves rages; Hudnut to continue ad campaign. *Printers' Ink, 240*, 37.

Toncar, M. F. (2001). The use of humour in television advertising: Revisiting the US-UK comparison. *International Journal of Advertising, 20*(4), 521–539.

Tormala, Z. L., & Petty, R. E. (2004). Resistance to persuasion and attitude certainty: The moderating role of elaboration. *Personality and Social Psychology Bulletin, 30*(11), 1446–1457.

Tungate, M. (2013). *Ad-land: A global history of advertising* (2nd Ed.). London, UK: Kogan Page.

TV code's bell warns of rise in ad disparagement; it's ultimatum: Cantz, agency exec says he'll fight move; says other Renault folk like copy. (1965, September 13). *Advertising Age*, 1, 8.

Tylenol exec speaks out on datril price ad. (1976, March 29). *Advertising Age, 47*(13), 115.

Unger, L. S. (1995). Observations: A cross-cultural study on the affect-based model of humor in advertising. *Journal of Advertising Research, 35*(1), 66–71.

Unsolicited ad idea problems, other woes get Four A's airing. (1975, November 24). *Advertising Age, 46*(47), 3.

Van Auken, S., & Adams, A. J. (2006). Developing perspectives into across-class associational advertising. *Journal of Promotion Management, 12*(2), 93–117.

Van Auken, S., & Adams, A. J. (2005). Validating across-class brand anchoring theory: Issues and implications. *Journal of Brand Management, 12*(3), 165–176.

Van Auken, S., & Adams, A. J. (1999). Across-versus within-class comparative advertising: Insights into prestige class anchoring. *Psychology and Marketing, 16*(5), 429–450.

Van Auken, S., & Adams, A. J. (1998). Attribute upgrading through across-class, within-category comparison advertising. *Journal of Advertising Research, 38*(20), 6–16.

Vaughn, R. (1980). How advertising works: A planning model. *Journal of Advertising Research, 20*(5), 27–33.

Venture North Law Limited. (2015). *Comparative advertising in Vietnam*. Retrieved from https://vietnam-business-law.info/blog/2015/4/7/comparative-advertising-in-vietnam

Vijayalakshmi, A., Muehling, D. D., & Laczniak, R. N. (2015). An investigation of consumers' responses to comparative "attack" ads. *Journal of Promotion Management, 21*(6), 760–775.

Voss, P. J. (1998). Books for sale: Advertising and patronage in Late Elizabethan England. *The Sixteenth Century Journal, 29*(Autumn), 733–756.

Vranica, S. (2008). *And in this corner.... Marketers take some jabs*. Retrieved from https://www.wsj.com/articles/SB122289868915095901

Walker, R. B. (1973). Advertising in London newspapers, 1650–1750. *Business History, 15*(2), 112–130.

Wasserman, T. (2001, October 8). Ailing tech sector eschews branding, breaks out the charts and jabs. *Brandweek, 42*(37), 8.

Watkins, J. L. (1959). *The 100 greatest advertisements: Who wrote them and what they did* (2nd Ed.). New York, NY: Dover Publications.

wcgabe. (2009, April 13). *DiGiorno Pizza* (Video file). Retrieved from https://www.youtube.com/watch?v=9GiKhAtFthM

Weinberger, M. G., & Campbell, L. (1991). The use and impact of humor in radio advertising. *Journal of Advertising Research, 31*(1), 44–52.

Weinberger, M. G., & Gulas, C. S. (1992). The impact of humor in advertising: A review. *Journal of Advertising, 21*(4), 35–59.

Weinberger, M. G., & Spotts, H. E. (1989). Humor in US versus UK TV commercials: A comparison. *Journal of Advertising, 18*(2), 39–44.

Weinberger, M. G., Spotts, H., Campbell, L., & Parsons, A. L. (1995). The use and effect of humor in different advertising media. *Journal of Advertising Research, 35*(3), 44–57.

Weiss, E. B. (1951, November 30). Advertisers forget Americans like good sports. *Printers' Ink, 237*, 39.

Wengrow, D. (2008). Prehistories of commodity branding. *Current Anthropology, 49*(1), 7–34.

Western Historical Society. (2017). *Art of the draw: Advertising posters from the McCormick-International Harvester Collection*. Retrieved from https://www.wisconsinhistory.org/museum/exhibits/artofthedraw/poster9.asp

Wheaton, K. (2015). *Ad review: In macro-micro battle, MillerCoors plays the scold: Brewer looking to rally team? Punching back is way to go*. Retrieved from http://adage.com/article/ad-review/ad-review-macro-micro-battle-millercoors-plays-scold/297030/

Wheaton, K. (2014). *Taco Bell's recycled Ronald gag likely to make a mark*. Retrieved from http://adage.com/article/ad-review/taco-bell-s-recycled-ronald-gag-make-a-mark/292378/

When you knock your competitor, you knock advertising. (1931, November 25). *Advertising & Selling, 18*, 17–18.

Whipple, T. W., & Courtney, A. E. (1980). How to portray women in TV commercials. *Journal of Advertising Research, 20*(2), 53–59.

Why we stopped advertising; created competition. (1925, June 25). *Printers' Ink, 131*, 104.

Wilkie, W. L., & Farris, P. W. (1975). Comparison advertising: Problems and potential. *Journal of Marketing, 39*(4) 7–15.

Wilson, L. (2000). *The advertising law guide*. New York, NY: Allworth Press.

Winters, P., & Wayne W. (1990, October 8). Coke seeks tough tv ad watchdog; Herbert criticizes comparative claim. *Advertising Age*, 1–2.

Wisconsin Historical Society (2017). *Art of the draw: advertising posters from the McCormick-International Harvester Collection*. Retrieved from http://www.wisconsinhistory.org/museum/exhibits/artofthedraw/poster9.asp

Wisdom, W. B. (1930, April 24). Putting punch in copy vs. punching competitors. *Printers' Ink, 151*, 114.

Witkowski, T. H., & Jones, D. G. B. (2006). Qualitative historical research in marketing. In R. W. Belk (Ed.), *Handbook of qualitative research methods in marketing* (pp. 70–82). Cheltenham, UK: Edward Elgar Publishing, Inc.

Wong, E. (2009). *Yogurt giant offers course in "Dannonomics."* Retrieved from http://www.adweek.com/news/advertising-branding/yogurt-giant-offers-course-dannonomics-105809

Wong, E. (2008). *Mm-mm militant: Campbell goes after Progresso*. Retrieved from http://www.adweek.com/news/advertising-branding/mm-mm-militant-campbell-goes-after-progresso-104585

Wood, S., & Fowle, J. P. M. (1961, April 3). British adman seeks to abolish ban on "knocking copy." *Advertising Age, 32*, 32.

Word of Mouth Marketing Association (2017). *About WOMMA*. Retrieved from womma.org/about-womma/

Word war; mayonnaise and salad dressing, steel and steel-wood motor bodies are arguing in public. (1933, Aug. 26). *Business Week*, 21–21.

Xangxin Partners PC (2009). *Playing with fire: The risks and rewards of comparative advertising in China*. Retrieved from https://www.lexology.com/library/detail.aspx?g=4a01fe64–7f14–420d-af0c-3b89acad1973

Yin, R. (2003). *Case study research: Design and methods* (3rd ed.). Thousand Oaks, CA: Sage Publications.

York, E. B. (2010). *So sue me: Why big brands are taking claims to court: When marketers hype ad battles, the public becomes ultimate judge*. Retrieved from http://adage.com/article/news/marketing-big-brands-taking-claims-court/141261/

York, E. B. (2009a). *The gloves are off: More marketers opt for attack ads: Comparison spots move the sales needle for Campbell, Domino's*. Retrieved from http://adage.com/print/136841

York, E. B. (2009b). *Despite sales success, Campbell puts an end to soup wars: New, positive campaign will aim to draw consumers to the category*. Retrieved from http://adage.com/article/news/sales-success-campbell-puts-end-soup-wars/138479

York, E. B. (2009c). *DiGiorno turns to twitter for flatbread-pizza launch: Kraft will deliver frozen pies to tweetups to generate word-of-mouth*. Retrieved from http://adage.com/article/digital/digiorno-turns-twitter-flatbread-pizza-launch/135876/

York, E. B. (2009d). *DiGiorno: An America's hottest brands case study*. Retrieved from http://adage.com/article/special-report-americas-hottest-brands-2009/digiorno-america-s-hottest-brands-case-study/140468/

Zanot, E. J. (1985). Unseen but effective advertising regulation: The clearance process. *Journal of Advertising*, *14*(4), 44–68.

Zhang, L., Moore, M., & Moore, R. (2011). The effect of self-construals on the effectiveness of comparative advertising. *Marketing Management Journal, 21*(1), 195–206.

Zhang, S., Kardes, F. R., & Cronley, M. L. (2002). Comparative advertising: Effects of structural alignability on target brand evaluations. *Journal of Consumer Psychology*, *12*(4), 303–311.

Zhang, Y. (1996). The effect of humor in advertising: An individual-difference perspective. *Psychology & Marketing*, *13*(6), 531–545.

Zhang, Y., & Zinkhan, G. M. (1996). Responses to humorous advertising: The moderating effect of need for cognition. *Journal of Advertising*, *25*(1), 15–32.

Zillman, D. (1983) Disparagement humor. In P. E. McGhee, & J. H. Goldstein (Eds.), *Handbook of humor research* (pp. 85–108). New York, NY: Springer-Verlag.

Zillman, D., & Cantor, J. R. (1976). A disposition theory of humour and mirth. In A. J. Chapman, & H. C. Foot (Eds.), *Humour and laughter: Theory, research and application* (pp. 93–116). London, UK: John Wiley & Sons.

Index

About the Author

Fred Beard, PhD, is a Gaylord Family Research Professor of Advertising in the Gaylord College of Journalism and Mass Communication, University of Oklahoma. His research interests include comparative advertising, advertising humor, advertising history, and advertising regulation. He is author of the well-reviewed *Humor in the Advertising Business: Theory, Practice, and Wit* (Rowman & Littlefield, 2007), which has been acquired by nearly 600 university, college, and public libraries worldwide. He has also written nearly 120 sole- and coauthored articles, abstracts, book chapters, and conference papers. His research has appeared in top journals in advertising, business, marketing, and journalism, including the *Journal of Advertising*, the *Journal of Advertising Research*, the *Journal of Business Ethics*, the *Journal of Business Research*, the *Journal of Macromarketing*, the *Journal of Historical Research in Marketing*, *Journalism and Communication Monographs*, *Journalism History*, and the *Journal of Marketing Communications*, among many others. He has also contributed chapters and essays to *Marketing Metaphors and Metamorphosis* (2008), *Advertising Principles & Practice* (2008), *The Dominant Influence of Marketing in the 21st Century: The Marketing Leviathan* (2013), and *The Routledge Companion to Marketing History* (2016).